RE-SIT

Re-Situating Identities:

The Politics of Race, Ethnicity, and Culture

Vered Amit-Talai & Caroline Knowles

broadview press

©1996 The authors

All rights reserved. The use of any part of this publication reproduced, transmitted in any form or by any means, electronic, mechanical, photocopying, recording, or otherwise, or stored in a retrieval system, without prior written consent of the publisher — or in the case of photocopying, a licence from cancopy (Canadian Copyright Licensing Agency) 6 Adelaide Street East, Suite 900, Toronto, Ontario M5C 1H6 — is an infringement of the copyright law.

Canadian Cataloguing in Publication Data

Re-situating identities

Includes index
ISBN 1-55111-071-7

1. Ethnic groups. 2. Ethnicity. I. Amit-Talai, Vered, 1955-
II. Knowles, Caroline, 1954-

GN495.6.R47   1996   305.8   C95-933386-X

Broadview Press
Post Office Box 1243, Peterborough, Ontario, Canada K9J 7H5

in the United States of America:
3576 California Road, Orchard Park, NY 14127

in the United Kingdom:
B.R.A.D. Book Representation & Distribution Ltd.,
244A, London Road, Hadleigh, Essex. SS7 2DE

Broadview Press gratefully acknowledges the support of the Canada Council, the Ontario Arts Council, and the Ministry of Canadian Heritage.

PRINTED IN CANADA

Contributors

Vered Amit-Talai, Associate Professor, Concordia University, Montreal, Canada.

Parminder Bhachu, Henry R. Luce Professor of Cultural Identity & Global Process, Clark University, Massachusetts, U.S.A.

Alrick Cambridge, Director, New Directions Project, London, U.K.

Anthony Cohen, Professor and Chair of Anthropology, Edinburgh University, Edinburgh, U.K.

Philip Cohen, Director, New Ethnicities Unit University of East London, London, U.K.

David Howes, Associate Professor, Concordia University, Montreal, Canada.

Tracy K'Meyer, Assistant Professor and Co-director, Oral History Center, University of Louisville, Kentucky, U.S.A.

Caroline Knowles, Associate Professor, Concordia University, Montreal, Canada.

Henri Lustiger-Thaler, Assistant Professor, Ramapo College, New Jersey, U.S.A.

Robert Miles, Professor and Chair of Sociology, University of Glasgow, Glasgow, U.K.

Val Morrison, Doctoral Candidate, Carleton University, Ottawa, Canada.

Robert Paine, Visiting Professor, McGill University, Montreal, Canada.

Anthony Synnott, Associate Professor, Concordia University, Montreal, Canada.

Rudy Torres, Associate Professor, California State University, Long Beach, U.S.A.

Acknowledgements

Our thanks to Francine Robillard for her help with the preparation of this manuscript. We would also like to thank the Social Science & Humanities Research Council, Concordia University, and the Canadian Ministry of Multiculturalism and Citizenship which supported our respective research projects. Most importantly, we would like to thank all our contributors for their participation in this collection.

Contents

INTRODUCTION
Vered Amit-Talai and Caroline Knowles
Against Parochialism and Fragmentation   9

Part I: Race and Racism
Introduction   21

CHAPTER 1
Robert Miles and Rudy Torres
Does "Race" Matter? Transatlantic Perspectives on Racism after "Race Relations"   24

CHAPTER 2
Caroline Knowles
Racism, Biography, and Psychiatry   47

CHAPTER 3
Phil. Cohen
Homing Devices   68

Part II: The Politics of Identity
Introduction   85

CHAPTER 4
Vered Amit-Talai
The Minority Circuit: Identity Politics and the Professionalization of Ethnic Activism   89

CHAPTER 5
Val Morrison
Mediating Identity: Kashtin, the Media, and the Oka Crisis   115

CHAPTER 6
Anthony Synnott and David Howes
Canada's Visible Minorities: Identity and Representation   137

CHAPTER 7
Alrick Cambridge
The Beauty of Valuing Black Cultures   161

Part III: Memory and Histories
Introduction   187

CHAPTER 8
Henri Lustiger-Thaler
Remembering Forgetfully   190

CHAPTER 9
Tracy E. K'Meyer
Shared Memory in Community: Oral History, Community, and Race Relations   218

CHAPTER 10
Robert Paine
Dilemmas of Discovery: Europeans and "America"   240

Part IV: Nationalism and Transnationalism
Introduction   265

CHAPTER 11
Anthony P. Cohen
Owning the Nation, and the Personal Nature of Nationalism: Locality and the Rhetoric of Nationhood in Scotland   267

CHAPTER 12
Parminder Bhachu
The Multiple Landscapes of Transnational Asian Women in the Diaspora   283

INDEX   304

Introduction: Against Parochialism and Fragmentation

Vered Amit-Talai and Caroline Knowles

Like its subjects, the study of race and ethnicity has combined an enthusiasm for invention and border crossings with an equally determined parochialism. For nearly three decades, anthropologists and sociologists have stressed the socially constructed and situationally contingent nature of racial and ethnic distinctions. With the end of the Cold War, more people moving than ever before, and the relentless innovation of communication technologies, the boundaries and identities of local political units appear increasingly uncertain. Indeed in the ensuing scholarly celebration of border zones, the Local sometimes seems in danger of a premature epistemological oblivion: people may still be living there but academics, and graduate students in particular, appear to have decamped to the Superhighway. In this de-anchored, hybrid and moving world, the ethnic Diaspora has taken on a new relevance, as a kind of metaphor for the late-twentieth-century human condition, writ large.

Associated with this effort to grapple with the displacements and uncertainties of the *fin de siècle* has been the argument for a shift in analytical levels away from the study of local ethnic and racial groupings to the study of the organization of diversity (Sanjek 1994:10). Hence the focus here tends to be on the impact of state formation (Williams 1989), the relationship between ethnicity and other forms of differentiation (Verdery 1994), racism as a global system (Sanjek 1994), repeat migration (Alvarez 1987), transnationalism (Hannerz 1992) and the margins or borders of state systems (Bhaba 1990; Rosaldo 1989).

Yet pick up one of the mountain of readers on race and ethnic relations in Canada or the United States, flip to its table of contents, and in most cases you are likely to find the very categories we were supposed to have left behind. In the United States, these will probably include Asian, Hispanic, Native and African Americans and perhaps in some cases references to white ethnic categories. In Canada a somewhat longer list of similar categories is carefully balanced with attention to official language distinctions and regional representativeness. This, we contend, is not an accidental parochialism born out of a lag between current research and the simplifications of undergraduate textbooks. It is a self-conscious and in some ways accurate depiction of academic territorial claims. Textbook inventories may not tell us very much about the social organization of ethnicity or the impact of racism but they do delineate the proliferation of ethnic studies chairs, native studies programs, and Hispanic or African American institutes. They reflect the organization of curriculum, hiring committees, university task forces, and mission statements. In short, these books sell, and they sell because they accurately read the institutional landscape of their principal patrons.

That landscape is increasingly being reshaped by identity politics that draw upon a conceptual convergence between cultural studies, multiculturalism, and political correctness. The conservatism engendered by this convergence is painfully ironic given the initial political and critical aspirations of cultural studies, which emerged as a transatlantic, multidisciplinary critique of representation. Drawing heavily on postmodernist and poststructuralist work in Britain, France, and more recently in North America, cultural studies was profoundly sceptical of traditional hierarchies of knowledge, power, and culture, hierarchies which privileged materialism over rhetorical forms, the market and society over everyday forms of life, and high versus popular culture. The politics associated with that critical challenge was conceived as egalitarian, levelling, and intellectually liberating; liberated from the constraints of a spurious base/superstructure, truth/representation polarity, the political imagination was now capable of conceiving radically new forms of social life (Ryan 1988).

Michael Ryan was based in an American university when he wrote this optimistic portrait of postmodern politics, but in the transatlantic passage from its British roots to an American efflorescence, the sense of political engagement which had originally inspired cultural studies diminished. Cultural studies "moved increasingly from the study of social action to the study of texts" (Knauft 1994:133). As Knauft continues, in British and even more so in American cultural studies,

> Concepts such as "hegemony", "resistance", "articulation", "war of position" and the "organic" nature of popular culture are too sweepingly and uncritically used and are only lightly underpinned by substantive social analysis.

And one can see the attraction of this textual preoccupation. At a time when intellectuals seem increasingly irrelevant to and powerless in the face of a global shift to the right, when a brutal economic reductionism has become enshrined in a sacred cult of deficit reduction, it's harder than ever to launch a politically engaged critique of representational icons. How comforting it is to feel that resistance can still be achieved through a hermeneutics that rarely requires straying from the university library or the television set or that the production of texts can stand in for effective political changes. In short, the struggle against "discursive hegemonies" has become a sardonic guide to 1990s radicalism. Let us be blunt. This is not only lazy radicalism; it is a politically emasculated intellectualism.

It is this postmodern husk, a ritual invocation of analytical terms reduced to slogans, which has bled into the academic politics of identity. It is a politics which attaches a pretentious importance to curricular reform, bland mission statements, and an obsessional preoccupation with naming. If former left-wing activists have indeed captured academe as critics like Richard Bernstein (1994) contend (although unfortunately we see little evidence of this), they're not manning the barricades, they're manning university program committees. This is not a right-wing nightmare; it's a reactionary's dream of co-optation come true. Sadly, it is not only Baudrillard who has ended up in "agentless apathy on the right" (Knauft 1994:131). Far too many of us have joined him. Academics may be trying to launch themselves onto a global landscape but their politics are becoming painfully localized to the academic bureaucracy.

These are not novel insights but they suggest a few twists and implications worth noting. The first is that while the accounts produced by academic identity politics distort the distribution and experience of racial and ethnic distinctions, this is not an innocent or unaware distortion. It is a politically astute calculation of opportunities and tactics within the academic infrastructure and must be countered as such. Second this form of deliberate parochialism is associated with a bureaucratic and disciplinary balkanization. We have long been aware that disciplinary boundaries, rigorously maintained, may soothe occupational insecurities and aid managerial control but do little to stimulate the development of sophisticated theoretical paradigms. Similarly, reproducing ethnic categories and groups as the product or object of study of a proliferation of academic programs, "experts" and owners may protect old and establish new occupational enclaves, but they have a theoretical "wheel-spinning" effect.

Curiously, some of those who have emphasized the emergent, invented character of ethnic or racial categories have also insisted on this kind of fragmentation. For Roger Sanjek, twenty-five years of anthropological writing on ethnic and social boundaries, on the organization of difference and the political construction of identity, have little contribution to make to the study of race and racism, which he construes as somehow entirely separate (1994:10). In Canada, this kind of attitude has meant a persistent lag between ethnic studies and theoretical developments in the social sciences and humanities. as Li (1990) has noted, far too many Canadian studies of ethnicity and race are still obsessively preoccupied with theories of assimilation and pluralism which were current in the 1960s and earlier. Other Canadian studies (Satzewich 1992) have become stuck in an equally outmoded Marxist groove which restricts their coverage to the significance of labour markets and what is often referred to as "institutional racism" in which race and ethnicity are grafted onto the more significant category of class. Still other studies are concerned with racism at the level of popular "attitudes" revealed in surveys (Henry et al. 1995). These have long ceased to be major concerns in recent cross-disciplinary efforts to rethink culture, identity, and structure.

In Britain, local investigations into the mobilization of racial and ethnic markers and belonging in local politics (Ball and Solomos 1990; Eade 1992), biography and boundary (Feuchtwang 1992), black phenomenology (Cambridge 1992), the racialization of social relationships (Miles 1989), urbanization as racialized space (Cross and Keith 1993) have generated a climate of interrogation and contestation around the race concept and its relationship to racism. The result is that British race sociology has developed a substantial theoretical literature where race and ethnicity are the object of continual scrutiny rather than taken as a "given" upon which the fragmentation of the field can be construed.

It is precisely this attention to theory and the importance placed on the analysis – if not always the political resolution – of racism as a set of concrete practices which delayed the fragmentation of British race sociology. Whatever the debates about the nature of race and racial exclusion, there was a broad consensus around the maintenance of the category "black" for social and political analysis. The insistence that "blackness" was necessary for political mobilization around anti-racist struggles survived the onslaught of African American and Black British feminists and the local mobilization of activists around identity and cultural politics. Fragmentation around identity politics and cultural expression really only made its way into mainstream (white-dominated) British race sociology in the late 1980s. Hall's (1992) "new" (fragmented) ethnicities for "old" may produce more authentic forms of representation of multiple black identities, but the advantages of this in tackling the social inequalities organized by race and ethnicity are not apparent. Hall's interjection signals a convergence between the British and the American literature. In the ensuing cultural celebration of difference, the fact that neither offers a mode of political engagement in anti-racist politics has been overlooked.

The debates of British race sociology highlight a key, indeed *the* key, dilemma of a politically engaged social analysis. How do we develop analytical categories that are intrinsically comparative and sufficiently comprehensive to address national, regional, and increasingly global trends? How do we contribute to the formation of constituencies inclusive enough to mount effective political challenges and enact social change? And how do we do this without undermining recognition of the particularity of local collective identities and while respecting the complexity and agency invested in selfhood (Cohen 1985, 1994)? In short, how do we move beyond the specific theoretical and ethnographic case without resorting to structural or cultural determinism and without treating human beings as if they are categorical signifiers rather than self-aware subjects?

This is surely not a new set of questions and certainly not one that has been restricted to British sociology or the study of race and ethnicity. It is, and in a sense has always been, the $64,000 question for the social sciences and humanities, continuously addressed and re-addressed under a variety of rubrics: macro/micro; global/local; critiques of grand narratives; appeals to cultural agency. The most significant contribution of postmodernism has been a revitalization of this central conundrum, a refreshed warning about the configuring power of representation and the dangers of naive renderings of "realism." But all too often, postmodernist analyses have appeared overwhelmed by the very challenges they pose. The ensuing postmodernist declarations about the "Death of the Subject," the exaggerated opposition between local stories and global histories (Benhabib 1992) and the exultation in fragmentation, have resulted in a dangerous political fatalism.

If we celebrate fragmentation as not only insurmountable but ethically virtuous, how can intellectuals speak to each other across the specificity of their research projects, across disciplines and countries? If we give in to the seduction of local incommensurabilities, then we negate our capacity and accountability as political agents and doom any possibility of new alliances. We are therefore arguing for a re-energized research project, one that resituates the production of identities in the systematic investigation of power relations, that pays heed to discursive hegemonies but not at the expense of rigorous, empirically grounded analysis and an insistence on concrete social change. If the study of race and ethnicity is to keep conceptual pace with the political and cultural developments of the late twentieth century, it must be able to mine but also to extend the reflexiveness and conceptual rethinking that have characterized the last few decades in sociology and anthropology as well as their sister disciplines. This is not to suggest, however, that once we have moved beyond the more glaring reifications of textbook ethnic catalogues, we have necessarily escaped their conflation of categories, groups, and individuals.

It is therefore not as redundant as we might have hoped to state the following obvious points. States are not political actors. Ethnic and racial groups are not political actors. Ethnic and racial categories are not political actors. People are political actors who produce, mediate, contest, and experience the outcomes of racial and ethnic distinctions. If we are going to have any hope of demystifying concepts as complex as race, ethnicity, and identity, then we need both to diversify and to resolutely populate the scenarios we examine. In the following chapters you will therefore encounter psychiatrists, explorers, minority lobbyists, singers, reporters, elected and appointed office holders, community organizers, theologians, historians, teachers, wedding service providers, and more. They operate in a multiplicity of political contexts including classrooms and courtrooms, Diaspora bases, a college lecture, intentional community, state memorials, historical discovery, media representations, and consultation exercises. The ensuing considerations of power and control are redolent of irony and contradiction. A teacher decides to make a stand against years of painful racial harassment, sacrifices his health, job, and peace of mind, but wins a Quebec Human Rights Commission ruling (Knowles, Ch.2). In the face of committed protest, a memorial to the extinguished pre-World War II Frankfurt Jewish community is eventually incorporated into the construction of a local utilities company branch. Meanwhile in other quarters, the Nazi past is being buried in a recasting of German history as the ascendant triumph of a reunited nation (Lustiger-Thaler, Ch.8).

Political impetuses, the following chapters illustrate, can come from a wide range of state, institutional, local, and transnational sources; like academic representations, their repercussions are more likely to be uneven and inconsistent than comprehensive and coherent. Thus official multicultural policies in Canada have encouraged the emergence of a small, select occupational network of professional activists but their impact on mass ethnic mobilization is far more nebulous (Amit-Talai, Ch. 4). The problem for nationalism, Anthony Cohen argues (Ch.11), is that to be compelling it must be mediated by the very local experiences it is attempting to supersede. Politicians, he suggests, overestimate their abilities to resolve this fundamental contradiction. What after all does the Local mean, and what influence does the nation-state have on its production when you are an Asian woman with a migration history that includes Asia, Africa, Europe, and North America (Bhachu, Ch.12)?

The authors of the twelve chapters in this book are sociologists, anthropologists, and cultural theorists situated in Canada, Britain, and the United States, and with one exception they report on or review research in these locales. Most, however, have studied, worked, and conducted research in two or sometimes all three of these countries. Our aim in framing the collection in these terms is to provide an opportunity not only for examples of varied ethnographic settings but for a cross-sampling of the theoretical, historical, and political debates occurring in these countries. We make no claim nor do we aspire to be exhaustive; in twelve chapters, we cannot hope to cover the complexity of issues, settings and actors which can and should be subsumed within this field. The essays in this book, therefore, don't summarize the study of race, ethnicity and identity. Instead, and more significantly, they expand it through expositions that are conceptually and politically provocative.

References

Alvarez, Robert R., Jr., (1987). "The Foundations and Genesis of a Mexican American Community: A Sociohistorical Perspective". In Leith Mullings (ed.), *Cities of the United States*. New York: Columbia University Press, pp. 176-197.

Ball, Wendy and Solomos, John. (Eds.) (1990). *Race and Local Politics*. London: Macmillan.

Barth, Fredrik. (1994). "Enduring and emerging issues in the analysis of ethnicity" In Hans Vermeulen and Cora Grovers (eds.), *The Anthropology of Ethnicity: Beyond "Ethnic Groups and Boundaries"*. Amsterdam: Het Spinhuis. pp. 11-32.

Bhaba, Homi K. (1990). "DissemiNation: time, narrative and the margins of the modern nation". In Homi K. Bhaba (ed.), *Nation and Narration*, London and New York: Routledge, pp. 291-332.

Benhabib, Seyla. (1992). *Situating the Self: Gender, Community and Postmodernism in Contemporary Ethics*. New York: Routledge.

Bernstein, Richard. (1994). *Dictatorship of Virtue: Multiculturalism and the Battle for America's Future*. New York: Alfred A. Knopf.

Cambridge, Alrick. (1992). "Cultural Recognition and Identity." In Alrick Cambridge and Stephan Feuchtwang (eds), *Where You Belong*. Aldershot: Avebury.

Cohen, Anthony P. (1985). *The Symbolic Construction of Community*. London: Tavistock.

_____. (1994). *Self Consciousness: An Alternative Anthropology of Identity*. London and New York: Routledge.

Cross, Malcolm and Keith, Michael. (1993). *Racism, the City and the State*. London: Routledge.

Eade, John. (1992). "Quests for Belonging." In Alrick Cambridge and Stephan Feuchtwang (eds.), *Where You Belong*. Aldershot: Avebury.

Feuchtwang, Stephan. (1992). "Where You Belong." In Stephan Feuchtwang and Alrick Cambridge (eds.), *Where You Belong*. Aldershot: Avebury.

Hall, Stuart. (1992). "New Ethnicities." In James Donald and Ali Rattansi, (eds.), *Race, Culture and Difference*. London: Sage.

Hannerz, Ulf. (1992). *Cultural Complexity: Studies in the Social Organization of Meaning*. New York: Columbia University Press.

Henry, Frances, Carol Tator, Winston Mattis, and Tim Rees, (1995). *The Colour of Democracy: Racism in Canadian Society*. Toronto and Montreal: Harcourt Brace.

Knauft, Bruce M. (1994). "Pushing Anthropology Past the Posts: Critical notes on cultural anthropology and cultural studies as influenced by postmodernism and existentialism." *Critique of Anthropology*. 14 (2): 117-152.

Li, Peter S. (1990). "Race and Ethnicity" In Peter S. Li (ed.), *Race and Ethnic Relations in Canada*. Toronto: Oxford University Press, pp. 3-17.

Miles, Robert. (1989). *Racism*. London: Routledge.

Rosaldo, Renato. (1989). *Culture and Truth: The Remaking of Social Analysis*. Boston: Beacon Press.

Ryan, Michael. (1988). "Postmodern Politics." *Theory, Culture and Society*. Special Issue on Postmodernism. 5 (2-3): 559-576.

Sanjek, Roger. (1994). "The Enduring Inequalities of Race" In Steven Gregory and Roger Sanjek (eds.), *Race*. New Brunswick, New Jersey: Rutgers University Press, pp. 1-17.

Satzewich, Vic. (1992). *Deconstructing a Nation: Immigration, Multiculturalism and Racism in '90s Canada*. Halifax, Nova Scotia: Fernwood.

Verdery, Katherine. (1994). "Ethnicity, nationalism and state-making *Ethnic groups and boundaries: past and future*." In Hans Vermeulen and Cora Grovers (eds.), *The Anthropology of Ethnicity: Beyond "Ethnic Groups and Boundaries."* Amsterdam: Het Spinhuis, pp. 33-58.

Williams, Brackette. (1989). "A Class Act: Anthropology and the Race to Nation Across Ethnic Terrain." *Annual Review of Anthropology*. 18: 401-444.

[Part I]

RACE & RACISM

Introduction

Contemporary accounts of race and racism frequently begin with what has become a mantra: statements of urgency and political potency urging the reader to understand the demands which race and racism make upon the lives and bodies of those whose social locations they frame. Despite more than thirty years of theoretical framing and reframing in the social sciences, racial distinctions and the social inequalities and forms of violence with which they are arranged are, as ever, pressing issues of social reform. Racism has eluded sustained attempts to understand it, and to challenge it. Racial and ethnic cleansing in various parts of the world have become familiar news items. Even genocide, it seems, has lost its horrifying novelty.

The United States, Britain, and Canada, the empirical contexts of the papers in this section, are places where race remains a focus for significant forms of social disadvantage – this is racism. But these are, of course, not the only places where immigration is being toughened up, where affirmative action is being dismantled, and where officious policing and the distribution of social resources generate and support racialized social distinctions – this too is racism.

These racialized forms of disparity in human rights are challenged on both sides of the Atlantic. But the mounting protests, led by successive generations of minority citizens, parallel two contradictory outcomes. The first is an explosion of discourse advocating human equality: policy statements, reports, and initiatives at all levels of public life, government, and administration. The second outcome is the subject of the mantra: the observation that the everyday lives of certain stigmatized and disadvantaged minority citizens, fissured by hostility, exclusion, and even physical violence, have failed to improve and may even have significantly deteriorated.

If it is the case that the more we have to say about race, the worse things become, then policy makers confront a "credibility gap" into which social and political analysts need to be careful not to fall. The papers in this section tread carefully around this credibility gap, detailing theoretical insights in everyday social and political contexts. They deftly manipulate the interface between individual and social scripts, and between everyday ideas about race on the one hand, and race as a concept developed in academic discourse on the other.

Robert Miles and Rudy Torres document some of the connections between the development of race in the United States and its development in Britain. Drawing on the work of the distinguished African American scholar Cornel West in *Race Matters*, they argue that the popular idea that races have a "real" basis in human physiology is sustained by sociologists continuing to address race as a significant dimension of social and political inequality. Popular ideas about race, they argue, are importantly legitimated by their continued examination in academic enterprise. We should consequently jettison race in sociology, but continue to study racism. This offers an important challenge to thirty years of sociological analysis in Britain and the United States to clarify the connections between race and racism and between popular/political and theoretical discourse.

Philip Cohen discusses the hidden symbolism and imagery of race and of racism in the ways in which territory and space have become racialized in East London. He shows how the racialization of territory invokes a re-invention, in popular narrative, of traditions of white living space. This is a space which is politically defended against alien invasion by the "other," those whose ancestral origins and belonging come from elsewhere. Combining an urban geography with an analysis of popular culture, Cohen discusses both the social contexts of racial mobilization and the internal lives of individuals who, as active social agents, construct racialized meaning in the everyday use of urban space. Cohen argues that racialized notions of "home," in which space is significant, help to frame notions of the "self"; and that which gives meaning to the self -

"otherness." Home, self, and otherness, he argues, are embedded in the symbolic order of culture.

Caroline Knowles' analysis of racism in Quebec similarly positions the dual analytic focus of individual black lives and their racialized social contexts. Exploring the life story of a Ghanaian teacher she traces the interface between "administrative racism" (the social policy contexts in which black people are "dealt with" as social problems), and the "existential" experience of racism. Knowles shows how in stories of the self, narrative constructions of race as blackness confront and negotiate both the cultural scripts of blackness and the administrative stories of psychiatric assessment. Racism, incremental, cumulative, and embedded in everyday life, is more than a series of outcomes. It is a dynamic in which black lives and the strategies used to manage them are constantly reconfigured.

Each of the three papers in this section confronts and explores the social construction of racism through different mechanisms. Space, the symbolic order of culture, psychiatry, the self, otherness, and the relationship between academic and popular/political discourse – these are all a part of an analysis which embraces the empirical, the theoretical, the micro and the macro dimensions of the social.

"We should jettison race in sociology but continue to study racism."

1

Does "Race" Matter?

Transatlantic Perspectives on Racism after "Race Relations"

Robert Miles and Rudy Torres

> The discourse promoting resistance to racism must not prompt identification with and in terms of categories fundamental to the discourse of oppression. Resistance must break not only with *practices* of oppression, although its first task is to do that. Resistance must oppose also the *language* of oppression, including the categories in terms of which the oppressor (or racist) represents the forms in which resistance is expressed. (Goldberg 1990:313-14)

In April 1993, one year after the Los Angeles civil unrest, a major U.S. publisher released a book with the creatively ambiguous title *Race Matters* by the distinguished scholar Cornel West. The back cover of the slightly revised edition published the following year categorized it as a contribution to both African American studies and current affairs. The latter was confirmed by the publisher's strategy of marketing the book as a "trade" rather than as an "academic" title: this was a book for the "American public" to read. And the American public was assured that they were reading a quality product when they were told that its author had "built a reputation as one of the most eloquent voices in America's racial debate."

Some two years later, the *Los Angeles Times* published an article by its science writer under the headline "Scientists Say Race Has No Biological Basis." The opening paragraph ran as follows:

> Researchers adept at analyzing the genetic threads of human diversity said Sunday that the concept of race – the source of abiding cultural and political divisions in American society – simply has no basis in fundamental human biology. Scientists should abandon it.

And on the same day (20 February 1995), the *Chronicle of Higher Education* reproduced the substance of these claims in an article under the title "A Growing Number of Scientists Reject the Concept of Race." Both publications were reporting on the proceedings of the American Association for the Advancement of Science in Atlanta.

If "the concept of race ... simply has no basis in fundamental human biology," how are we to evaluate Professor West's assertion that "Race Matters"? If "race" matters, then "races" must exist! But if there are no "races," then "race" cannot matter. These two contributions to public political debate seem to reveal a contradiction. Yet within the specific arena of academic debate there is a well-rehearsed attempt to dissolve the contradiction, which runs as follows. It is acknowledged that, earlier this century, the biological and genetic sciences established conclusively in the light of empirical evidence that the attempt to establish the existence of different types or "races" of human beings by scientific procedures had failed. The idea that the human species consisted of a number of distinct "races," each exhibiting a set of discrete physical and cultural characteristics is therefore false, mistaken. The interventions reported as having been made in Atlanta in February 1995 only repeat what some scientists have been arguing since the 1930s. Yet the fact that scientists have to continue to assert these claims demonstrates that the contrary is still widely believed and articulated in public discussion.

Because this scientific knowledge has not yet been comprehensively understood by "the general public" (which not only persists in believing in the existence of "races" as biologically discrete entities but also acts in ways consistent with such a belief), it is argued that social scientists must employ a *concept* of "race" to describe and analyze these beliefs, and the discrimination and exclusion that are premised on this kind of classification. In other words, while social scientists know that there are no "races," they also know that things believed to exist (in this case "races") have a real existence for those who believe in them and that actions consistent with the belief have real social consequences. In sum, because people believe that "races" exist (i.e. because they utilize the *idea* of "race" to comprehend their social world), social scientists need a *concept* of "race."

Or do they? This chapter will explore the reasons why this question needs to be asked. It will also answer it by suggesting that social scientists do not need to, and indeed should not, transform the *idea* of "race" into an analytical category and use "race" as a *concept*. Pre-eminent amongst the reasons for such an assertion is that the arenas of academic and political discourse cannot be clinically separated. Hence Professor West, in seeking to use his status as a leading Afro-American scholar to make a political intervention in current affairs by arguing that "Race Matters," is likely to legitimate and reinforce the widespread public belief that "races" exist irrespective of his views on this issue. For if this belief in the existence of "races" was not widespread, there would be no news value in publishing an article in a leading daily U.S. newspaper that claims that "Race Has No Biological Basis."

Criticizing "Race" as an Analytical Category

We begin this exploration by crossing the Atlantic in order to consider the issue as it has been discussed in Britain since the early 1950s. As we shall see, the development of the British discussion has in fact been influenced substantially by the preconceptions and language employed in the U.S.: the use of "race" as an analytical category in the social sciences is a transatlantic phenomenon.

It is now difficult to conceive, but forty years ago no one would have suggested that "Race Matters" *in* Britain. The idea of "race" was employed in public and political discussion, but largely only in order to discuss "the colonies": the "race problem" was spatially located beyond British shores in the British Empire and especially in certain colonies, notably South Africa. It is relevant to add that this too had not always been so. During the nineteenth and early twentieth centuries, it was widely believed that the population of Britain was composed of a number of different "races" (e.g., the Irish were identified as being "of the Celtic race") and, moreover, migration to Britain from central and eastern Europe in the late nineteenth century was interpreted using the language of "race" to signify the Jewish refugees fleeing persecution (e.g., Barkan 1992:15-165). But, as the situation in the port city of Liverpool after the First World War suggested (e.g. Barkan 1992:57-165), the language of "race" used to refer to the interior of Britain was to become tied exclusively to differences in skin colour in the second half of the twentieth century. What, then, was the "race" problem that existed beyond the shores of Britain?

Briefly expressed, the problem was that, or so it was thought, the colonies were spatial sites where members of different "races" (Caucasian, White, African, Hindoo, Mongoloid, Celts: the language to name these supposed "races" varied enormously) met and where their "natures" (to civilize, to fight, to be lazy, to progress, to drink, to engage in sexual perversions, etc.) interacted, often with tragic consequences. This language of "race" was usually anchored in the signification of certain forms of somatic difference (skin colour, facial characteristics, body shape and size, eye colour, skull shape) which were interpreted as the physical marks which accompanied, and which in some unexplained way determined, the "nature" of those so marked. In this way, the social relations of British colonialism were explained as being rooted simultaneously in the biology of the human body and in the cultural attributes determined by nature.

But the "race" problem was not to remain isolated from British shores, to be contained there by a combination of civilization and violence. All Her Majesty's subjects had the right of residence in the Motherland, and increasing numbers of them chose to exercise that right as the 1950s progressed. Members of "coloured races," from the Caribbean and the Indian subcontinent in particular, migrated to Britain largely to fill vacancies in the labour market but against the will of successive governments (Labour and Conservative) who feared that they carried in their cheap suitcases not only their few clothes and personal possessions but also the "race problem" (e.g., Joshi and Carter 1984, Solomos 1989, Layton-Henry 1992). By the late 1950s, it was widely argued that, as a result of "coloured immigration," Britain had imported a "race" problem: prior to this migration, so it was believed, Britain's population was "racially homogeneous," a claim that neatly dispensed with not only earlier racialized classifications of both migrants and the population of the British Isles but also the history of interior racisms.

The political and public response to immigration from the Caribbean and the Indian subcontinent is now a well-known story (e.g., Solomos 1989, Layton-Henry 1992), although there are a number of important by-ways still to be explored. What is of more interest here is the academic response. A small number of social scientists (particularly sociologists and anthropologists) wrote about these migrations and their social consequences using the language of everyday life: *Dark Strangers* and *The Colour Problem* were the titles of two books that achieved a certain prominence during the 1950s, and their authors subsequently pursued distinguished academic careers. Considered from the point of view of the 1990s, these titles now seem a little unfortunate, and perhaps even a part of the problem insofar as they employ language that seems to echo and legitimate racist discourses of the time.

But can the same be said for two other books that became classic texts within the social sciences: Michael Banton's *Race Relations* (1967) and John Rex's *Race Relations in Sociological Theory* (1970)? Both were published in the following decade and were widely interpreted as offering different theoretical and political interpretations of the consequences of the migration to, and settlement in, Britain of British subjects and citizens from the Caribbean and the Indian subcontinent. And indeed they did offer very different analyses. Notably, Rex sought to reinterpret the scope of the concept of racism to ensure that it could encompass the then contemporary political discourses about immigration. Such discourse avoided any direct references to an alleged hierarchy of "races" while at the same time referring to or implying the existence of different "races." Banton interpreted this shift in discourse as evidence of a decline in racism, a conclusion that was to lead him to eventually reject the concept of racism entirely (1987).

But what is more remarkable is that, despite their very different philosophical and theoretical backgrounds and conclusions, they shared something else in common. Both Banton and Rex mirrored the language of everyday life, incorporated it into academic discourse and thereby legitimated it. They agreed that Britain (which they both analyzed comparatively with reference to the U.S. and South Africa) had a race relations problem, and Rex in particular wished to conceptualize this problem theoretically in the discipline of sociology. In so doing, both premised their arguments on the understanding that scientific knowledge proves that "races" do not exist in the sense widely understood in everyday common sense discourse: if "race" was a problem, it was a social and not a biological problem, one rooted in part at least in the continued popular belief in the existence of "races." Indeed, John Rex had been one of the members of the team of experts recruited by UNESCO to officially discredit the continuing exploitation of nineteenth-century scientific knowledge about "race" by certain political groups and to educate the public by making widely known the more recent conclusions of biological and genetic scientists (Montagu 1972).

The concept of "race relations" seemed to have impeccable credentials, unlike the language of "dark strangers," for example. This is in part because the notion was borrowed from the early sociology of the "Chicago School" in the U.S. which, amongst other things, was interested in the consequences of two contemporaneous migrations: the early twentieth-century migration from the southern to the northern states of "Negroes" fleeing poverty (and much more besides) in search of wage labour and the continuing large-scale migration from Europe to the U.S. As a result of the former migration, "Negro" and "white races" entered, or so it was conceptualized, into conflicting social relations in the burgeoning industrial urban areas of the northern states and sociologists had named a new field of study. "Coloured migration" to British cities after 1945 provided an opportunity for sociologists to import this field of study into Britain: Britain too now had a "race relations" problem.

Moreover, for Rex at least, "race relations situations" were characterized by the presence of a racist ideology. Hence, the struggle against colonialism could now be pursued within the Mother Country "herself": by intervening in the new, domestic race relations problem on the side of the colonized victims of racism, one could position oneself against the British state now busily seeking a solution to that problem through the introduction of immigration controls intended specifically to prevent "coloured" British subjects from entering the country. Such was the rush to be on the side of the angels that few, if any, wondered about what the angels looked like and whether there was any validity in the very concept of angel.

There was a further import from the U.S. that had a substantial impact on the everyday and academic discourses of race relations in the late 1960s and early 1970s in Britain: the struggle for civil rights and against racism on the part of "the blacks" in the U.S. (the notion of "Negro" had now run its course and, like "coloured" before it, it had been ejected into the waste-bin of politically unacceptable language). This movement had the effect of mobilizing not only many blacks in Britain but also many whites politically inclined towards one of several competing versions of socialist transformation. And if radical blacks were busy "seizing the time" in the names of anti-racism and "black autonomy," there was little political or academic space within which radically-inclined white social scientists could wonder about the legitimacy and the consequences of seizing the language of "race" to do battle against racism. For it was specifically in the name of "race" that black people were resisting their long history of colonial oppression: indeed, in some versions of this vision of liberation, contemporary blacks were the direct descendants and inheritors of the African "race" which had been deceived and disinherited by the "white devils" many centuries ago. In this "race war," the white race was soon to face the day of judgement.

Possession of a common language and associated historical traditions can blind as well as illuminate. It is especially significant that both the Left and the Right in Britain looked across the Atlantic when seeking to analyze and to offer forecasts about the outcome of the race relations problem that both agreed existed within Britain. The infamous speeches on immigration made by the MP Enoch Powell in the late 1960s and 1970s contained a great deal of vivid imagery, refracting the current events in U.S. cities and framing them as prophecies of what was inevitably going to happen in due course in British cities if the "alien wedge" was not quickly "repatriated." At the same time, the Left drew political inspiration from the black struggle against racism and sought to incorporate aspects of its rhetoric, style, and politics. Hence, while there was disagreement about the identity of the heroes and the villains of race relations in the U.S., there was fundamental agreement that race relations there provided a framework with which to assess the course of race relations in Britain. Even legislation intended to regulate race relations and to make racialized discrimination illegal refracted the "American experience."

As a result, the academic response to the race relations problem in Britain was largely isolated both from the situations elsewhere in Europe – and particularly in northwest Europe which was experiencing a quantitatively much more substantial migration than that taking place in Britain – and from academic and political writing about those situations. Two features of those situations are pertinent to the argument here.

First, the nation states of northwest Europe had recently experienced either fascist rule or fascist occupation, and therefore had suffered the direct consequences of the so-called "final solution to the Jewish question" which sought to eliminate the "Jewish race." Hence, the collective historical memory of most of the major cities of northwest Europe was shaped by the genocide effected against the Jews and legitimated in the name of "race," even if that historical memory was now the focus of denial or repression. Second, this experience left the collective memory especially susceptible to the activities of UNESCO and others seeking to discredit the idea of "race" as a valid and meaningful descriptor. Hence, the temporal and spatial proximity of the Holocaust rendered its legitimating racism (a racism in which the idea of "race" was explicit and central) an immediate reality: in this context, few people were willing to make themselves vulnerable to the charge of racism, with the result that suppressing the idea of "race," at least in the official and formal arenas of public life, became a political imperative.

The political and academic culture of mainland northwest Europe has therefore been open to two developments which distinguish it from that existing in the British Isles. First, in any debate about the scope and validity of the concept of racism, the Jewish experience of racism is much more likely to be discussed, and even to be prioritized over any other. Second, the idea of "race" itself became highly politically sensitive. Its very use as a descriptor is more likely to be interpreted in itself as evidence of racist beliefs and, as a result, the idea is rarely employed in everyday political and academic discussion, at least not in connection with domestic social relations. However, in Britain, given the combination of the colonial migration and the multiple ideological exchange with the U.S., there were far fewer constraints on the everyday use of the idea of "race" and on a redefinition of the concept of racism. As a result, the latter came to refer exclusively to an ideology held by "white" people about "black" people which was rooted in colonial exploitation and in capitalist expansion beyond Europe.

Having recognized the relative distinctiveness of the political and academic space in northwest Europe and then having occupied that space, one can view those social relations defined in Britain and the U.S. as race relations from another point of view. For there is no public or academic reference to the existence of race relations in contemporary France or Germany. It then becomes possible to pose questions that seem not to be posed from within these intimately interlinked social and historical contexts. What kinds of social relations are signified as race relations? Why is the idea of "race" employed in everyday life to refer only to certain groups of people and to certain social situations? And why do social scientists unquestioningly import everyday meanings into their reasoning and theoretical frameworks in defining "race" and "race relations" as a particular field of study? As a result, what does it mean for an academic to claim, for example, that "race" is a factor in determining the structure of social inequality or that "race" and gender are interlinked forms of oppression? What is intended and what might be the consequences of asserting as an academic that "race matters"?

These are the kinds of question that one of the present authors has been posing for nearly fifteen years (e.g., Miles 1982, 1984, 1989), influenced in part by the important writing of the French theorist Guillaumin (1972, 1995). The answers to these questions lead to the conclusion that one should follow the example of biological and genetic scientists and refuse to attribute analytical status to the *idea* of "race" within the social sciences, and thereby refuse to use it as a descriptive and explanatory *concept*. The reasoning can be summarized as follows (cf. Miles 1982:22–43; 1993:47–9).

First, the idea of "race" is used to effect a reification within sociological analysis insofar as the outcome of an often complex social process is explained as the consequence of some thing named "race" rather than of the social process itself. Consider both the recent publication of *The Bell Curve* (1994) by Richard J. Hernstein and Charles Murray and the authors' common assertion that "race" determines academic performance and life chances. The assertion can be supported with statistical evidence that demonstrates that, in comparison with "black people," "white people" are more likely to achieve top grades in school and to enter the leading universities in the U.S. The determining processes are extremely complex, including amongst other things parental class position, active and passive racialized stereotyping, and exclusion in the classroom and beyond. The effects of these processes are all mediated through a previously racialized categorization into a "white/black" dichotomy which is employed in everyday social relations. Hence, it is not "race" that determines academic performance; rather, academic performance is determined by an interplay of social processes, one of which is premised on the articulation of racism to effect and legitimate exclusion. Indeed, given the nineteenth-century meanings of "race," this form of reification invites the possibility of explaining academic performance as the outcome of some quality within the body of those racialized as "black."

Second, when academics who choose to write about race relations seek to speak to a wider audience (an activity which we believe to be fully justified) or when their writings are utilized by non-academics, this unwittingly legitimates and reinforces everyday beliefs that the human species is constituted by a number of different "races," each of which is characterized by a particular combination of real or imagined physical features or marks and cultural practices. When Professor West seeks to persuade the American public that "Race Matters," there is no doubt that he himself does not believe in the existence of biologically defined "races," but he cannot control the meanings attributed to his claim on the part of those who identify differences in skin colour, for example, as marks designating the existence of blacks and whites as discrete "races." Unintentionally, his writing may then come to serve as a legitimation not only of a belief in the existence of "race" as a biological phenomenon but also of racism itself. He could avoid this outcome by breaking with the race relations paradigm.

Third, as a result of reification and the interplay between academic and common sense discourses, the use of "race" as an analytical concept incorporates a notion which has been central to the evolution of racism into the discourse of antiracism, thereby sustaining one of the conditions of the reproduction of racism within the discourse and practice of antiracism.

For these reasons, the idea of "race" should not be employed as an analytical category within the social sciences, and it follows from this that the object of study should not be described as race relations. Hence, we reject the race relations problematic as the locus for the analysis of racism. But we do not reject the concept of racism. Rather, we critique the race relations problematic in order to retain a concept of racism which is constructed in such a way as to recognize the existence of a plurality of historically specific racisms, not all of which employ explicitly the idea of "race." In contrast, the race relations paradigm refers exclusively to either black/white social relations or social relations between "people of colour" and "white people," with the result that there is only one racism, the racism of whites which has as its object and victim people of colour (e.g., Essed 1991). Moreover, as is increasingly recognized in the academic literature of the past decade, many recent and contemporary discourses which eschew use of the idea of "race" nevertheless advance notions that were previously a referent of such an idea. We can only comprehend contemporary discourses that dispense with the explicit use of the idea of "race" and those discourses which naturalize and inferiorize white populations if we rescue the concept of racism from the simultaneous inflation and narrowing of its meaning by the intersection of the academic and political debates that have taken place in Britain and the U.S. since the end of the Second World War.

Reflections on the Racialization of the U.S. by the American Academy

When one views the contemporary academic debate about racism in the U.S. both from this analytical position and from Europe, one is struck by the following things. First, when compared with the mid- and late 1960s, it is now an extremely contested debate, and one in which many voices are heard arguing different positions. On the one hand, writers such as Wellman (1993) continue to assert that racism remains the primary determinant of social inequality in the U.S., while on the other writers such as Wilson claim that the influence of racism has declined substantially, to the point where it cannot be considered to be a significant influence on current structures of inequality (1987). Between these two positions, one finds writers such as West who assert that the continuing impact of racism has to be assessed in terms of its relationship with the effects of class, sexism, and homophobia (e.g., 1994:44). Moreover, it is a debate in which the voices of "Afrocentrists" (e.g., Karenga 1993) and "black feminists" (e.g., hooks 1990) have become extremely influential over the past two decades, while at the same time a "black" conservative intellectual tradition has emerged and attracted increasing attention (e.g., Sowell 1994).

Second, it remains a debate in which it is either largely taken for granted or explicitly argued that the concept of racism refers to an ideology and (in some cases) a set of practices, of which black people are the exclusive victim: racism refers to what "white" people think about and do to "black" people. While the concept of institutional racism goes further by eschewing any reference to human intentionality, it retains the white/black dichotomy in order to identify beneficiary and victim. Thus the scope of the concept of racism is very narrowly defined: the centrality of the white/black dichotomy denies by definition the possibility that any group other than white people can articulate, practise or benefit from racism and suggests that only black people can be the object or victim of racism.

Some of West's writing illustrates this difficulty. He clearly distinguishes himself from those he describes as black nationalists when he argues that their obsession with white racism obstructs the development of the political alliances that are essential to effecting social changes, changes that will alleviate the suffering of black people in the U.S., and that white racism alone cannot explain the socio-economic position of the majority of black Americans (1994:82, 98-99). Moreover, he goes so far as to suggest that certain black nationalist accounts "simply mirror the white supremacist ideals we are opposing" (1994:99). Yet he seems reluctant to identify any form of racism other than white racism. In his carefully considered discussion of what he describes as "Black-Jewish relations," he employs a distinction between black anti-Semitism and Jewish anti-black racism (1994:104; see also Lerner and West 1995:135-56) which suggests that these are qualitatively different phenomena: Jews articulate racism while blacks express anti-Semitism. This interpretation is reinforced by his assertion that black anti-Semitism is a form of "xenophobia from below" which has a different institutional power when compared with "those racisms that afflict their victims from above" (1994:109-110) even though he claims that both merit moral condemnation.

A similar distinction is implicit in the recent writing of Blauner (1992) who, partly in response to the arguments of one of the present authors, has revised his position significantly since the 1960s. Blauner returns to the common distinction between "race" and ethnicity, arguing that the "peculiarly modern division of the world into a discrete number of hierarchically ranked races is a historic product of Western colonialism" (1992:61). This, he argues, is a very different process from that associated with ethnicity. Hence, Blauner refrains from analyzing the ideologies employed to justify the exclusion of Italians and Jews in the U.S. in the 1920s as racism: these populations are described as "white ethnics" who were "viewed racially" (1992:64). Concerning the period of fascism in Germany, Blauner refers to genocide "where racial imagery was obviously intensified" (1992:64), but presumably the imagery could never be intensified to the point of warranting description as racism because the Jews were not "black." Yet, as we shall see shortly in the case of West's writing, Blauner comes very close to breaking with the race relations problematic when he argues that

> Much of the popular discourse about race in America today goes awry because ethnic realities get lost under the racial umbrella. The positive meanings and potential of ethnicity are overlooked, even overrun, by the more inflammatory meanings of race. (1992:61)

Third, it is a debate which is firmly grounded in the specific realities of the history and contemporary social structure of the U.S., or rather a particular interpretation of those particular realities. It is perhaps not suprising therefore that scholars of racism in the U.S. have shown so little interest in undertaking comparative research, although there are important exceptions. Some comparative work has been undertaken which compares the U.S. with South Africa (e.g., van den Berghe 1978; Fredrickson 1981), and a comparison between the U.S. and England achieved prominence some twenty years ago (Katznelson 1976; for a recent analysis, see Small 1994). More recently, the "neo-conservative" Sowell (1994) has chosen a comparative international arena to demonstrate what he sees as the explanatory power of his thesis, although it is arguable whether this constitutes a contribution to the sociology of racism. But the vast bulk of work on racism by scholars in the U.S. focuses on the U.S. itself. This may be explained as the outcome of a benign ethnocentrism, but one wonders whether it is not also a function of the limited applicability of a theory of racism that is so closely tied to the race relations paradigm and a black/white dichotomy that it has limited potential to be used to analyze social formations where there is no "black" presence.

Yet there is evidence of an increasingly conscious unease with this race relations paradigm and the black/white dichotomy. For example, as we have already noted, West argues in a recent book that "race matters":

> Race is the most explosive issue in American life precisely because it forces us to confront the tragic facts of poverty and paranoia, despair and distrust. In short, a candid examination of *race* matters takes us to the core of the crisis of American democracy. (1994:155-56)

But he also argues that it is necessary to formulate new frameworks and languages in order not only to comprehend the current crisis in the U.S. but also to identify solutions to it (1994:11). Indeed, he asserts that it is imperative to move beyond the narrow framework of "dominant liberal and conservative views of race in America," views which are formulated with a "worn-out vocabulary" (1994:4). But it seems that West does not accept that the idea of "race" itself is an example of this exhausted language, for he employs it throughout with apparently little hesitation, despite the fact that he believes that the manner in which "we set up the terms for discussing racial issues shapes our perception and response to these issues" (1994:6). Later in the book, he seems to be on the verge of following through the logic of this argument to its ultimate conclusion when he argues that the Clarence Thomas/Anita Hill hearings demonstrate that "the very framework of racial reasoning" needs to be called into question in order to reinterpret the black freedom struggle not as an issue of "skin pigmentation and racial phenotype" but, instead, as an issue of ethics and politics (1994:38). And yet West cannot follow through the logic of this argument to the point of acknowledging that there cannot be a place for the use of "race" as an analytical concept in the social sciences.

But there is a transatlantic trade in theories of racism and this is now a two-way trade. Some scholars in the U.S. are not only aware of debates and arguments generated in Europe, (including those contributions which question some of the key assumptions that characterize the debate in the U.S.), but some have also acknowledged and responded to one of the present authors, who has criticized both the use of "race" as an analytical concept and the way in which the concept of racism has been inflated (e.g., Miles 1982, 1989, 1993). Recent contributions by Wellman (1993), Blauner (1992), Omi and Winant (1993, 1994) and Goldberg (1993) all refer to and comment on these arguments, with varying degrees of enthusiasm. Interestingly, they all seem to ignore the writing of Lieberman and his associates (e.g., Lieberman 1968; Reynolds 1992) in the U.S., who argue for a position which overlaps in important respects the one outlined here.

Goldberg offers perhaps the most complex and thoughtful response in the course of a wide-ranging and, in part, philosophically inspired analysis of contemporary racisms and of the conceptual language required to analyze them. His important analysis requires a more extended evaluation than is possible in the limited space available here, so we have chosen to focus instead on the work of Omi and Winant. This is in part because their writing has already had considerable influence in both the U.S. and Britain, partly because of the way in which some of their key concepts have parallels in the equally influential work of Gilroy (1987).

And this influence is deserved. There is much to admire and to learn from their theoretical and conceptual innovations. We prefer to employ a concept of *racialized* formation (rather than racial formation), but we agree that racialized categories are socially created, transformed, and destroyed through historical time (1994:55). We can recognize that it is essential to differentiate between "race" (although we do not use "race" as a *concept* but rather we capture its use in everyday life by referring to the *idea* of "race") and the concept of racism, a distinction that allows us to make a further distinction between racialization and racism (although Omi and Winant refer to this as a distinction between racial awareness and racial essentialism; (compare Omi and Winant 1994:71 with Miles 1989: 73-84). And we also agree that it is essential to retain the concept of racism to identify a multiplicity of historically specific racisms, with the consequence that there is "nothing inherently white about racism" (Omi and Winant 1994:72; see also 1994:73, and compare with Miles 1989:57-60; 1993). Wellman (1993:3) is simply mistaken when he claims that Miles argues that racism is not a useful concept.

It is important to highlight these areas of agreement prior to considering Omi and Winant's defence of the use of the idea of "race" as an analytical concept in the social sciences in order to indicate both the innovations that they have effected within the discussion in the U.S. about racism and their failure to pursue the logic of these innovations to their ultimate conclusion. Partly as a result of their emphasis upon the way in which the idea of "race" has been socially constructed and reconstructed, there is now a debate within the literature in the U.S. about the theoretical and analytical status of the idea of "race." Other scholars in the U.S. have made important contributions to the development of this debate, notably Lieberman (1968), Fields (1990), and Roediger (1994). Fields' work is especially significant because it reaches a conclusion that is close to that reached by one of the present authors (see Miles 1982; 1993:27-52). Omi and Winant have criticized Fields' conclusions in the course of defending their continued use of "race" as analytical concept and it is therefore important to reflect upon the arguments and evidence that they have employed.

Omi and Winant offer two criticisms of the position that the idea of "race" should be analyzed exclusively as a social or ideological construct (1993:5). First, they suggest that it fails to recognize the social impact of the longevity of the concept of "race." Second, they claim that, as a result of this longevity, "race is an almost indissoluble part of our identities," a fact that is not recognized by those who argue that "race" is an ideological construct. They are mistaken on both counts. The writing of Miles highlights the historical evolution of the meanings attributed to the idea of "race" and, for example in his discussions of colonialism and of the articulation between racism and nationalism, stresses the way in which the idea of belonging to the "white race" was central to the construction of the identity of the British bourgeoisie and working class (1982, 1993). Indeed, these claims can be refuted simply by citing a quotation from Fields (1990:118) that Omi and Winant themselves reproduce (1993:5). Fields writes:

> Nothing handed down from the past could keep race alive if we did not constantly reinvent and re-ritualise it to fit our own terrain. If race lives on today, it can do so only because we continue to create and re-create it in our social life, continue to verify it, and thus continue to need a social vocabulary that will allow us to make sense, not of what our ancestors did then, but of what we choose to do now.

Thus Fields certainly does not deny that in the contemporary world people use the idea of "race" to classify themselves and others into social collectivities and act in ways consistent with such a belief, actions which collectively produce structured exclusion. And, hence, Omi and Winant's critique is shown to be vacuous. Fields' key objective is to critique the way in which historians invoke the idea of "race" to construct explanations for events and processes in the past, and her critique applies equally to the work of sociologists such as Omi and Winant who have reinvented and re-ritualized the idea of "race" to fit their own terrain within the academy (which is after all only one more arena of social life). Let us examine how Omi and Winant reinvent and thereby reify the idea of "race" in the course of their sociological analysis. Consider the following claim: "One of the first things we notice about people when we meet them (along with their sex) is their race" (1994:59). Elsewhere, they argue that "To be raceless is akin to being genderless. Indeed, when one cannot identify another's race, a microsociological 'crisis of interpretation' results ... " (1993:5). How are we to interpret this assertion? While they also claim that "race is ... a socially constructed way of differentiating human beings" (1994:65), the former assertion is at the very least open to interpretation as suggesting that "race" is an objective quality inherent in a person's being, that every human being is a member of a "race," and that such membership is inscribed in a person's visible appearance. It is in the interstices of such ambiguity that the idea of "race" as a biological fact does not just "live on" but is actively recreated by social scientists in the course of their academic practice.

This argument commonly stimulates incomprehension on the part of scholars in the U.S., who echo arguments employed in some critiques of this position in Britain. Thus, it is often said, "How can you deny analytical status to the idea of race and ultimately the existence of race when blacks and whites are so obviously different and when all the evidence demonstrates that their life chances differ too?" In responding to this question, it is necessary first to problematize what it takes for granted, specifically that the "black/white" division is *obvious*. The quality of *obviousness* is not inherent in a phenomenon, but is the outcome of a social process in the course of which meaning is attributed to the phenomenon in a particular historical and social context. The meaning is learnt by those who are its subject and object. They therefore learn to habitually recognize it, and perhaps to pass on this signification and knowledge to others, with the result that the quality of obviousness attributed to the phenomenon is reproduced through historical time and social space.

Skin colour is one such phenomenon. Its visibility is not inherent in its existence but is a product of signification: human beings identify skin colour to *mark* or symbolize other phenomena in a historical context in which other significations occur. When human practices include and exclude people in the light of the signification of skin colour, collective identities are produced and social inequalities are structured. It is for this reason that historical studies of the meanings attributed to skin colour in different historical contexts and through time are of considerable importance. And it is in relation to such studies that one can enquire into the continuities and discontinuities with contemporary processes of signification which sustain the obviousness of skin colour as a social *mark*. Historically and contemporarily, differences in skin colour have been and are signified as a mark which suggests the existence of different "races." But people do not see "race": rather, they observe certain combinations of real and sometimes imagined somatic and cultural characteristics which they attribute meaning to with the idea of "race." A difference of skin colour is not essential to the process of marking: other somatic features can be and are signified in order to racialize. Indeed, in some historical circumstances, the absence of somatic difference has been central to the powerful impact of racism: the racialized "enemy within" can be identified as a threatening presence even more effectively if the group is not "obviously different" because "they" can be imagined to be everywhere.

Omi and Winant reify this social process and reach the conclusion that all human beings belong to a "race" because they seek to construct their analytical *concepts* to reproduce directly the common sense ideologies of the everyday world. Because the idea of "race" continues to be widely used in everyday life in the U.S. (and Britain) to classify human beings and to interpret their behaviour, Omi and Winant believe that social scientists must employ a *concept* of race. This assumption is the source of our disagreement with them. We argue that one of the contemporary challenges in the analysis of racisms is to develop a conceptual vocabulary that explicitly acknowledges that people use the *idea* of "race" in the everyday world while simultaneously refusing to use the idea of "race" as an analytical *concept* when social scientists analyze the discourses and practices of the everyday world. It is not the *concept* of "race" that "continues to play a fundamental role in structuring and representing the social world" (Omi and Winant 1994:55) but rather the *idea* of "race," and the task of social scientists is to develop a theoretical framework for the analysis of this process of structuring and representing which breaks completely with the reified language of biological essentialism. Hence, we object fundamentally to Omi and Winant's project of developing a critical theory of the *concept* of "race" (1993:6-9) because we also recognize the importance of historical context and contingency in the framing of racialized categories and the social construction of racialized experiences (cf. Omi and Winant 1993:6): we believe that historical context requires us to criticize all concepts of "race," and this can be done by means of a concept of racialization. Omi and Winant's defence of the concept of "race" is a classic example of the way in which the academy in the U.S. continues to racialize the world.

Furthermore, the concept of racialization employed by Omi and Winant is not fully developed, nor do they use it in a sustained analytical manner, because it is grounded in "race relations" sociology, a sociology that reifies the notion of "race" and thereby implies the existence of "racial groups" as monolithic categories of existence. Additionally, they fail to take into account the impact of the social relations of production within the racialization process. We, on the other hand, advance the position that the process of racialization takes place and has its effects in the context of class and production relations and that the idea of "race" may indeed not even be explicitly articulated in the racialization process (see Miles 1989, 1993).

Conclusion

West begins the first essay in his book *Race Matters* with a reference to the Los Angeles riots of April 1992. He denies that they were either a "race riot or a class rebellion." Rather, he continues,

> ... this monumental upheaval was a multi-racial, trans-class, and largely male display of social rage ... Of those arrested, only 36 percent were black, more than a third had full-time jobs, and most claimed to shun political affiliation. What we witnessed in Los Angeles was the consequence of a lethal linkage of economic decline, cultural decay, and political lethargy in American life. Race was the visible catalyst, not the underlying cause. (1994:3-4)

And he concludes by claiming that the meaning of the riots is obscured because we are trapped by the narrow framework imposed by the dominant views of "race" in the U.S.

The *Los Angeles Times* Opinion Editor, Jack Miles, rendered a different version of the narrow framework of the black/white dichotomy. In an essay in the October 1992 issue of the *Atlantic Monthly* entitled "Blacks vs Browns," Miles suggested that Latinos were taking jobs that the nation, by dint of the historic crimes committed against them, owed to African Americans. He blamed Latinos for the poverty in African American communities – a gross misattribution of responsibility – while reinforcing "race" as a relevant category of social and analytical value. His confusion was revealing: the "two societies, one black, one white – separate and unequal" dichotomy made famous by the 1968 report of the National Advisory Commission on Civil Disorders cannot provide an analytical framework to deconstruct the post-Fordist racialized social relations of the 1990s.

The meaning of West's argument is constructed by what is not said as much as by what is. There is a silence about the definition of "race riot": presumably, the events of April 1992 would have been a race riot if the principal actors had been "blacks" and "whites." Hence, West refers only to "race" as the visible catalyst: Rodney King was "obviously black" and the policemen who arrested him were "obviously white."

But the riots themselves did not fit the race relations paradigm because the rioters and those who became the victims of the riot were not exclusively blacks and whites. Indeed, as the media were framing the events of April 1992 in black/white terms in the great melodrama of race relations, the first image across the airwaves was of men atop a car waving the Mexican flag! Thus, "Hispanic" may signify presumptively as "white" in the ethno-"racial" dynamics that rest on a system of neat racialized categories, but this has little to do with the popular understanding and experience of Latinos. The outcome of such practices has led to superficial analysis of the full impact of the riots within the context of a changing political economy. The analytical task is therefore to explain the complex nature of the structural changes associated with the emergence of the post-Fordist socio-economic landscape and the reconfigured city's racialized social relations.

Perhaps half of the businesses looted or burned were owned by Korean Americans and another third or so were owned by Mexican Americans/Latinos and Cuban Americans. Those engaged in the looting and burning certainly included African Americans, but poor, recent, and often undocumented immigrants and refugees from Mexico and Central America were equally prominent. Of those arrested, 51% were Latinos and 36% were African Americans. And, of those who died in the civil unrest, about half were African Americans and about a third were Latinos. All this is only surprising if one begins with the assumption that the events were or could have been "race riots." But such an assumption is problematic for two reasons.

First, academics, media reporters, and politicians "conspired" to use the vocabulary of "race" to make sense of the Los Angeles riots because it is a central component of everyday, commonsense discourse in the U.S. And when it became overwhelmingly apparent that it was not a black/white riot, the language of "race" was nevertheless unthinkingly retained by switching to the use of the notion of "multiracial" in order to encompass the diversity of historical and cultural origins of the participants and victims. Therefore while the race relations paradigm was dealt a serious blow by the reality of riots, the vocabulary of "race" was retained. But – and here we find the source of West's unease – the idea of "race" is so firmly embedded in common sense that it cannot easily encompass a reference to Koreans or Hispanics or Latinos, for these are neither black nor white. It is thus not surprising that pundits and scholars such as West stumble over "racial" ambiguity. The clash of racialized language with a changing political economy presents challenges for scholars and activists alike.

Second, if one had begun with an analysis grounded simultaneously in history and political economy rather than with the supremely ideological notion of race relations, one would have quickly concluded that the actors in any riot in central Los Angeles would probably be *ethnically* diverse. Large-scale inward migration from Mexico and Central America and from southeast Asia into California has coincided with a restructuring of the Californian economy, the loss of major manufacturing jobs, and large-scale internal migration within the urban sprawl of "greater" Los Angeles, with the consequence that the spatial, ethnic, and class structure that underlay the Watts riots of 1965 had been transformed into a much more complex set of relationships. The most general conditions were structural in nature, and thus the decline and shift in the manufacturing base in Los Angeles was not unique but represented a shift in the mode of capital accumulation worldwide (from Fordist to Flexible). In order to analyze those relationships, there is no need to employ a concept of "race": indeed, its retention is a significant hindrance. But it is also necessary to draw upon the insights consequent upon the creation of the concept of *racisms*. The complex relationships of exploitation and resistance, grounded in differences of class, gender, and ethnicity, give rise to a multiplicity of ideological constructions of the racialized Other. For, while the idea of "race" does not matter outside the process of racialization, to which academics are active contributors, the racisms employed in Los Angeles and elsewhere to naturalise, inferiorize, exclude, and sustain privilege certainly *do* matter.

References

Banton, M. (1967). *Race Relations*. London: Tavistock.
___. (1987). *Racial Theories*. Cambridge: Cambridge University Press.
Barkan, E. (1992). *The Retreat of Scientific Racism: Changing Concepts of Race in Britain and the United States Between the Wars*. Cambridge: Cambridge University Press.
van den Berghe, P.L. (1978). *Race and Racism: A Comparative Perspective*. New York: John Wiley.
Blauner, B. (1992). "Talking Past Each Other: Black and White Languages of Race," *The American Prospect*. 10: 55-64.

Essed, P. (1991). *Understanding Everyday Racism: An Interdisciplinary Theory.* Newbury Park, Cal.: Sage.

Fields, B.J. (1990). "Slavery, Race and Ideology in the United States of America," *New Left Review* 181: 95-118.

Fredrickson, G.M. (1981). *White Supremacy.* New York: Oxford University Press.

Gilroy, P. (1987). *"There Ain't No Black in the Union Jack": the Cultural Politics of Race and Nation.* London: Hutchinson.

Goldberg, D. T. (1990). "The Social Formation of Racist Discourse." In D.T. Goldberg (ed.), *Anatomy of Racism.* Minneapolis: University of Minnesota Press.

____. (1993). *Racist Culture: Philosophy and the Politics of Meaning.* Oxford: Blackwell.

Guillaumin, C. (1972). *L'Idéologie Raciste.* Paris: Mouton.

____. (1995). *Racism, Sexism, Power and Ideology.* London: Routledge.

hooks, b. (1990). *Yearning: Race, Gender and Cultural Politics.* Boston: South End Press.

Joshi, S. and, Carter, B. (1984). "The Role of Labour in the Creation of a Racist Britain." *Race and Class* 25(3): 53-70.

Karenga, M. (1993). *Introduction to Black Studies.* Los Angeles: University of Sankore Press.

Katznelson, I. (1976). *Black Men, White Cities.* Chicago: University of Chicago Press.

Layton-Henry, Z. (1992). *The Politics of Immigration.* Oxford: Blackwell.

Lerner, M. and, West, C. (1995). *Jews and Blacks: Let the Healing Begin.* New York: G.P. Putnam's Sons.

Lieberman, L. (1968). "The Debate Over Race: A Study in the Sociology of Knowledge."*Phylon.* 39: 127-41.

Miles, R. (1982). *Racism and Migrant Labour: A Critical Text.* London: Routledge and Kegan Paul.

____. (1984). "Marxism versus the 'Sociology of Race Relations.' *Ethnic and Racial Studies* 7(2): 217-37.

____. (1989). *Racism.* London: Routledge.

____. (1993). *Racism After "Race Relations."* London: Routledge.

Montagu, A. (1972). *Statement on Race.* London: Oxford University Press.

Omi, M. and Winant, M (1993). "On the Theoretical Status of the Concept of Race." In C. McCarthy and W. Crichlow (eds.), *Race, Identity and Representation.* New York: Routledge.

(1994). *Racial Formation in the United States: From the 1960s to the 1990s*, 2nd. ed. New York: Routledge.

Rex, J. (1970). *Race Relations in Sociological Theory*. London: Weidenfeld and Nicolson.

Reynolds, L.T. (1992). "A Retrospective on 'Race': the Career of a Concept." *Sociological Focus*. 25(1): 1-14.

Roediger, D. (1994). *Towards the Abolition of Whiteness: Essays on Race, Politics and Working Class History*. London: Verso.

Small, S. (1994). *Racialized Barriers: The Black Experience in the United States and England in the 1980s London*. Routledge.

Solomos, J. (1989). *Race and Racism in Contemporary Britain*. London: Macmillan.

Sowell, T. (1994). *Race and Culture: A World View*. New York: Basic Books.

Wellman, D. (1993). *Portraits of White Racism*, 2nd. ed. Cambridge: Cambridge University Press.

West, C. (1994). *Race Matters*. New York: Vintage Books.

Wilson, W.J. (1987). *The Truly Disadvantaged*. Chicago: University of Chicago Press.

2

Racism, Biography, and Psychiatry

Caroline Knowles

Conceptualizing Racism

Racism is embedded in political discourses and actions (Knowles 1992, Back and Solomos 1992), in the procedures and practices of public and social policies (Cambridge and Feuchtwang 1990), in national identities (Feuchtwang 1992:129), and in the many forms of collective representation of the "other." Racism concerns the exclusions, the marginalization, and the social inequities attached to imagined collectivities and identified through the visibility of bodies. This paper explores, through the narratives of a black teacher living in Québec, some of the interconnections between two dimensions of racism: the administrative and the existential.

Administrative racism consists of a multifaceted series of "inventions of blackness" in which black lives feature as problematic in some way: as criminal, as insane, as in need of social welfare intervention, special provision and so on. Blackness itself has acquired an edifice of social meanings through racism, in the apparatuses through which black people are dealt with as problematic populations in racist societies. Narratives locating the social significance of blackness as an administrative invention are generated and sustained in professional practices. Thus this paper is concerned with psychiatry, and in passing with law and employment. Racism has existential dimensions which transcend its administrative details, and these are explored here through biography and individual testimony. Black lives, reconfigured in narrative, can be understood through the stories which are told about them (Ricoeur 1991:26, 31), and it is through narrative that the existential – ways of being – is played out. The lived dimensions of racism are not reducible to the administrative actions in which blackness is conceptualized and dealt with; an investigation of racism requires that it be grasped at the micro level, at the interface between the existential and the administrative. What does (administrative) racism at the micro level consist of? And how do black people interpret and live with this racism? For a white author to ask these questions of a black life is highly problematic. My co-author (William Kafe[1]) and I live on different sides of a significant social divide. While I re-arrange his life story, rendering it part of an analysis of racism, I benefit from the same social systems and practices which have excluded and abused him and which necessarily feature in my rendering of his story.[2]

Lived or existential racism takes many forms and operates at a dynamic interface with administrative racism. This paper shows how administrative racism is forced to negotiate the existential responses it invokes. Living with racism demands personal and political strategies by those directly involved. Some strategies are subtle and conciliatory and some are more confrontational, but all are forms of self-defence. In our research in Montreal[3] we have encountered people who deal with racism by wearing designer clothes, by educating themselves, by joking and teasing, by drawing on the strength of networks of friends and intimate relationships, by ignoring it, and also by a range of confrontational means, from vigilante action to legal redress. William Kafe lives at the confrontational end of this "lived racism" spectrum. The richness of his story lies in the multiple layers of administrative and popular racism it reveals, as well as in the interactive relationship between the administrative and the lived dimensions of racism. Kafe's strategy of self-defence, his response to living with racism, played an important part in intensifying the administrative actions and strategies which were used to deal with him.

Also forming an important part of the social and political context in which William Kafe lives is multiculturalism, an official, legislative response to the racial and ethnic plurality of Québécois and Canadian society, and something which is especially pertinent to the ethnic and cultural diversity of Montreal.[4] Legislated multiculturalism incorporates sentiments on human equality – diversity within a framework of equal rights – and is a central constituent of the official version of Canadian national identity:

> Whereas the Government of Canada recognizes the diversity of Canadians as regards race, national or ethnic origin, colour and religion as a fundamental characteristic of Canadian society and its commitment to a policy of multiculturalism designed to preserve and enhance the multicultural heritage of Canadians while working to achieve the equality of all Canadians in the economic, social, cultural and political life of Canada. (Canadian Multiculturalism Act 1988)

Official federal multiculturalism is significantly dissected by its "Québec version," which is more aggressively assimilationist in its construction and defence of Québec as a distinct society or nation-in-waiting. But the Québec variant of multiculturalism still respects the rights of minorities and is, therefore, at odds with the treatment of William Kafe. Legislated multiculturalism provides redress for those whose rights are violated. This legal apparatus ensuring human rights works – sometimes. William Kafe fought, and won, his racial harassment case through the Québec Human Rights Commission, yet Kafe's victory was a hollow one. He won his case but he has lost his job and will never again work as a teacher in Québec.

The problem with multiculturalism is that it really only supports the expression and celebration of private forms of difference: in family, food, religious conventions, and so on. It is an expression of "nation as a unity of human difference" which lacks a real conception of how tensions arising from those differences can be managed. It is a limited strategy which fails to admit a limitedness, which is constantly being revealed in practice, through debates around the acceptability of Muslim dress in schools or turbans at the legion, and in incidents of racial harassment, for example. Multiculturalism lacks a conception of power and because of this treats all symbols of difference as equally valid. It lacks a means of discussing which symbols and practices dominate crucial areas of social policy decision-making. Thus multiculturalism is also a limited strategy for dealing with racism. Although it stigmatizes the overt verbalization of racial bigotry and provides a limited means for its redress, the climate of political correctness it supports conceals, rather than confronts, popular feelings and beliefs about race. The fettered voice of racial bigotry is not long silenced by posturing on human rights; it breaks out verbally, physically, and administratively. As the story of William Kafe shows, Canadian and Québécois multiculturalism are an optimistic fantasy of human community.

William Kafe's Story: Racism and Resistance

William Kafe occupies a strategic point in a confluence of narratives about race. Three key narratives have a bearing on his situation: his conception of himself; dominant, shared, cultural images from the area about what it means to be "African"; and the narratives of the various psychiatrists who were asked to report on him, and who offer competing interpretations of his personality, competence, and "place" in Canadian society. This paper is about the ways in which Kafe's self-defence campaign against racial persecution became conceptualized as a dangerous form of madness in psychiatric narratives, issues to which we will return.

William Kafe's story of himself starts like this. He is a Ghanaian whose training as a Catholic priest brought him first to the United States and later (in 1969) to Montreal. After successfully pursuing a number of degrees in Canadian universities he took a job as a probationary high school teacher with the Deux Montagnes School Commission outside Montreal. But stories of the self have also to negotiate stories told by others. The most significant of these for our purposes are "categorical" stories which construe imagined groups of people in narrative – Africans, blacks, women, and so on – and which in the process invent notions of race, ethnicity, and culture. As a black African working in the education system of Oka (just outside of Montreal and, significantly, also the site of an earlier racialized struggle between native and other local people over the use of a burial ground for a golf course) where few other black people worked, Kafe was seen as "exotic." He draws upon this image in presenting himself as an African with a proud ancestral heritage, whilst at the same time acknowledging the consequences of exotica by also describing himself as "a poor citizen of Black African origin." It was clear from the start that Kafe would never be absorbed into the cultural landscape of Oka. The crucial issue is how he would negotiate his existence within it, an existence to which he was entitled by official multiculturalism, by Québec immigration policy which had permitted him entry, and by the Québec Code of Human Rights. What forms would his exclusion take? And how would he live with this exclusion? These are crucial questions in understanding racism in this (dynamic) context in which the existential and the administrative are always being reconfigured.

Kafe soon became enmeshed within a system of racially construed markers and exclusionary practices. These were organized almost "incidentally" in the schools in which he worked and by the school commissions which ran them. He experienced the refusal to constitute his probationary committee at the appropriate time; the repeated allocation to him of slow learners and disruptive students; untenable teaching loads spread over two sites; mix-ups over textbooks, which antagonized his students; and the refusal of the school management teams to confront the issue of racial violence and harassment, at various points both denied and acknowledged, in the schools in which he worked. Individually these are fairly ordinary things which can happen to any teacher in even the best-run schools. But their convergence upon one black teacher is highly suspicious. Racism in this case was incremental, cumulative, and embedded in the everyday "administrative" fabric of Kafe's professional life. Kafe himself sees his treatment as unfair discrimination by some, but not all, of those involved. He carefully distinguishes between colleagues and superiors who were helpful, and those who were indifferent or hostile.

The legitimation conferred by Kafe's treatment in the "administrative" apparatus of the local education system of Oka importantly sustained the daily explicit incidents of racial violence and harassment which Kafe suffered at the hands of students, and which he endured over a fifteen-year period. He gives moving testimony of some of these incidents, recognizing the extent to which they were management-supported:

> ... the principal also supported a student who gave me blows all the way from the third floor to his own office on the ground floor. He also refused to punish the student who flooded my classroom with fire extinguishers shouting 'Pour inonder le nègre' and held my tie and pulled me around like a dog.... The horrible barbaric things he (principal of one of the schools) did to me are beyond description ... like my whole self was destroyed by what was going on there.

Kafe also recalls being shouted down in class by students asserting "You are not supposed to be my teacher, you are supposed to be my slave. Didn't you watch *Roots*?" He remembers being kicked to shouts of "If the nigger dies what does it matter?" Another common chant was "Nigger crisis; the niggers are everywhere." His students once took soap and a face cloth to scrub away the blackness because "blacks are dirty." The message was unequivocal: "We don't want a black teacher; do you understand?"

What do we learn from these routine ugly instances about popular racism? Kafe's presence had unleashed local white fears about blackness as invasion, servility, and dirt. He was confronted with categorical, cultural narratives: others' views of him which spelled out some of the social significance invented around blackness, and which significantly contradicted his notions of a proud African heritage as well as notions of Human Rights embedded in the multiculturalism act. Kafe's adolescent students were giving voice to what was unspoken in the adult world around them. Theirs was the raw voice of racial hostility which is either unconscious of, or unconcerned with, the posturing on human rights required by political correctness. The voice that could, unselfconsciously, shout "brûle le nègre" is the voice of local popular racism which is fuelled by white fantasies and fears about blackness, and which is sometimes silenced by official multiculturalism.

Kafe's story reveals multiple dimensions of racism. It shows how racial harassment, exclusion, and marginalization were embedded in the daily practices around which his teaching career revolved. His story also indicates points of contestation and convergence negotiated around cultural, administrative, and "self" narratives. In Kafe's own account racism is construed ambiguously as a litany of abuses and mistreatment as well as an unspeakable, shadowy horror.[5]

The multiple dimensions of racism with which Kafe's professional life was enmeshed intensified with his resistance. His adoption of a policy of self-defence is highly significant in the generation of narratives offering alternative explanations of him, and in organizing the social consequences of those narratives. He contested his treatment by his employers through the teachers' union. He brought and won a case against the School Commission at the Québec Human Rights Commission in 1993. He managed to publicize his case, co-operating in a television documentary, and seems to have had sporadic support from the Ghanaian and other black "cultural communities" organizations, as they are known in Québec. All of this activity has generated the extraordinary archive of written records, reports, tape recorded conversations, videotapes, and interviews which have made it possible for me to write this story of his story. Indeed, his story is an archive of racism in Québec.

But Kafe's resistance to racism had two significant consequences in his personal biography. It led the School Commission to redouble its efforts to get rid of him, and this in turn led to an intensification of stress and depression, the consequent deterioration of his health, and increasingly lengthy absences from work. Both of these consequences led Kafe to the domain of psychiatric reporting. The story of how Kafe became an object of psychiatric scrutiny shows clearly the operation of this form of administrative racism and its interface with lived experience.

Psychiatrization and the Lived Experience of Racism

Kafe's story is bound up with three strands of psychiatric investigation. The first was a personal one, initiated by Kafe's decision to consult a black psychiatrist whom he trusted, to guide him through the stress and depression symptoms produced by his rapidly deteriorating working conditions. He says of these:

> I was very much sick, physically weak ... the school board was harassing me so much, I use the word torture but people in this part of the world don't like that word because it is too strong ... feeling weak, feeling anguished, sometimes my voice is choked, sometimes they [students] throw objects at me and I have bruises with blood sometimes.... I wasn't the same person, even physically, always very weak, having difficulty to sleep, concentration was very low.

Kafe's own account of his health powerfully makes the point that existentially the consequences of racial abuse are played out in the terrain of personal sanity and health.

The second and third strands can be treated together and arise from the elaborate system of psychiatric reporting required by the School Commission to cover Kafe's periods of absence. Looking for grounds to terminate his employment, the School Commission instigated psychiatric investigations to determine whether he was competent to teach, arguing that it was his poor teaching skills and not racial abuse which led to his confrontations with students. Realizing that this was the School

Commission's strategy, the teachers' union instigated a third round of psychiatric consultations to counteract any adverse findings by the School Commission and to mount a defence of Kafe on psychiatric grounds. As a result of this Kafe was, by 1985, the object of extensive psychiatric scrutiny which generated a series of narratives exploring his personality, his actions, and his relationship to Québec society. More of this later.

Kafe felt intense frustration at being an object of such scrutiny. This, combined with his lengthening periods of absence from work, his poor health, and an increasing sense that he was being abused by a society which also refused to "hear" him, culminated in a desperate letter sent to various Montreal officials headed "Please help avoid a shooting rampage in Verdun." This letter threatened the life of the School Commission's psychiatrist, Guérin, whom Kafe saw as construing him as "mad," something which would have important and serious career consequences. A peculiar combination of local circumstances ensured that this letter was taken to indicate that Kafe was dangerous. Arrested and refused bail on the (contested) psychiatric evidence of dangerousness, Kafe subsequently spent four months in secure psychiatric detention. During this time the psychiatric reporting on him refocused from an investigation of his competence to teach to an investigation of the danger he posed to Québec society. At his trial, in a bizarre juxtaposition of circumstances, Kafe was found guilty of threatening behaviour. He had already been fired by the School Commission and had won his case at the Québec Human Rights Commission. His career as a school teacher in Canada is over and he no longer wishes to live here. He is currently serving a two-year suspended sentence which requires him to see a psychiatrist, implicitly identifying him as mad and potentially dangerous. The consequences of this decision have altered not only Kafe's life, but also the way he himself perceives his life.

Indeed, Kafe's life story as he tells it has been reconfigured to become the story of his treatment by the Deux Montagnes School Commission and its supporting cast of legal and psychiatric personnel. All of his self stories now connect with this all-consuming drama. But as he tells his story his narrative style is depersonalized. He tells it as though he were talking about someone else, recounting the "facts" point by point in the mode of a courtroom presentation. The facts are the pieces of evidence – tape-recorded conversations with officials at the school board or the union, letters and reports written by psychiatrists, and so on. However, his legalistic presentation does not betray the litany of abuse, professional humiliation, and pain he has suffered; on the contrary, his personal and video-taped appearances convey the impression of someone in shock: the victim of some horrible accident. His story has a strict temporal and thematic organization which hinges on the sequential actions of key protagonists and events and which cannot be disrupted. To whom is he speaking as he is telling his story? He is at various points addressing "Québec society," "Canadian society," and "the entire humanity of the globe," thus garnering a "listening" constituency of those who are opposed to social injustice.

There are three central themes of Kafe's story embedded in his documentation of key events. First, Kafe has a distinct sense of the differences in racial terms between himself and the majority community in Québec. His narrative contains an ambiguous and multifaceted conceptualization of race which is both highly individual and personal, but which at the same time draws on the collectivity of blackness, the categorical. He speaks of the "black race" as though races had an ontological existence as sub-categories of humanity. He refers to himself as "African" and speaks of his "ancestors" and his "black mother," category memberships to which he is in various ways connected. Race in his narrative is also individual and metaphysical. He speaks of society's attempts to annihilate, through medical and psychiatric persecution, his "black body" which he sees as the only concrete proof of human existence. In his videotape he presents a shocked black body detailing the facts of his persecution, the result of which is to deprive him of his "humanity," his "membership in the human race." Blackness here is the categorical sign for physical and spiritual annihilation:

> My human rights have been violated and my human dignity has been taken away. I have been reduced to an animal level. My spiritual, moral and physical life has been destroyed together with my reputation and my reason of being (rationality)... I want my human life back.

The second theme of Kafe's story concerns his own identity as a missionary, informed by his strong religious convictions and by biblical references from his early training in the priesthood:

> ... I tell myself we are not in the dark ages, we are in the 20th century and this [racism] should not go buried. I know that in Canada racism must be

kept in silence, you see and I say to myself I am not that kind of person, I gave myself a mission ..."

Kafe's "mission" was to stay and fight the School Commission and, later, the courts and psychiatrists. It is an honourable stand, not just for himself but for other black people living in Québec. It is a stand for which he has paid a high price with his health, career, living space, and peace of mind.

The third, also a religious theme, is the martyrdom of victimization. Kafe is victimized both by his students and by the broader "Québec society." This, supporting the missionary theme, demands that Kafe stay and "suffer" racial persecution. His narrative reveals the significance of religious thinking in the construction of himself and the political stance he took in adopting the more confrontational strategy of self-defence in place of the alternatives.

Grand Narratives of Psychiatry

The stories Kafe tells about himself take into account, sometimes by opposing and sometimes by incorporating, the professional, administrative, and popular stories told about him by others. These include stories about his competence as a teacher, his dangerousness, and some of the local and cultural associations and meanings attributed to blackness. The most powerful stories about Kafe, because they are used as a source of reference by other agencies and because of their potential outcomes, are those told by psychiatry.

The grand narratives[6] (Bernstein 1991:108-9, 113) of psychiatry occupy a central position in the social domain. They mobilize the power to judge individual competence, to name with diagnostic labels, and to "manage" with a pharmacological armoury. The mental pathologies named with diagnostic categories are social and historical productions invested with chronicity, dangerousness, incurability and so on (Barham 1984:22). Most importantly, for the purposes of this paper, psychiatric narratives are racialized social productions (Knowles 1991, Harrison et al. 1988, Bebbington et al. 1981, Fuller Torrey et al. 1987). Psychiatry contains a series of powerful, racialized narratives which dictate the terms on which certain lives will be lived and judged.

The psychiatric reports dealing with Kafe, of which there are more than twenty between 1985 and 1993, are a certain kind of narrative enterprise. They begin with previous psychiatric and medical judgments which are used to confirm or vary a diagnosis. Selected elements of Kafe's story are then retold in the third person along with the stories of others who provided alternate versions of "reality" against which the veracity of Kafe's story is checked. To this is added the psychiatrist's story; a brief review of his childhood and family life and the circumstances of his immigration are edited selections of his story deemed to have special significance. The psychiatrist's interpretation of the assembled stories precedes the diagnosis, which is the temporary end of the story. It is a delicate positioning of the mental pathology in its social context, a positioning from which treatment can proceed.

In diagnosing Kafe, psychiatrists had to make sense of his story of racial persecution. Was this the story of a rational or a deluded mind? None of the psychiatrists who examined Kafe was Ghanaian or even African,[7] and none of them reported any anxiety about being able to interpret his story and his subsequent behaviour.

Competence as a teacher

Because of the way his story developed Kafe was a moving psychiatric target. Official psychiatric intervention initiated by the School Commission in 1985 was intended to assess his competence as a teacher: " ... the school board wanted to find out if I was mentally sick."

There are two contradictory stories concerning Kafe's competence as a teacher. His own story is that his absences were the result of the stress and consequent poor health caused by constant racial harassment in the classroom. In his letter of 25 December 1992, Kafe wrote:

> I have been the target of abominable racial harassment at work for over twelve years because the students don't want a black teacher and the school board have been supporting the students against me. I have also been the target of constant torture by the School Board ... a dehumanizing medical plot to turn me into a psychiatric patient for their own interest.

However, the School Commission's story was that Kafe's difficulties were those of a poor teacher trying to control his students. A great deal was at stake in establishing the veracity of these stories; for Kafe, his job held the key to his income, his lifestyle, and his occupational and personal identity. It is not clear why psychiatric, and not teaching expertise, was brought to bear on this issue of teaching competence. But psychiatric opinion held the key to Kafe's continued employment prospects, and such opinion was divided on the issue.

Majority psychiatric opinion supported Kafe's account of himself: that he was a victim of racial harassment and that this was a critical factor affecting his teaching, his health, and his subsequent absence record. Dr. Neree, a psychiatrist appointed by the School Commission, diagnosed anxiety depression arising from a stressful work situation: "The intensity of rejection and harassment of which he has been a victim, however have taken their toll on his health and ended up causing his problems of adaptation and defence" (Neree 1985).

Dr. Jean, a doctor appointed by the School Commission, concurred that his was "a complex case of depression and is complicated further by a delicate social problem [racism]," adding that Kafe's problem was not medical, but administrative, arising through his conflict with the School Commission (1988). Dr. Grégoire, objecting that "It is not up to me to evaluate Mr. Kafe's competence as a teacher," in line with the other School Commission-appointed psychiatrists, ruled out serious mental illness in part on the ground that Kafe's story was fully supported with evidence and validated by the Québec Human Rights Commission:

> Mr. Kafe does not seem to be a victim of severe mental illness accompanied by delirious ideas since most of the complaints that he is voicing are supported by written proofs or other types of documents and that an Inquiry of the Human Rights Commission has, to a certain degree, ruled in his favour. (Grégoire, 1989)

But the psychiatric (grand) narratives in which William Kafe was administratively invented as a "pathological" teacher were produced by Dr. Guérin, the threatened target of the "Verdun shooting rampage." Although Dr. Guérin had himself previously ruled out mental pathology, his diagnoses following Kafe's arrest for threatening behaviour were reconfigured to support his view that Kafe was dangerous. Guérin's delineation of the "normal" from the "pathological" hinged on the legitimate interpretation by a teacher of his students' behaviour.

> In his case, when they play dirty tricks on him, he interprets that as a sign of racism on the part of the children. Well this is his interpretation. Obvi-

ously, we cannot deny that the kids, undoubtedly use racist expressions ... this is inevitable and it is going on everywhere, but when this occurs with a normal teacher, he doesn't take it personally, he knows very well that it is part of the problems related to adolescence, and in turn, he treats them as discipline related problems and not as something personal. Whereas the paranoid takes this as a personal attack on his own person because he perceives himself as being greater than the others and consequently, he is more likely to be attacked or be the target of attacks. (Guérin 1993)

Kafe's pathology, then, consisted in his failure to see racial abuse in the way the psychiatrist sees it – as a "normal" dimension of adolescent behaviour. Just as Kafe was a shifting target for psychiatric assessment, the context of his psychiatric assessment had also significantly shifted. The veracity of contested accounts of Kafe's competence as a teacher was no longer being fought out between the teachers' union and the School Commission. The stakes were now somewhat higher: following Kafe's arrest, the judicial arena became the arbiter of conflicting psychiatric stories.

A number of psychiatrists could have given evidence at Kafe's trial, for by this time he had been an object of psychiatric scrutiny for over seven years with no hint of mental pathology. But the "star" expert witness at Kafe's bail hearing and subsequent trial was the psychiatrist whose story dominated other psychiatric stories; he was the psychiatrist who reported on Kafe to the School Commission, the psychiatrist whom he most mistrusted, the psychiatrist who was the target of his "threatening" letter, and the only psychiatrist to report that Kafe was delusional: the psychiatrist was Dr. Guérin.

The weight attached to Guérin's testimony raises important questions about the racism embedded in the Québec judicial system and its readiness to believe that a black man was, by the colour of his skin alone, to be considered dangerous.

Dangerousness

The crucial part of Guérin's construction of Kafe at this stage was no longer that he was a "pathological teacher" but that he was "dangerous." Dangerousness is construed through a diagnosis of delusion and paranoia, which had three key elements in Kafe's case.

First, as far as Guérin was concerned, "grandeur" was a key element in the diagnosis: "I noticed significant elements of grandeur.... Grandeur is always at the bottom of it" (1993). His evidence for this consisted of Kafe's insistence that he was well known as a teacher of English as a second language, and that he had given conference papers in other countries on issues of pedagogy, which indeed he has. Grandeur consists of an exaggerated or inappropriate self-importance. So what level of self-importance is permissible for a black immigrant teacher of English in Québec? And might not self-importance also be a form of self-defence from professional humiliation?

Excessive writing was seen as the second significant symptom of Kafe's pathology, a reference to his growing collection of documents relating to the case:

> What sergeant Poirier [the arresting police officer] explained to us earlier is that his apartment was full of documents. When they reach the acute phase, paranoids write a lot, they write and write and can write 60 page letters sometimes. (Guérin 1993)

Again the psychiatrist's assessment hinges on what constitutes appropriateness, and fails to take into account the situation in which Kafe finds himself. Kafe's collection of documents had proven to be an appropriate form of self-defence at the Québec Human Rights Commission, and at least one other psychiatrist had discounted paranoia because of the extent to which Kafe's story was supported by this kind of evidence.

The third and most significant element in the psychiatric construction of paranoia was Kafe's "over-interpretation" of the actions of others: "you could see there was a problem with his character ... he had a tendency to insinuate, to interpret things his way" (Guérin 1993). As with grandeur and excessive writing the difference between interpretation and over-interpretation is a matter of degree, and a matter on which the psychiatrist assumed the power of arbitration. Presumably over-interpretation is that which goes beyond authorial intent. The sources of authorial intent in question are Kafe's students and Guérin himself.

We have already seen in Guérin's construction of the "pathological teacher" his claim that racial harassment by Kafe's students is an expected, and, by implication, normal and acceptable feature of adolescence and the social context in which it operates. If paranoia is interpretation which goes beyond authorial intent, then it is not clear how Guérin is in a position to judge this from his interviews with Kafe, rather than with his students. Moreover, the claim that racism is a normal and acceptable feature of society in general, and of adolescent behaviour in particular, most certainly clashes with Canada's multiculturalist framework and contravenes Kafe's human rights, as the Québec Human Rights Commission judgement in his favour suggests. Furthermore, to assert that Kafe behaved unreasonably in objecting to racial abuse by his students is preposterous. By this logic the unofficial, operational version of Canadian multiculturalism is this: if you are lucky enough to be let in don't have the bad manners to complain about the way you are treated.

Most significant evidence of Kafe's paranoia was his "over- interpretation" of his consultations with Guérin himself. Kafe began to see Guérin as part of a "medical plot" to undermine his teaching career. In the reports which Guérin made it is clear that his "discovery" of paranoia parallels Kafe's increasing realization that Guérin himself was an important part of the reporting process which fed into the School Commission's deliberations about his future as a teacher. As Guérin was sending his reports to the School Commission, which was engaged in an effort to fire Kafe and contest his case at the Québec Human Rights Commission, Guérin is surely not denying his part in this drama. He must then be objecting to Kafe's refusal to see him as a "neutral" expert commentator on mental pathology. Is then the ultimate proof of madness the patient's failure to share the psychiatrist's view of himself?

Having established Kafe's pathology and its symptoms, at Kafe's bail hearing Guérin went on to describe his paranoia as a "capsuled delirium," one which "attacks certain restricted areas of the personality." Most importantly, Kafe's condition was pronounced both acute and incurable, recalling Barham's (1984) argument that diagnostic categories in mental illness are social productions invested with meaning and arrived at by reviewing psychiatric evidence in a particular way. Acuteness and incurability pave the way for the construction of dangerousness, which enters the narrative not through the paranoia itself but through the psychiatrist's clinical experience with "similar" cases.

> ... Mr. Kafe is like all paranoids who lose control ... there's a real danger of losing control of their behaviour and their emotions. The danger is significant then. It is a type of danger that is normally limited by time ... during the acute phase the level of danger is significant. (Guérin 1993)

Dangerousness also enters the narrative through a reference to the tragic consequences of failing to identify it.

> We know that these people do regrettable things in extreme cases. We have seen what Mr. Fabrikant[8] did not long ago, this is a similar case, a case of a guy who sees himself as a victim of society.... This is the same kind of pathology. (Guérin 1993)

Dangerousness, then, is what the psychiatrist "knows" and the public "fears." The right to assert dangerousness ultimately rests on the imagined social consequences of not doing so.

Incidentally, Kafe's account of his conversations with Dr. Guérin, who refused to allow Kafe to tape any of their sessions, are rather different. Referring to one meeting he says:

> During the so-called examination which lasted 15 minutes, he asked me some childish, unprofessional, irrelevant questions such as 'What will you do if you lose in court?' 'Do you really think that I want to destroy you?' Since I refused to answer these questions, he said that I was not in my right mind.

Race and Diagnosis

Racism is central to the psychiatric narratives of this case which hinge on the appropriateness of Kafe's behaviour. Race and racism feature in ambiguous and contradictory ways in both the silences and the explicit statements which surround the investigation of "dangerous paranoia." Guérin's strategy was to deny the centrality of racism as an issue. His narrative carefully avoids racialization, although dangerousness emerges from the silences in his narrative as implicitly black. He advances two contradictory theories of racism.

First, racism is embedded in the everyday and is therefore unremarkable: "we all know that racism exists so there isn't anything bizarre in that *per se*." But racism also features as the fantasy of a black delusional mind: "... one has to understand that to him [to Kafe, but not, by implication, to anyone else] this [being a victim of racism] is a reality" (Guérin 1993). So racism is at once an unremarkable feature of the social fabric *and* the substance of a paranoid delusion. It is, indeed, an ambiguous resource which can be deployed in any number of constructions of blackness. What links these contradictory interpretations is the inappropriateness of responding. It would be equally absurd to respond to something which was either unremarkably common or the product of a deluded mind. Self-defence from racial hostility with its attendant notions of self- and social worth, the documentation of incidents of racial harassment, and the interpretation of the acts of others as racist – these all emerge from this narrative as a diagnosable psychiatric pathology with some very serious consequences.

Guérin's diagnosis, his conception of racism, and the legitimacy of responding to racism through self-defence were all contested by other psychiatric assessments. For some of the psychiatrists involved in this case racism described a legitimate, lived experience with important psychological and political consequences.

> ... he admitted to being very sensitive to the general issues and problems affecting the Black population in society in general, and to his own experience as a 'Nigger.' He seems to have had the impression that his opportunities were limited because of his race and that it was his duty to defend himself as a victim. This is in part what propelled him to take legal action with the teachers' union, with the commission itself and with the Human Rights Commission ... This was as if his duty to stand up and defend the Black race was more important than his individual right to protect himself against persecution. (Sanchez 1993)

In this psychiatrist's assessment, dangerousness is construed as vulnerability, and racial disadvantage and harassment as a provocation of inner suffering. Dr. Sanchez further suggests that becoming a target for racial abuse inflicted "an important narcissistic wound" which could only be healed by "being heard." Part of being heard required self-defence, which was an understandable, even "healing," political reaction to the "interior" effects of racism which left him feeling "devalued and insulted."

Conclusion

William Kafe's story offers significant insights into the life of a black school teacher in Québec, a life lived at a particular administrative/existential interface. The administrative and popular racial abuse Kafe suffered was embedded in the everyday social relationships and practices of school education. There was the overt and crude racial taunting and physical attacks of his students which became embedded in a dispute about appropriate teacher-student relationships and behaviour codes. There was the complicity of the school management team in failing to confront this behaviour. There was the day-to-day administration of the school which added layers of difficulty to Kafe's already stressed professional life. And there was the failure of the higher level of school management to confront the source of Kafe's ill health and absences from school.

Psychiatry took up this dispute in a particular way. At each stage in this story there is a dynamic reconstruction of events and significance as blackness and black self-defence acquire further layers in an edifice of social meanings. Psychiatry consists of contested accounts of the individual which make use of racial and cultural markers in different ways, and certainly this story suggests that a central problem for psychiatry is racism and not simply cultural difference. Psychiatric diagnoses are racialized social productions in which racial markers can be deployed in any number of ways to understand, to accommodate or to punish black people. There is evidently no single way in which race is deployed and construed in psychiatric narratives.

From William Kafe's story we learn how racial demarcations and distinctions operate in the minutiae of the social fabric. In employment practices, in the unions, in psychiatry, and in the judicial system, racial demarcations are invented around practices which have nothing essentially to do with race but which, although contested, provide the opportunity for the unequal treatment of black people. All of these practices are obvious targets for social reform. Kafe could have emerged from this as the victim in a narrative of racial persecution. Instead he was administratively and popularly constructed as a (black) troublemaker and a poor teacher who was mad and dangerous. Kafe's story casts a critical light upon many dimensions of the social. It points to the need to reform the way psychiatry operates with black patients. It points to the need to reform the centrality of psychiatry as an authoritative voice in a web of social practices. And most of all it points to the pressing need to confront racism throughout our education system in Québec. Kafe's narrative, in other words, holds up a mirror to Québec society into which we are entitled to look with a certain discomfort.

Personal, biographical narrative offers an existential dimension in the analysis of race. Kafe tells us what effect racism had on his health, his body, his dignity, and his humanity in a way which no other more abstracted form of analysis can. In his story we see a number of encounters between the administrative practices of racism and the effect this has on a life. Racial demarcation has an ontological reality in his narrative: it invokes the moments in which the inhumanity of whiteness is made explicit, the moments in which it negates the humanity of blackness. In deciding to contest this and defend himself (other black teachers have resigned in a similar position), William Kafe powerfully confronts us with the myth that Québec is a multicultural society in which the rights of minorities are protected.

Acknowledgements

I would like to thank William Kafe for the time he took to tell us his story and for his tolerance of what this analysis has "done" to that story. For someone's life story to be wielded as support for an analysis of racism is to do it a great injustice, and for this I apologize. I should like to thank Olivia Rovenescue and Clifford Ruggles for introducing me to William Kafe, and for the numerous discussions of Montreal race politics. Pascale Annoual did much of the research which made it possible to write this paper as well as offering comments and suggestions. I also thank David Mofford for his comments and suggestions and Francine Robillard for her work on the manuscript. Finally, I should like to thank the Social Science and Humanities Research Council and Concordia University for financial support.

Notes

1. The usual conditions of anonymity are not applied in this paper. William Kafe wanted this story to be told using his real name and the real names of the psychiatrists involved. Their reports are, anyway, now matters of public record.
2. Unlike in papers where the identities of informants are disguised I negotiated the evolving contents of this paper with William Kafe. My concerns were twofold: that the story as I retold it was accurate in terms of key event sequences and details, and that he would still recognize this as "his" story. As the paper developed the analysis of racism to some extent eclipsed the life story on which it is based. As William Kafe expressed it in a letter to me (16.11.94) "Your work is not aimed at telling the story as such, but it is rather critical analysis." This story, then, is the product of contradictory objectives; his was to give an account of a particular part of his own life and

mine was to make an analysis of racism. William Kafe has been generous in accommodating my agenda, and I am aware that in rendering his life story a part of an analysis of racism I do it a great injustice.
3. Interviews with black psychiatric nurses about their work and lived experiences of racism were conducted in Montreal by Pascale Annoual during 1994.
4. The population of Montreal which contains the bulk of all recent (black) immigrants to Québec and most of the Anglophone population is demographically quite distinct from the Québec population as a whole which is 85% (white) Francophone.
5. Videotape produced by Kafe, 1993.
6. Bernstein (1991:107-8) says that grand narratives are interpretations of a special sort – impossible positions (racial identities) from which we must speak and act, and the "excesses" through which humanity explains itself in the slow exposure of meaning.
7. The appointment of a Ghanaian psychiatrist from Toronto was blocked.
8. Valery Fabrikant is the Concordia University professor who shot dead four other professors and injured a secretary in August 1992. Part of the debate which subsequently erupted was about the need to predict this kind of dangerousness through behaviour signs and psychological testing. This case has no connection at all with William Kafe save in the narratives of the psychiatrist Guérin who used this reference to convince a court that Kafe too could be dangerous.

References

Back, L., and J. Solomos (1992). "Black Politics and Social Change in Birmingham, U.K.: An Analysis of Recent Trends." *Ethnic and Racial Studies* 15.

Barham, P. (1984). *Schizophrenia and Human Values*. Oxford: Blackwell.

Bebbington, P.E., *et al.* (1981). "Psychiatric Disorders in Selected Immigrant Groups in Camberwell." *Social Psychiatry* 16:43-51.

Bernstein, J.M. (1991). "Grand Narratives." In David Wood (ed.), *On Paul Ricoeur*. London: Routledge.

Cambridge, A.X., and S. Feuchtwang, (eds.) (1990). *Antiracist Strategies*. Aldershot: Avebury.

___. (1992). Conclusion. *Where You Belong*. Aldershot: Avebury.

Canadian Multiculturalism Act (1988). Revised Statutes of Canada vol. 24, 4th Supplement. Ottawa: The Queen's Printer.

Fuller Torrey, E. (1987). "Prevalence Studies in Schizophrenia." *British Journal of Psychiatry* 15:598-603.

Grégoire, M. (1989, Jan. 17). Psychiatric Assessment of William Kafe.

Guérin, M. (1993, Mar. 9). Psychiatric Evidence, Bail Hearing for William Kafe.

Harrison, G., *et al.* (1988). "A Prospective Study of Severe Mental Disorders in Afro-Caribbean Patients." *Psychological Medicine.* 18:643-657.

Jean, C.F. (1988, March). Medical Evaluation of William Kafe.

Knowles, C. (1991). "Afro-Caribbeans and Schizophrenia: How Does Psychiatry Deal with Issues of Race, Culture and Ethnicity?" *Journal of Social Policy* 20(2):172-190.

___. (1992). *Race, Discourse and Labourism*. London: Routledge.

Neree, A. (1985, Nov. 14). Psychiatric Evaluation of William Kafe.

Ricoeur, Paul (1991) 'Life in Quest of Nawatwe' David Wood (ed.) *On Paul Ricoeur*. London: Routledge.

Sanchez, M.A. (1993, Apr. 7). Psychiatric Evaluation of the Admission of William Kafe to the Philippe Pinel Institute.

3

Homing Devices

Phil Cohen

> *All that defines a reticular space – where everyone for a time is master of their niche, and where each centre, distributed, produces its local power by identification inside and expulsion outside, where every group is found in its place, is not only a moral precept, or a truth value, but everything that delights or disquiets the body.*
>
> ∽ MICHEL SERRES, *The Parasite*

The Hearth of the Nation

The work of Benedict Anderson (1983) has helped us to recognize some of the more intimate registers through which imagined communities of "race" and "nation" are lived through in everyday life. Reading the newspaper, listening to the radio, or watching TV, in the apparent "privacy" of one's own home – it is in these small quiet moments of "withdrawal," as much as in the grand occasions and narratives of history that the work of nation-building goes on. And this should maybe alert us to the fact, which has perhaps been insufficiently explored, that domestic metaphors and images of privacy are frequently used in constructing common-sense arguments for the exclusion of those who are held not to belong within the public domains of the body politic.

Here is a typical example:

> This great influx is driving out the native from hearth and home. Some of us have been born here. Others have come here when they were quite young children, have been brought up and educated here. Some of us have old associations here of such a nature that we feel it hard to be parted from them. And all this is being jeopardized by those who come amongst us with their alien ways, and who dare to claim our native heath as their own.

This statement was made in 1880 against Jewish immigration into the East End of London, but similar sentiments were being voiced against the Bangladeshi community in the same area a century later, and indeed this refrain can be heard in every European country, when and wherever resentment is expressed by self-proclaimed "natives" against immigrants and ethnic minorities.

The power of this kind of statement derives in part from the ease with which the boundaries of state and nation are pinned to those of the neighbourhood and family within the single rhetorical space of race. The elision between hearth and heath, inside and outside, native and nature, is produced through a succession of homely images, the fond memories of happy childhoods blurring into the nostalgic reminiscences of old age, an organic image of life and landscape now threatened by the alien presence.

What is conveyed by these means is a pervasive sense of privacy invaded as well as of tradition undone, and this is intimately connected to the gendering of the metaphor. If women's place is "in the home," then the man's place is clearly to be out there protecting her from unwelcome visitors of the opposite sex. The "hearth" which is being protected signifies the man's place in the home – metaphorically, the "home fires" of his sexual passion which it is the wife's duty to keep burning, and in a more literal sense, a place of repose after the day's labours. It is this "productive erasure" of women's work from the male discourse of home which makes possible the focusing of desires on the possession/protection of the female sex. The gendering of home, its invention as a space of threatened privacy and public intervention, is a necessary condition for its mobilization in discourses of racism and nationalism, and these discourses in turn reinforce the patriarchal closure.

In France, Jean-Marie Le Pen makes constant use of domestic imagery:

> Imagine that you have forgotten your house keys. You go home and find a family of immigrants sleeping on your floor. What do you do? Call the police, of course, and have them removed.

This homely analogy between domestic and public order has a precise and brutal aim: to secure popular support for a program of forcible repatriation by playing on the anxieties associated with losing one's own home. It is calculated to win the sympathy of respectable and well-to-do householders who may well be inclined to dissociate themselves from the actions of the storm troopers who firebomb the homes of those targeted as "undesirable aliens." Yet the message is the same in both cases: foreigners go home.

There are two senses of home being invoked here; one relates to the nation as a homeland, a place of birth which is also a politico-legal identity based on some invented tradition of exclusive ethnic origin, a locus of *jus soli*. The other sense belongs to a discourse in which race functions as a primordial way of being at home in one's own body, while trying to make the Others feel uncomfortable in theirs. Here we have the locus of *jus sanguine* as an imagined community of kith and kin.

The evocation of home does not have to be confined to these terms, of course. Indeed, the multiplicity of meanings and diversity of investments which are today concentrated in the word militate against its permanent annexation by any one ideology. Nevertheless there are aspects of this image complex which lend it to processes of racialization or nationalization.

Marx was one of the first to point out the role which the private abode plays as a safe haven for asylum seekers and refugees from the storms and stresses of everyday life in the marketplaces of capitalism. He did not perhaps anticipate the extent to which daydreams of the domestic interior would become furnished through the most advanced technologies of popular consumption to fabricate not just ideal homes but also the social desirability of whole neighbourhoods. Nor did he imagine in his wildest nightmares the extent to which every Englishman's home would remain his castle, or at least some scaled-down approximation in the form of a suburban villa or cottage. We only have to look as far as the advertisements in yesterday's papers or on TV to see the domestic seat of ancient liberties (if not the New Jerusalem) being built again upon a largely feudal, or at least pre-industrial, idyll of England's green and pleasant land, now postmodernized throughout with the latest gadgetry of do-it-yourself individualism.

If it were not for the pervasive idealization of the home in such terms, the rhetoric of homely racism would lose much of its popular appeal. As it is, domestic metaphors have become increasingly important devices for elaborating scenarios of racial threat in which the barbarians have already broken and entered the gates, invaded the privacy of the master bedroom, occupied and laid waste desirable residential areas, before finally besieging and occupying the citadels of power.

Race and Space

This kind of topography entails a specific racialization of space. For example, it involves the colour-coding of particular residential areas, housing estates, or public amenities as "white" or "black" in a way which often homogenizes ethnically diverse neighbourhoods and turns relative population densities into absolute markers of racial division. This process is usually articulated through images of confrontation – "front lines," "no-go areas," and the like – which serve to orchestrate moral panics about "invasion" and "blacks taking over."

These can become self-fulfilling prophecies when they also entail a spatialization of "race." In this case structural inequalities of resource and access become metaphors of racial location, in a way that both legitimates and perpetuates processes of discrimination. What the Rookeries did to the Irish and the Ghetto to Jews in the Victorian city, the "Inner City" now does to Blacks. Initially constructed as sites of internal regulation over "dangerous" or migrant populations, they also serve as informal exclusion zones for the rest of society. But what turns these areas into places of entrapment within cycles of degradation and despair for so many of their inhabitants are the very strategies of self-improvement and social amelioration which are introduced to enable a minority within the ethnic minority to move outwards and upwards into the wider society.

For even (and especially) when this relatively affluent, socially mobile, faction remains locally "in place," in private rather than public housing, their very presence may serve less as an example *pour encourager les autres* than as an incitement to crime amongst those who remain disadvantaged. Under these conditions the project of turning defensible spaces into training grounds for more collective and political ambitions becomes all too easily displaced into local demarcation disputes over spheres of influence.

On the other side of the tracks, the phenomenology of white flight follows an even more complicated pattern of meaning. The term itself is something of a dangerous misnomer, since it tends to conjure up an image of panic-stricken white residents driven out of "their areas" by a black "invasion," legging it to the safety of the suburbs. In fact what is usually involved is a calculated move on the part of those involved to reinvent traditions of white territorial dominance associated with "old" working-class neighbourhoods; at the same time, they shift from public to private housing and join the imagined community of the middle class.

If home is where the heart is, it is also where structures of national and racial sentiment are connected to daydreams of self-empowerment. Such dreams are associated with having a "property," which holds the connotation of permanent and desirable residence, as opposed to living in a "dwelling," which does not. We must remember that today housing has taken on all the symbolisms of the body and psyche; external physical features and address are primary markers of social status, while the interior has become a site for the expression of individual personality. Amongst other things, this makes possible a process of splitting whereby the external environment can come to be seen as uniformly undesirable and dangerous; meanwhile, behind the symbolic lace curtains, "personal standards are maintained." The sense of home shrinks to that space where some sense of inherent "order and decency" can be imposed on that small part of a chaotic world which the subject can directly own and control. At the same time, for those who do not own their own homes, and do not exert any real control over the political ecology of their neighbourhood, the issue of "who belongs" directly resonates with the question "Who rules round here, Us or Them?"

In all these ways, the idealization of the domestic interior as a space of privatized transcendence serves to intensify the racialization of public space. There comes a point, however, when the social stigma associated with living in what has come to be seen as a "black area" overcomes the internally defended "white space." In the folklore of white flight this moment is often reached as a result of some traumatic incident, a mugging or break-in which is attributed by gossip or rumour to blacks. It is at this point, where the split can no longer be maintained, *and precisely in order to maintain it elsewhere, on a more global scale,* that people pick up and go. What they are fleeing from is not "black muggers" but that home truth. When they arrive in their new white space, it is only to discover that everywhere outside "the blacks have taken over."

Michael Balint (1974) has provided us with a useful model for mapping some of these processes. He suggests there are two basic kinds of imaginary geography. In the first the environment is experienced as a basically friendly and supportive site of personal exploration, but also as containing within it certain zones which are dangerous or forbidden, and which may be treated as a source of fear, fascination, and risk-taking. In the second kind of space the environment is felt to be basically hostile and dangerous, but within it there are certain sites which are safe from attack. Survival consists in moving as quickly as possible from one safe place to another, taking a risk in trying to enlarge the boundaries of the safe home base.

How does this work in terms of the racialization of space? Space might correspond to a situation where a white working-class community feels it is basically in control of its neighbourhood, but there are certain places within it which have been colonized by "immigrant" populations (certain street corners or cafés, corner shops or pubs). But from the perspective of the "immigrants" the situation is the opposite. What the whites construct as dangerous no-go areas or "breeding grounds of vice and crime," are for them warm and friendly places, defensible spaces carved out of a basically hostile racist environment. Now there may be some whites who will feel especially drawn to these black territories. Out of a mixture of bravado and resentment they seek to invade these spaces, either passively, by trying to adopt their habits or characteristics, or aggressively, by attacking and trying to drive out their inhabitants. In the course of this some of the whites may flip over into the second spatial mode and come to experience the whole area – and by extension the whole society – as having been taken over by blacks and transformed into a hostile and alien environment, while they themselves occupy small, "safe," all-white enclaves within it. This construction is closely related to the phenomenology of white flight which we have just discussed.

As these examples show, population flows and patterns of residential segregation are not the sum of individual consumer choices or the simple result of structures of discrimination impacting on market forces. The political ecologies of migration and settlement are traversed by landscapes of symbolic meaning which are themselves sedimentations of diverse material and cultural histories. But what role does the discourse of home play in the racialization of this process?

Safe as Houses / Living Room

Homely racism both makes and seeks to break the link between the general right of abode within a country, which is usually tied to universalistic definitions of citizenship, or denizenship, and the specific right of individuals to take up local residence, in terms of living in a particular area, or neighbourhood of their choice. In Britain that link is in principle (but not always in practice) substantive. The local state has the statutory obligation to house legal immigrants whose point of arrival in this country falls within their boundaries. In other countries there is no such coincidence. A permit of residence issued by the central state does not entail specific rights or obligations in respect of local housing or other social services. But while the question of specific legal entitlements is crucial for immigrants themselves, for those who see their very presence as an affront it signifies only the proverbial truism, "give them an inch and they'll take a mile."

Popular racism operates a legal fiction which assumes an absolute correspondence between the local and the global. The fact that a Bangladeshi or Moroccan family moves in next door or across the street is made to signify the migration of entire Muslim or Arab populations across borders on a national or international scale. And of course there is a whole image repertoire centred on the theme of promiscuity, breeding, and powers of social combination to underpin the assertion that to house one such family here today will mean having to live with a thousand like them tomorrow. Therefore, according to this perverse logic, to get that one family to move out of that flat or house is not only to free it for a white resident, it is to communicate a message to all who are defined as not British (or European) that they are not wanted here.

At the level of rhetorical realities, the imagery conjured up by the discourse of homely racism often makes connections between the language of reasonable and respectable racism, the racism which speaks of the need for cultural assimilation or the danger of swamping, and the violent aversive racism of "wogs go home." It does so according to what might be called a homespun philosophy of habitation which argues as follows:

> Our habits have developed over a long period, and have been formed by a privileged organic relation to our habitats. This indigenous status entitles us to priority. We were here first or at least before the others, and it is only fair that resources should be allocated on the basis of 'first come first served.' These others, with their foreign habits cannot claim any such privileged link to habitat. Irrespective of how long they have actually lived in the country they are squatters, people who have wilfully made themselves homeless by leaving their country of origin and who now occupy places in society which do not belong to them. Whatever the actual state of affairs, they are presumed to have no right to housing, residence, or any wider accommodation to their existence in civil society. They must never be allowed to settle, to establish a home away from home. And yet they have also already insinuated themselves into the most intimate and interior spaces of the political and domestic landscape, not only dispossessing their rightful inhabitants, but rendering familiar habitats unrecognizable by their alien way of life.

In my view even where no explicit reference is made to the problematics of home it remains an implicit, or hidden, anchorage of racialist argument. When, for example, the objection to immigration or the ethnic minority presence is couched in terms of its presumed effect on jobs, crime, or education (the old refrain "they are taking our jobs, our property, our exams"), there is always an underlying sense that an environment is being polluted, a generation disinherited, honour or habitat defiled. The implicit storyline is that once upon a time before these Others came, there was home, a secure world made perfect in our own image, as it will be again once they have been removed from our midst.

The rationale of homely racism is thus usually linked to the assertion or defence of relative privilege, but couched in the language of relative deprivation. It is founded on a deeply held belief in domestic order as the centre of social aspiration, and an equally profound sense that the indigenous are being deprived of their "natural" patrimony. If immigrants put down roots, if ethnic minorities make a home from home, then they are perceived to threaten the privileged link between habit and habitat upon which the myth of indigenous origins rests. If, on the other hand, they are forced to remain migrants, kept on the move through continual harassment and lack of legal protection or rights, then their "nomadism" makes them a threat to the stability of the social order. That is the vicious double bind at the heart of the injunction to "go home."

The irony of the injunction is that the "homelands" of these groups have been rendered uninhabitable either as a direct result of European colonization, or through civil wars generated by internal lines of division which are part of the colonial legacy. This should alert us to the fact that domestic metaphors are not confined to internal racisms, directed against immigrants or ethnic minorities in the "home country." They are equally present in the rhetorics of expansionist nationalism and settler colonialism. But this also obliges us to consider the reverse connection, the link between a certain imperial legacy and the intimate registers of homely racism which are now resurgent in the post-imperial era. And it is to this we must now turn.

Home but Not Alone, or Racism – Not in My Back Yard

The language of barricades and front lines, mobilizations, and "they shall not pass" seems to belong to another era, another kind of urban space, where large crowds were more than a collective pose for the mass media, but were direct agents of the historical process. Nevertheless, in a "postmodern" world supposedly dominated by global flows of human and cultural capital, where these kinds of political protest rooted in stable communities of local interest have supposedly been rendered obsolete, the most obdurate struggles continually break out in and around the front doors and back yards of whatever is called home. More often than not, people are arrested for obstruction and the bulldozers are sent in. Meanwhile the local itself has become a kind of global "non-place" realm; at stake are identities which transcend their immediate anchorage and become metaphors of membership in imagined communities whose networks of affiliation stretch across fixed boundaries and act at a distance from one side of the world to the other.

The centrality of the domestic interior to these rhetorics of local/global resistance might at first sight appear to be little more than an archaic survival, a nostalgic retrieve of a "world we have lost." But if we consider that the home, in its identification with the maternal body, and lap remains an irreducible paradigm of human scale, we can see its continued salience as a means of measuring up against economic and political forces which would otherwise appear overwhelming; it helps to cut them down to size. What I have called homely racism, and its philosophy of habitation, is thus fundamentally a humanism, a way of imposing an anthropomorphic model on a spatial economy which obeys quite other principles. The question is this: are there alternative ways of doing the same thing?

The popularity of the recent *Home Alone* movies gives us some indication of which way the wind is blowing. The story line of the first movie in the series is simple: In the rush to go on vacation a family living in an affluent suburb leave their youngest son behind. At first he is jubilant at the sudden freedom, but then some crooks turn up to try to steal the house contents and he has to single-handedly defend the family property. The film revolves around the usual battle of wits between Young Hero and Adult Villain, but what is unusual is the way the house itself becomes a protagonist in the story. Whose side is it on? Does it obstruct the crooks, or offer them an easy way in? Does it lend itself to the boy's ingenious stratagems to keep them out, or does it trip him up? At one level, then, the film speaks to the anxieties of Middle America surrounding the incipient breakdown of its domestic order and the invasion of privacy by forces of urban degeneration. Race, of course, is never mentioned, but it is implicit. This is an all-white film set in an all-white neighbourhood, and the racial analogy is clear enough to all who know the place and time in which the film is set. At another level it portrays the male fantasy of what might happen once good, safe, internal objects associated with the maternal body are put at the mercy of persecutory or envious external objects – these objects representing the split off components of aggressive drives linked to anxieties of separation, abandonment, and loss. Linking the outer and inner environments are the fear and fascination which all children have of being "home alone."

The wider issue indirectly raised by the film is whether it is possible to find a way of containing these fears and fantasies, in some way that does not lend itself to racist resolution. Under what conditions might it be possible to mobilize rules and rituals of territoriality to establish firm boundaries against racism? To make our neighbourhood, our street, our workplace an exclusion zone? Or to formulate this demand in the language of public propriety, to express civic pride in the fact that practices of discrimination have no place in the local body politic?

One way to do this might be to appeal to the contemporary rhetorics of "Not in My Back Yardism." NIMBYism is an expression of a pervasive feeling that to travel hopefully is no longer better than to arrive. The goal of life is to achieve some kind of domestic security in an increasingly chaotic and dangerous world, rather than to take risks in building a new one. The first and last priority is to prevent the intrusion of any outside forces which would disturb that sense of internal order. NIMBYism is the ideology of the little man and woman against the big guns of corporate capitalism and the state. As such it is closely associated with the libertarian philosophies of the New Right, and, in Britain, with certain invented traditions from the "freeborn Englishman." But does it have to take this form?

The antiracist movement could usefully develop its own version. The basic message to be conveyed is that "Those Others Over There" (on the other side of the street, or town, in the next neighbourhood, region, or country) may be racist (which only confirms how stupid and uncivilized they are), but at least "Us Lot Over Here" know better than to behave like that because we are taking active steps to put our own house in order. And it is in our own self-interest to do so, because there are also material incentives for complying with anti-discriminatory policies.

The success of contract compliance as a means of implementing equal opportunities policies is a good example of antiracist NIMBYism in action. It does not rely on ideological commitment to The Cause, or even limited altruism – just economic self-interest on the part of contractors. At the same time NIMBYism can sublimate local prides of place in a kind of political peer-group rivalry aimed at establishing the exemplary nature of one's own practices.

Of course, the strategy only works if it is symmetrical and there are similar initiatives in the next street, town, region, and country saying and doing the very same thing back. And that requires a degree of coordinated effort which may be hard to sustain. There is a further risk that it may encourage complacency, especially in "white highlands" areas, where the assumption often is "No Blacks, No problem." Yet of course it is precisely in these no-go areas for ethnic minorities that racism is most deeply entrenched.

Despite the risks and limitations, such an approach does at least start from where many people are at in a world dominated by individualism. It also speaks to the home truth that local, regional, and national particularisms do exist within the antiracist movement; everyone secretly believes that their own experience of racism is definitive and that others should learn from their example. Better to work through these rivalries than rationalize them ideologically or hide them under a pious universalism which fools no one.

There are other strategies of containment which rely on more spontaneous gestures of self-interest. A story from the East End of London may illustrate how this may work. In 1936, Moseley's British Union of Fascists proposed to march through the heart of the Jewish community in Whitechapel at a time of rising antisemitism throughout East London. The Moseleyite action provoked a counter-mobilization from left and anti-fascist organizations, which was also supported by sections of the local labour movement. The organizing slogan was "They Shall Not Pass." It was to be a trial of political strength with national as well as local implications, and things came to a head in the famous battle of Cable Street, where the BUF was finally stopped.

Now at that time there lived near Cable Street a working-class family who were well-known for their antisemitism. Some members of the family were active trade unionists and had supported restrictive practices to prevent Jews being taken on in East End trades. The younger members had been involved in street brawls with the local Jewish gang. It might have been anticipated that they would welcome Moseley's intervention. But not a bit of it. Like many east-enders, then and since, they were fiercely patriotic in both a local and national sense. They regarded fascism as a foreign ideology and Moseley's march as an invasion of their territory. On the day of the march, the entire family stationed themselves on top of one of the Jewish houses overlooking Cable Street. They spent their time ripping the slates off the roof and hurling them down onto the heads of the Blackshirts, yelling "They may be Yids, but they're our bloody Yids." In this way they managed to simultaneously attack Jewish property and protect Jewish lives, making their area an exclusion zone for fascism, whilst at the same time asserting their claims as an imaginary ruling class to exercise a form of quasi-colonial jurisdiction over its "native" inhabitants.

This was a highly ambivalent response, in which the desire to maintain territorial hegemony temporarily suspended other allegiances, and where the internal contradictions of this type of racism succeeded in neutralizing its local effect. No one is suggesting that an effective antiracist strategy could be built around such instances – but the lesson they have to teach is that we always have to deal with impure realities which do not always fit into neat categories of what (or who) is racist or antiracist. And there may be situations in which even these reality principles can be re-articulated, as in the following case.

HOMING DEVICES 79

Mrs. Ntolo came to London from the Cameroons in the 1960s, and she now lives in a council house on the Becontree Estate in Dagenham, East London, a predominantly white working-class suburb, close to the main Fords factory. She belongs to the Essene Community, a group of black Jews who settled in Africa after the fall of the first Temple, and who have been practising a unique syncretic form of Judaism ever since. Part of the requirement of her religion is that certain observances such as ritual purification and the burning of mourning bands should be carried out in an Oracle built on specially consecrated ground outside the house, to allow the observant to be in physical contact with the earth. In Africa there is no problem with building the Oracle: the word is put around the village that it will be built on such-and-such a day and everyone puts aside some time to help. It is built of mud and straw and the structure is made to last for several generations. As Mrs. Ntolo found out, putting up a structure in her own back yard in England is not such a straightforward procedure.

When she wrote to the planning department explaining at length her reasons for wanting to put up this structure and why it had to be built of mud, she at first got an enthusiastic response. The department even rang the local papers to tell them all about it. But when the man from Housing arrived on the scene it was very different story. They couldn't have their tenants putting up mud huts all over the place. What would people think? The neighbours had already complained; after all, this was Essex, not Africa. Why couldn't she assimilate like other people? If she were white, it might be different, but if they allowed her to go ahead it would set a bad example to other black tenants. In any case, they had had a look at it and it was definitely a dangerous structure, unfit for human habitation. And so on.

It did not stop at insults. The Council sent in workmen to knock the Oracle down. They had quite a job, even with an earth digger, because they did not understand the principles of its construction. Mrs. Ntolo got a petition from the neighbours supporting her right to have the structure stay. The local synagogue and the black community rallied round. The press ran the story, completely ignoring the religious and cultural politics of the issue, presenting it instead as a bad case of homesickness: Mrs. Ntolo was putting up a mud hut to remind her of her happy childhood in the Cameroons! No doubt the intention of this "human angle" was to win sympathy, but the effect was the opposite. Hate mail poured in, suggesting that she be helped to go back to the jungle where she belonged. Meanwhile, the Council decided to take her to Court, to get a possession order to evict her from the house, as well as an injunction preventing her from erecting a similar structure.

They had not reckoned on the extent to which the rights of private property are associated with the freedom of the individual in English common law. The judge was not amused. In his view the Council had behaved outrageously; it was the right of every freeborn Englishman – and woman – to practise his or her religion in the privacy of his or her own home. The garden was still a private space and the Oracle was interfering with no one, and in no way could it be considered a dangerous structure. Still, local feelings had to be taken into account: Mrs. Ntolo could rebuild the Oracle, using the original materials, provided the structure was encased in concrete. So on the outside it would look like a modern European type of building, while on the inside it would still be an African mud hut. That way everybody would be happy: Mrs. Ntolo could carry out her religious observances, and the neighbours would not be offended – typically "English" compromise, but one which perhaps raises a number of wider issues.

Is it possible that people can stop thinking of home as a container or enclosed space defined by fixed coordinates or boundaries, and thus something which can be occupied, invaded or possessed? If so, under what circumstances? Would this be an effective way of undermining the deep structure of racist and nationalist discourses? What role could the feminist movement play in such a radical "deconstruction?"

Certainly the strategy of containment implied by historical compromises illustrated in the Ntolo case can at best (or worst) only be holding operations which are ultimately doomed to failure. Returning to the fate of Mrs. Ntolo's project we may reflect that earth expands as it fills with organic life; concrete is brittle and crumbles easily; the walls of the Oracle will expand over time and break through the thin concrete shell which is designed to render it invisible. The sacred will invade the profane. At that point it will truly become a dangerous structure!

Acknowledgements

I would like to thank Michael Rustin for reading and commenting on various parts of this chapter. Also my colleagues in the New Ethnicities Unit for the seminars and informal discussions in which many of these ideas were first argued over. Thanks also to Caroline Knowles for her encouragement and support in completing the text.

References

Anderson, B. (1983). *Imagined Communities: Reflections on the Origins and Spread of Nationalism*. London: Verso.
Balint, M. (1974). *Thrills and Regression*. London: Tavistock.
Serres, M. (1982). *The Parasite*. Lawrence R. Schehr, trans. Baltimore: Johns Hopkins University Press.

[Part II]

THE POLITICS
OF IDENTITY

Introduction

As a term, the "politics of identity" has become popular only over the last few years. Ethnic politics, however, is hardly new (Esman, 1994) nor is the notion of collective identity as a political resource. Earlier constructions regarded ethnicity as a resource for group mobilization in pursuit of members' common political interests. Ethnic boundaries emerged and were perpetuated through the competition between ethnic groups for scarce resources, often distributed and controlled by state agencies (Cohen 1969; Glazer & Moynihan 1965; Keyes 1981). In this version, ethnic politics operated in the shadows with little or no official acknowledgement. In the more recent exegesis of identity politics the locus has shifted to the centre of the public stage where social movements based on race, ethnicity, and gender are viewed as having replaced or at least overshadowed class-based political pressure groups (Knopff and Morton 1992). In spite of, or perhaps because of, the passions that surround this form of political representation, this is precious little information about its workings and a baffling tendency to treat its rhetorics at face value. Thus Stanley Aronowitz (1992) can invoke notions of social movements, the emergence of new historical agents, and political resistance to characterize the contemporary politics of identity without, it would seem, a corresponding urgency to explore its mechanics. In contrast, the four chapters in this section aptly illustrate the contribution which can be gained by moving beyond ideological generalities to a review of who, what, where, and when.

Vered Amit-Talai traces the institutionalization of a round of minority consultation exercises which she refers to as the Montreal Minority Circuit. The proliferation of government and institutional committees, task forces, hearings, and programs ostensibly concerned with increasing opportunities for minority representation have instead augmented the usefulness of a small, select, identifiable cadre of professional ethnic spokespersons. As it has solidified, the Minority Circuit has become increasingly independent from the minority populations which continue to provide it with a rationale. The existence of the Circuit, however, is belied by political rhetorics which represent its constituent activities as singular events, its patrons and clients as icons, respectively of the "majority" and the "minorities." Academic treatises on multiculturalism have more often buttressed than penetrated these representations. This largely uncritical treatment can only be understood, Amit-Talai argues, within the context of academia's own implication in identity politics.

Like Amit-Talai, Valerie Morrison is also concerned with media representations, but in this case as they articulate with the apparatuses of popular music promotion and packaging. Her chapter focuses on Kashtin, an Innu musical duo who, over the last few years, have enjoyed considerable success in Québec, their home province, but also across Canada as well as internationally. In Québec, Kashtin's rise coincided with the growing popularity of "world music" as well as with an expansion of the musical styles portrayed by the local industry as authentically Québécois. This confluence allowed Kashtin to be the first act to be publicly accorded the status of Québécois even when they were not ethnically Québécois and did not sing in French. What the media bestow, however, they can also revoke. In 1990, during an armed confrontation between Mohawks from two Québec reservations and first police and then the armed forces, Kashtin's music was boycotted by several French language radio stations in the province, and suddenly Kashtin became quite "Native, period."

Amit-Talai's and Morrison's papers advance portrayals of ethnic politics beyond chessboard encounters between monolithic groups and train our attention instead on the circumstances, mythologies, and power imbalances of official and popular representations of categorical identities. These are not one-dimensional tales of victimization and imposition. The Minority Circuit clients and Kashtin's Florent Vollant and Claude McKenzie are active agents in at least some stages of these processes of identity construction. Significantly, however, they do not control the terms of engagement, and that crucial limitation acts as an important brake on enthusiastic claims for the transformative potential of identity politics.

The starting premise of Anthony Synnott and David Howes' critical deconstruction of the term "visible minority" is precisely this issue of control and definition. Over the last decade, as this concept has become jurally entrenched in successive employment equity and multiculturalism legislation, it has become much more than a descriptive reference term – it has become an important instrument of government policy. Synnott and Howes question the emphasis on visibility as an effective gauge of stigma and disadvantage. They note that there is very little research on the impact and meaning of visibility, that those attitudinal surveys that do exist do not support a simple equation of colour with negative prejudice, and that the concept in fact lumps together two quite different criteria of national origin and colour. The classification aggregates categories with quite distinct socio-economic profiles, immigration histories, and associated stigmas while excluding a wide range of linguistic, religious and chronological minorities who may have experienced significant disadvantage. Given these contradictions, Synnott and Howes doubt the effectiveness of visible minority as a descriptive category and as a policy instrument. They urge a reappraisal of the cultural significance of the visual and a reformulation of policy initiatives.

If Synnott and Howes are concerned with the imposition of political categories, Alrick Cambridge directs his criticism against the imposition of political agendas. Cambridge argues that unreflective and repetitive homages to fashionable concepts such as ambivalence, hybridity, and representation allow black cultural critics to avoid revealing the principles guiding their evaluations. This silence permits analysts to avoid accountability for their own premises, values which are then projected onto black cultures. The result is a distortion of multifaceted, variable, and complex cultures into one-dimensional political manifestoes. In sharp contrast, Cambridge himself argues that cultures are moved by a cluster of shared and emotively charged norms. Norms, however, do not have to be internalized to be effective; they are rules which specify how to obtain social recognition and validation of significant identities. Yet identities and roles can change, and when they do, different norms may become relevant. Black people, Cambridge argues, are not cardboard cutouts simply responding to the prevailing capitalist winds. They are cultural creators, historically encumbered but far more than the mechanical sum of their social identities and roles. Cambridge's analysis places priority on cultural agency, "on black people as active creators of whatever forms of life they employ for their spiritual human needs and self-realization."

References

Aronowitz, Stanley (1992). *The Politics of Identity: Class, Culture, Social Movements.* New York and London: Routledge.

Cohen, Abner (1969). *Custom and Politics in Urban Africa.* Berkeley and Los Angeles: University of California Press.

Esman, Milton J. (1994). *Ethnic Politics.* Ithaca and London: Cornell University Press.

Glazer, Nathan, and Daniel P. Moynihan (1965). *Beyond the Melting Pot: The Negroes, Puerto Ricans, Jews, Italians and Irish of New York City.* Cambridge, Mass.: M.I.T. Press.

Keyes, C.F. (ed.) (1981). *Ethnic Change.* Seattle: University of Washington Press.

Knopff, Rainer, and F.L. Morton (1992). *Charter Politics.* Scarborough, Ont.: Nelson Canada.

4

The Minority Circuit:

Identity Politics and the

Professionalization of Ethnic Activism[1]

Vered Amit-Talai

Within the metropolitan district of Greater Montreal, there are many hundreds of ethnic voluntary organizations. Small, large, ephemeral or enduring, single purpose or comprehensive, this extraordinarily varied array of associations involves thousands of organizers and volunteers. This chapter is *not* about these participants. It is, instead, concerned with a small, select set of high-profile Montreal activists, numbered in the dozens rather than the hundreds, who are regular players in an ongoing if somewhat inchoate circuit of public exercises in ethnic minority consultation and representation. While most of these events and many of its principal protagonists are publicized and contested, the political "ethnoscape" (Appadurai 1991) which they constitute is rarely accorded public acknowledgement in its own right. In the discourses of identity politics which percolate through the popular press, academic journals, and parliamentary statements, the very existence of the Circuit tends to be dissolved in strident disputes over the legitimacy of its activist members or generalized polemics on the value of Canadian multiculturalism. Far from illuminating the consequences of numerous significant governmental interventions, this rush of rhetorics amplifies a process in which representation has increasingly become its own object. And it is this fetishization which has been critical in the proliferation of official vehicles for representation and in the development of a professional cadre of minority "spokespersons" to occupy them. This chapter will examine some of the political ironies entailed in the emergence of this occupation and the challenges it poses to the conceptualization of ethnicity and political representation.

Multiculturalism and Identity Politics

There is certainly no shortage of literature on race and ethnic relations in Canada (Bolaria and Li 1985; Li 1990; Anderson and Frideres 1981; Bienvenue and Goldstein 1985; Herberg 1989; McCall 1990; Juteau 1991) are only a very few examples). But there has been relatively little attention paid to a public policy of multiculturalism which is into its third decade at the federal level, with analogous programs by provincial and major municipal governments (Roberts and Clifton 1990:120). Beyond interest in relevant legislation such as the Multiculturalism Act or the Charter of Rights, there is little concerted analysis of grant disbursement to academic, ethnic, and rights organizations; of hiring practices in government departments, crown, and parapublic agencies; negotiations with "community" associations; consultation exercises or the numerous advisory ethnic committees and positions which have been established at every level of government.[2]

Ironically, this analytical indifference to the complex infrastructure of state multiculturalism appears to be fuelled by its evocativeness as a political symbol. Like other key words such as democracy or liberty (Parkin 1978; Cohen 1985), multiculturalism's symbolic effectiveness derives from its ambiguity. Vague notions of ethnic, cultural or communal pluralism conflate with references to constitutional and civil rights, social justice, electoral strategies, and government policy to yield a symbolic bundle that is as politically charged as it is indeterminate. Far from untangling this mélange, a recent flurry of scholarly and popular writing, both denouncing and defending the policy, complicates it even further by associating it with a series of equally evocative and ambiguous themes: nation-building, equality, and participation or inclusion (Bibby 1990; Abu-Laban and Stasiulis 1992; Fleras and Elliott 1992; Wilson 1993; Bissoondath 1994).

Multiculturalism either makes Canada pioneering or mediocre; unifies or divides; ghettoizes or includes ethnic minorities; promotes acceptance of diversity or facilitates assimilation. The dramatic sweep of these claims does not seem to occasion much in the way of correspondingly generous data, clearly defined terminology or rigorous analysis. At least some of the authors even appear to have eschewed the presentation of their own data in favour of presenting political positions so general they inevitably assume a polemical cast. Seymour Wilson, for example, makes a point of noting that for two and a half years he has been conducting an extensive archival search of private and public government documents (1993:663). Yet in lieu of this material, he opts for a personal statement which is remarkable chiefly for the excitement with which a predictable and already well-documented conclusion is presented:[3]

> I am therefore faced with an enormous amount of evidence demanding some personal conclusion. And the only conclusion I can, with any sincerity, arrive at is one which states categorically that ethnocentrism of the worst variety, namely racism, was a widespread characteristic in the halls of decision-making in the Canada of yesteryear. This does not condemn everybody, it simply states a fact. For those who find the fact unpalatable I urge you not to shoot the messenger because of his message.

The policy of multiculturalism may not have succeeded in provoking the investigative curiosity of scholars and writers, but in recurrent echoes of Wilson's dramatic flourish, it does appear to have aroused their political passions, in the process assuming an iconic status. For Yasmeen Abu-Laban and Daiva Stasiulis, an attack on the multicultural policy is often a "thinly veiled" attack on demands for full civic membership by ethnic and particularly racial minorities and is but one instance of a "backlash against pluralism, ethnic and racial diversity and immigration that is besetting most advanced capitalist countries in the late 20th century" (1992:381). But for Augie Fleras and Jean Elliott, Canada's official multiculturalism is a last-ditch hedge against the American cultural pull and also a source of international prestige (1992:279). The issue being debated, then, is not how an official policy of multiculturalism actually works but whether one is for or against it and the political values with which either position is identified.

This kind of ideological positioning has resonances in the similar, if often more strident, iconic use of affirmative action and multicultural education programs in the United States. For Evelyn Hu-Dehart, a "war" is being waged on American university campuses (1994:243). The prize is the academic curriculum and the contenders are the multiculturalists and the antimulticulturalists or "triumphalists." In a line of argument strongly reminiscent of Abu-Laban and Stasiulis' conclusions, Hu-Dehart calls triumphalists "neoconservatives" who are reacting defensively and arrogantly to the attempts by people of colour to "reclaim their proper place in U.S. history, culture and institutions" (1994:252).

What is particularly interesting about this kind of political reading is its persistent appropriation of familiar dichotomies under the new labels of identity politics. In place of conservative/liberal or right/left, we now have the triumphalists and the multiculturalists or, in another version, privileged whites on the one hand and subordinated racial minorities and women on the other (Rosaldo 1994). One side is always conservative or neo-conservative, the other progressive or radical. Beyond its obvious over-simplifications, there are several critical problems involved with treating a public policy or an ascribed identity as an emblem of political affiliation.

The first is that it does little to promote debate, research or analysis. Renato Rosaldo is unapologetically blunt in this regard. For him, the challenge to white supremacy requires that people in relatively privileged positions – and social analysts are included in this category – be quiet and listen attentively to subordinated people (1994:223). But characterizing criticism of Canadian or American multicultural policy as reactionary opposition to the full enfranchisement of ethnic and racial minorities also does little to encourage thoughtful discussion. In such a totalizing equation, critics appear to have an unhappy choice between, at worst, accusations of racism or, at best, admonishments of naïveté in aiding and abetting racist detractors. How successful this accusation has been in stifling debate is exemplified in a recent paper by Katherine Verdery. After noting with concern the "new essentialism" of American identity politics, "the positing of difference of all kinds as inherent and imperative" (1994:54), Verdery argues for a cautious use of such insights. For in spite of the unsavouriness of this essentialism,

> [f]rom the point of view of empowering disadvantaged groups, scholars in a 'Barthian mode' [which she lauds] who challenge 'ethnic culture' as arbitrary and invented, or who refuse to consider identities as imperative, risk undermining political possibilities that might have progressive social effects. (55)

Surely this raises a critical question: what precisely are the social effects of the policies and ideas which have been associated with the politics of identity? Since the iconization of particular policies and identities has been far more conducive to polemic than to inquiry or analysis, it is difficult to see how anthropologists are to meet the challenge of studying the *"new* 'new ethnicity'" (Verdery 1994:55) without taking on the histrionics with which it has often been defended or attacked.

One of the most serious consequences of the reductionism and essentialism of identity politics has been the ways in which it has obscured the emergence of new political and ethnic forms, alliances, and convergences. Delineating, as Rosaldo does, political camps in terms of gender and race elides the emergence of what Dana Takagi refers to as a "vocal sector of minority conservatives" (1994:231). Painting identity politics as a struggle between neo-conservatives and progressives masks the convergent incorporation of race, ethnicity, and gender into the agendas of most major political parties in both Canada and the United States. Rhetorical invocations of minority inclusion or participation grossly minimize the paradoxes and limitations of political representation within state frameworks. In the following, I therefore examine the consequence of the increasing ubiquity of staged, official tableaus of representation and the concomitant pressure to find people to occupy them. In particular I focus on the emergence of a selective cadre of "representatives" and an occupational culture to service this circuit of events.[4]

Committees and More Committees

If you conducted a tour of public and semi-public events in Montreal that concern ethnic and racial minorities you would probably start off by feeling somewhat overwhelmed. There are frequent formal consultation hearings sponsored by all three levels of government or occasionally by autonomous public agencies: hearings on immigration levels, employment equity programs, police/minority relations, health and social services, and so on. There are the more private but regular meetings of the plethora of ethnic and racial advisory committees now serving virtually every government department, crown corporation and major parapublic agencies such as hospitals or school boards. There are frequent lectures or conferences which are sponsored by ethnic voluntary associations, often in conjunction with university departments. For example in 1993, the Congress of Black Lawyers and Jurists of Québec sponsored a conference in collaboration with two departments of the Université du Québec à Montréal (UQAM), as well as the Joint Concordia/UQAM Chair in Ethnic Studies, entitled "Youth of Black Minorities."

In addition, there are press conferences called by a variety of organizations to announce new initiatives, press demands or respond to particular events. There is a dizzying array of board committee meetings or training sessions of short- and long-term alliances. Thus the few ongoing ethnic coalitions or "regroupements" such as the Table de Concertation des réfugiés de Montréal or ACCESSS (Alliance des Communautés Culturelles pour Egalité et Services Santé and Sociaux) sponsor regular board and information meetings. While they exist, there are meetings sponsored by the more common, shorter term ad hoc coalition committees such as one established, in the wake of the Meech Lake and Charlottetown rounds of constitutional negotiations, to address the related concerns of Québec minorities. There are one-off meetings such as the 1993 conference of activists, political appointees, and academics, carefully planned and organized by two Montreal ethnic associations, with funding from the Federal Multicultural Department, to discuss the future of minorities in Québec. During the discussion period, the concept of a permanent umbrella organization for Québec ethnic and racial minorities was broached. While the idea died on the vine, in the days that followed the conference it continued to generate considerable discussion and not a little controversy among the participants. And there are more hastily organized crisis sessions such as a 1992 meeting to discuss a mooted municipal reorganization of positions dealing with ethnic minorities.

Without even including the committees and board meetings of ethnic community associations into our tour, you might still feel initially overwhelmed by the volume of activities, the range of institutions and associations which they involve, and the ethnic groups or categories invoked. Yet it would also not be surprising if shortly after you started making the rounds, you started getting a sense of déjà vu: reappearing faces, recurring names, repeated motifs.

> Ce que je me rends compte c'est que ce sont à peu près les mêmes personnes, des convertis que j'appelle et qui se rencontrent dans les mêmes forums, séminaires, colloques. C'est à peu près les mêmes militants et militantes qu'on rencontre.

What you've encountered is the official ethnic minorities Circuit. It has a small number of regular participants who are easily identifiable to each other, to more incidental players, and to the institutions which fuel and fund the Circuit. When I first encountered it in the mid-1980s, many of these key participants earned their living elsewhere and attended the Circuit events as volunteers. In the mid-1990s, most now make their living through its sponsoring agencies. They are employment equity officers, race relations advisors, intercultural training consultants or political attachés; they teach university courses on immigration or work as the staff of ethnic minority and civil rights associations. A growing number are running for and a few have succeeded in being elected to public offices.

On an institutional level, therefore, it may still be possible to locate a distinction between the government and organizational patrons of the Circuit and its client associations. But in terms of the individuals actually participating in these events, the distinction is nebulous, context-specific, and therefore constantly shifting. The government official or appointee responsible for organizing a consultative committee or hearing may once have been on the other side of the table and may still be involved, depending on the terms of his or her employment, either officially in client associations or informally with activist networks. The politician may have launched his or her career through the contacts and publicity of Circuit appearances. The client appearing on the Circuit or appealing to its sponsoring institutions may on another occasion be hired for short-term contract work, act as a consultant or serve as an appointee on commissions and committees.

The language with which Circuit events and players are described in press statements, media reports or by participants themselves gives little indication of this complexity and ambiguity. Portrayals tend to depict sharply demarcated boundaries and obscure the overlap between clientage and patronage while imparting a coherence and consolidation to the two camps that belies their internal differences. An example may help to highlight this public marketing of ethnic politics.

On November 11, 1991, Yves LaFontaine, a recently appointed Director of the Québec Human Rights Commission, suggested in a newspaper interview that minority leaders and the anglophone media were exaggerating the levels of racism in Québec. The comments were widely reported in both the French and English media and reaction came quickly. In the view of one prominent Circuit player, the first responses were too hasty. Without "consulting with anyone else," two individuals issued statements demanding the resignation of LaFontaine and provoking, she felt, a media backlash: "They said the minorities are against the French." Meanwhile, two other activists were talking on the phone. The two came from very different ethnic backgrounds and associations but they were well used to working with each other on other projects and committees. They decided to adopt a two-stage approach: first to demand a meeting with LaFontaine to see if there was any common ground, and only if this failed would there be a move to the second stage of demanding his resignation. A press conference sponsored by two organizations followed, a few other organizational spokespersons were interviewed individually, and a meeting with LaFontaine was demanded both publicly as well as privately. The Québec Minister of Cultural Communities and Immigration issued a press release urging the concerned parties to meet as soon as possible and clarify the situation. After some initial reluctance, LaFontaine agreed. He met with twenty-six individuals on November 14, 1991. According to one participant, they demanded a public apology and the establishment of a committee that would advise the Commission on minority relations. After a three-hour meeting, LaFontaine issued an official apology and promised to set up a Committee. He refused to meet with reporters, but "three spokespersons from the minority groups" (*The Gazette*, Nov. 15) held a news conference, to say that while remaining vigilant they were willing to try and work with the Commission Director. On November 23, *La Presse* reported that the Québec Human Rights Commission had given the green light to the formation of a nine member committee on inter-ethnic and inter-racial relations. The committee would include five 'representatives of ethnic communities.'

In press reports, there were references to "les leaders des communautés culturelles de Montréal" (the current official Québec euphemism for ethnic minorities), "26 angry members of minority groups," to the creation of a committee following "une demande des communautés culturelles." A prominent activist spoke publicly of the relations of confidence which had to be established between the groups of cultural communities and the institutions of the majority societies, and later, when the advisory committee had been established, of a "rapprochement entre la majorité et les communautés."

A dramatic scenario thus emerges of confrontation and subsequent reconciliation between the ethnic minorities of Montreal and the majority institutions. The individuals who marched into LaFontaine's office or issued statements to the press become the public face of ethnic minorities in Montreal, the director of one institution representing the majority. One doesn't have to examine this depiction very closely to see why it is such a convenient fiction for all concerned. Rather than deal with the various and contradictory views of the sometimes inarticulate, inaccessible or just downright disinterested thousands who can be classified under the general rubric of ethnic minorities, the reporters, politicians and managers can interact instead with a few eloquent, well-educated, highly politicized professionals. In the place of a myriad different demands and grievances, all that needs to be addressed are the two readily fulfilled requests for a public apology and the establishment of an advisory committee. With the establishment of the committee, the Commission Director and the reified majority with which he is being identified, are redeemed; meanwhile, the number of "representatives" shrinks from 26 to an even more manageable five. Nor does one have to mine very far to discern the rewards for the implicated activists: public recognition as "leaders," considerable press attention before and during the meeting, and an image of moderation and problem solving. It is probably not irrelevant that the three most active spokespersons have all since sought election to public office, albeit with varying degrees of success.

Omitted from this tale of majority, minorities, and their leaders are the structures and career paths engendered by this form of public relations. With one exception, all the minority "leaders" publicly profiled in this incident were of ethnic origins other than British or French. They also all had some kind of organizational affiliation, but these were not necessarily community associations serving or representing a particular ethnic group. A number, including many of the most visible, headed generic minority aid, rights or antiracist organizations. These also included one person whose ethnic constituency was somewhat hazy but whose personal reputation for accomplished multi-ethnic networking had long superseded the official identity of the association she headed. Not only were these individuals simply lumped in with the more ethnic-specific associations, but in some cases their organizational credentials were reworked. Therefore, one newspaper referred to a person who heads a general immigrant aid association as a representative of the black community. In other words, the organizational and ascriptive identities of these individuals were often treated as interchangeable, buttressing their concomitant identification as leaders of minority ethnic communities.

It might also appear from the press reports that with the final establishment of an advisory ethnic committee, the Human Rights Commission had embarked on a new era of minority relations. Yet this was but one of several similar bodies concerned with ethnic minorities or racism operating under Commission auspices before, during, and since the LaFontaine incident. Minority activists have, on occasion, served as Commissioners, a part-time paid position. Many of the "leaders" demanding a new Committee have consistently identified, in both public and private statements, several Commission employees as persons involved in the "cultural community sector." I was urged to interview these people for my own study. When much the same network involved in this affair protested the failure to include representatives of the ethnic and racial minorities on a provincial inquiry into the political and constitutional future of Québec, they put forward the names of three high-ranking Human Rights Commission employees as suitable nominees in this regard. In short, the people meeting with LaFontaine in November 1991 were well used to working with this organization; the establishment of yet another committee marked a continuation of ongoing relations, a structure in a series of similar structures rather than a point of departure.

I have dealt with this particular incident in some detail because it illustrates several important processes endemic to the Minority Circuit. First, the Circuit is punctuated and legitimated by regular "crises." The crises can run the gamut from the shocking to the predictable, from the deaths of unarmed civilians at the hands of the police to the ritual rediscovery that ethnic minorities are inadequately represented in one branch or another of the public service. They are, however, commemorated and defined as crises through press conferences and statements. But crises need responses and resolutions, and it is this contrived cycle of crisis/response that provides the praxis and pretext for ongoing Circuit events and structures. Here's how "Bill," a minority activist, describes the pattern of Circuit events:

> Ten years ago, I was very distrustful of government. Now I find myself more and more in advisory committees and being co-opted or asked to sit on consultative committees on specific issues so that's how I got into the ... committee and how I've got involved in the ... committee, where they all start, first of all from some kind of clash and they end up being basically

a way of either co-opting you or trying to solve the problem, so you cannot say no, basically, and so yeah, I work very closely with, in my work, I work very closely with certain departments.

Second, crises tend to be "resolved" by the establishment of committees and inquiries. Committees pile up on top of other committees, often repeat work or recommendations of previous committees, and draw upon the membership of previous incarnations. They are, however, publicly portrayed by activists, government officials, politicians, and reporters as special responses to a particular event or issue rather than institutionalized exhibitions of representation. It is as if the actors in a long-running Broadway play pretended that each night's performance was a singular event.

Third, the proliferation of committees both encourages and is supported by the selectiveness of their membership. The more frequent the exercise, the more useful the access to a small, identifiable, and increasingly professional set of generic minority activists becomes. It is a selectiveness that is useful both to patrons and clients. Activists are as likely to draw upon and recommend a small list of familiar allies as are the politicians and bureaucrats sponsoring the committees. It is too difficult and time-consuming, explained several activists, to start from scratch in each new instance:

> Mais on préfère que ce soit toujours les mêmes pour une raison bien simple. C'est parce qu'on a un dialogue plus ouvert et plus constructif avec quelqu'un avec qui on a l'habitude de travailler. Quand il arrive quelqu'un de nouveau dans le dossier, il faut refaire le tour. Il faut refaire l'histoire. Il faut tout redire, donc on se perd toujours en conjecture en racontant, en faisant l'historique et ça nous laisse très peu de temps parfois pour arriver au vif du sujet.

Finally, while the LaFontaine incident involved a provincial parapublic agency, I could equally well have used examples from every level of government and major institutions. In spite of the much trumpeted and oft-proclaimed ideological differences between Québec and Canada in attitudes toward pluralism, the two levels of government support very similar infrastructures. Whether the policy is cultural convergence, integration or multiculturalism, the sponsored frameworks are similar not only in structure; they also draw upon and fund the same network of people. The head of a federal task force on minority relations, and a former provincial employee, becomes a municipal advisor. The deputy director of a provincial council of cultural communities runs for federal office. By the same token, changes in political parties may result in a shuffle of faces and changes of titles, but they rarely result in a complete reinvention of the supporting structures. The ubiquity of minority committees, departments, action plans, and race relations advisors by now supersedes party politics.

The Circuit is therefore far more institutionalized and continuous than official representations of its constituent events would suggest. I have already noted the political rewards entailed in this public version of events, but as 'Bill's' comments above and 'Susan's' below indicate, Circuit participants still have to constantly wrestle with its contradictions.

> I guess in a sense it's natural because once, I mean, I don't know why do I get named on different committees because maybe I happen to be on that committee and so the word gets around so okay, from this core or this pool of people there are these people and if I want to form a committee, from this pool I invite or nominate. So, in a sense perhaps, it's not as interesting if you look farther or you look more harder, you know, maybe for some people, maybe less known but they have very interesting experiences but they don't market themselves or you don't have contact enough to be known, but they have very interesting ideas or experiences, you know, we can learn from or exchange with. But I think again, I guess, it's how, maybe it's something to do with so called 'old boy's club', you know, so the same people you think of, of course the same idea. But that is also a little unfortunate because you then recycle same idea, same people. I'm not saying that people don't learn or anything but somehow you want a new blood, you know, just like any organization or any evolution of new things.

It's difficult to entirely ignore the ironies of these practices: the exclusivity of a round of activities supposedly constituting opportunities for inclusion; that the need for representation is formulated in demands for committees and meetings at which the same group of actors discuss, over and over again, the need for representation and inclusion; that the professionalization of a cadre of spokespersons is claimed as a necessity born out of institutional constraints but which obviates the need to reform these institutions; that one of the few growing fields for minority employment in the Québec and Canadian public infrastructures has been in lobbying for and advising on increasing minority employment. The effect of these incongruities continually resonates in the dialectics underpinning Circuit careers, between praise and accusation, competition and interdependence, mission and profession.

Circuit Careers

A government employee describes his difficulties in trying to put together a special advisory committee which, he had been instructed, was to include four ethnic community representatives:

> ... well then I had to figure out something because you can never get it down to four and what I attempted to do was just try and find some names out there of their people that, how will I put it, enough people didn't actively dislike. It was more like a negative process than a positive process. It was funny testing some names of people that, say, [a few years ago] would've been seen as sort of up-and-comers and stuff; "Oh no, not him, he's got a government job now so he's just finished." And the fact that he succeeded in whatever the game is that he succeeded at, sort of disqualified him from being seen as a credible spokesman any more for his community. So, I don't know if you want me to name the name or not but I think that you can guess that a former leader from ... who was someone who, if we had this conversation 6 or 7 years ago, would have been identified as a new voice and this and that but who's gone on...

The person in question was not a community spokesperson; he had, at one point, been associated with a general antiracist organization. Many other Circuit clients have taken government jobs without censure, but he was far from being the only high-profile activist to be denounced by his peers for opportunism and self-aggrandizement following a cycle in which they were praised, sought after as allies, and recommended for committees. Intervals of successful networking and increasing public attention seem to alternate with periods of condemnation and even exclusion. For some affected individuals, the criticism is relatively subdued, privately expressed, and has little overall affect on their activities. Others do appear to drop off the Circuit map ... for a while. Even the hapless individual referred to above seems to be resurfacing.

It is likely that at least some of this alternation of praise and reproach reflects the tension between the inevitable competition among Circuit players and their mutual interdependence. Clients are competing for political appointments, jobs, organizational funds, and media attention. At the same time, a significant measure of their success as lobbyists stems from their ability to establish, maintain, and mobilize networks of political contacts with activists of other organizations and ethnic identities. In the LaFontaine example, it was this kind of ongoing relationship between two activists and their networks of colleagues from an ever wider range of affiliations that generated newsworthy responses to the Director's comments. One person meeting with LaFontaine would have been unlikely to generate much media coverage; twenty-six makes for an interesting story.

When you rely on the people with whom you compete, loyalty is a crucial but uncertain quality.

> quand on est trahi par quelqu'un comme ça, on se sent plus mal que si on était trahi par son propre père ou sa propre mère. Ce sont des gens avec lesquels on décide des choses vraiment de sa vie, vous voyez, des gens qu'on a fait entrer dans sa vie, par besoin ou bien par nécessité, donc on se dit que cette personne-là est la meilleure avec laquelle je peux fonctionner. Donc vous voyez une trahison de la part d'un militant, c'est grave.

Loners can generate heat, as the complaint at the start of the LaFontaine incident that "they didn't consult anybody" indicates, but a masterful networker can similarly evoke suspicion and resentment.

> Nobody would invite her. Well, at one point, *everybody* invited her and liked her but she profited from us quite often. People did not like that. I think she had a lot to contribute but I think she systematically undercuts her rivals. She's very insecure and that has caused her to be unpopular.

In a sense, however, the successful Circuit player is precisely someone who can "profit" from their network of contacts with clients and patrons in order to head a coalition initiative, mount a bid for office or secure a political appointment. It's almost inevitable, therefore, that movement through the occupational rungs associated with the Circuit will stir an irreconcilable brew of admiration and reproach.

But the tension of Circuit affiliations is prompted as much by these institutionally structured conflicts as by a more general ambivalence about the very notion of a career based on advocacy. In interviews with 35 individuals who operate, in some fashion, on the Circuit, 26 derived all or a significant portion of their income from this work. Two had worked in this sector previously but had moved onto public service jobs in other fields while continuing to participate in the Circuit as volunteers. For an additional three, contact with Circuit clients constituted a more incidental or sporadic element of their work. The majority of these respondents were, therefore, employed in this field. Yet there were few unequivocal expressions of belief either in the importance of this kind of career opportunity or in its viability. For some, such a career was simply unlikely or too difficult to realize. For others, it was the passion and the overtime, the volunteered extra that made an activist, not the formal career structure. For still others, professionalization and activism were simply incompatible:

> C'est le moment où c'est devenu une profession que c'est fini.
>
> Du militantisme doit être bénévole. Il faut que ça change quelque chose autrement ça devient une profession.
>
> Je pense que si quelqu'un se fait un plan de vie comme ça, c'est déjà pas bon.
>
> Un militant est bénévole par définition.
>
> It's very, very dangerous to do that, careerism.

Underlying this ambivalence are the difficulties of juggling competing images of advocacy as mission and advocacy as a profession. It's not easy to reconcile the image of an activist passionately committed to a cause with that of an ambitious professional seeking out career opportunities in the very system s/he is trying to reform. To the extent that Circuit clients promote the greater worth of the former, they can end up colluding in a peculiar kind of self-entrapment. The very qualities of professionalism and drive which were critical to their own advancement are devalued as potentially corrupting. It is therefore not surprising to find these activists taking their respective turns at denouncing and inevitably being themselves denounced for opportunism.

A Field of Political Action

Let us stop for a moment and consider what is new here and what is familiar from earlier work on urban ethnic movements. There is a long history of social science research which has noted the frequent marginalization of ethnic elites or "leaders" from their own groups. For Kurt Lewin, writing in the early 1940s, this kind of peripheral status rendered American ethnic leaders unreliable as strategists and spokesmen (Lewin as cited in Higham 1978). More recently, Pnina Werbner has noted the "deep suspicion" with which ethnic representatives are regarded by members of their own British Asian and Caribbean ethnic communities; their access to state patronage makes them suspect even as it functions as a primary source of their intracommunal influence and prestige (1991:17-18).

There are certainly aspects of this marginalization and brokership also operating in the Montreal situation I have described. In a sense the Circuit is first and foremost an institutionalized form of patronage. But unlike the ethnic brokers operating on the American political machine which Ulf Hannerz described over twenty years ago (1974), the Circuit clients cannot deliver votes or political support from an ethnic client population. While they are often very proficient in securing government funds for their respective organizations, these tend to be small operating or project grants which don't offer much in the way of welfare provisions, jobs or political perks.

> I don't have a lot of resources where I can reward board members, although it's starting to come my way because people call me up and they want names for nominations ... you know, people want to be, sometimes they ask me for nominations to commissions.... Theoretically, like I said there should be a way where a lot of the people move up and out and when people who are in contribute and give their time and there's no reward, they tend to stay because they're waiting for the reward and they get pissed off afterwards when they don't get the reward and they turn on you. So you know, it pays me to have, you know, this is why I play the political game, 'cause I tell those guys, you want, you know one of the ways to solve this dilemma is that you've got to recognize community

leaders in the sense you've got to listen to them when there's a crisis, you've got to give the appearance that there's some sort of communication and you got to give us some resources so that we can play the role of leader.

Those relatively few ethnic organizations which are more prosperous rely on private capital. The capacity of Circuit agents to mobilize ethnic populations through dispensation of government patronage is therefore extremely limited. Nor in many cases is there any deliberate attempt to do so, particularly in the case of the many players who work in public service jobs or for generic rather than ethnic-specific minority associations. These are not mass populists so much as ==public relations experts.== ※ This is therefore ==brokership in the political art of appearance.== Probably the most important asset that most Circuit agents offer their organizations, government or ethnic, is their knowledge of and contacts with external agencies: in short, their political network. In return, the organization gets enough public profile to help ensure its funding base or its place at significant political events.

The marginalization described by Kurt Lewin over fifty years ago has clear resonances in this scene as well. At least half of the Circuit players I interviewed expressed significant ambivalence about their membership in an ethnic community.

> Yes, as a matter of fact, I think I'm more respected and well loved by people from all the other groups than in my own. You know, that's where I have my friends. Most of the people who are considered my peers, who consider me their peer are people from all the other ethnic leaderships... There's a lot of wonderful people out there and like I say, I know pretty well anyone who's been active in the dossier for the last 10, 12 years.... I know where they're coming from, they know where I'm coming from. So, and so yeah but I really am serious. I mean in the ... community there's so much internal rivalry and jealousy that anybody who appears a little to go beyond the norm, right away is seen with a lot of jealousy and attacked from all fronts so a lot of people hate my guts in the ... community but you know I still work away.

If other players were somewhat more temperate in their comments, these remarks are part of ==two more general trends: the leitmotifs of friendship, even family, combined with professionalism which weave==

THE MINORITY CIRCUIT 105

through descriptions of personal Circuit networks; and the tendency for people to characterize their activism in universalist terms. These tendencies suggest that there is something here that diverges from the stock ambivalences of ethnic brokership.

I am not arguing for a literal treatment of these kinds of descriptions. Expressions of fellowhood and universalism take on a sardonic edge in the context of the competition and denunciations that are equally integral to the Circuit. But they do point to the emergence of a field of political action that is increasingly independent of the ethnic groupings which serve as its rationale. Within this field, a minority ethnic background may facilitate entry and legitimate participation. However, those players who cannot or do not wish to move beyond this entry point, i.e. beyond their own ethnic category, remain on the fringes of the Circuit. To advance, participants have to show themselves capable of operating on a broader transethnic basis. Civil servants and political appointees are usually assigned general dossiers – race relations, employment equity, cultural community council – or the files of ethnic "communities" of which they are not members. Given the nature of Canada's parliamentary system and the dispersal of most minority ethnic populations across several ridings, to be elected, an activist usually has to mobilize support across ethnic lines. A minority ethnic identity is, therefore, a useful calling card but it cannot function as the *sine qua non* of active and continued participation in the Circuit. Rather than representing specific communities, members use particular ethnic categories to launch themselves onto the Circuit, and adopt a generic minority rights rhetoric as an occupational vernacular.

Politicians use a variety of ascribed characteristics and social networks to launch their political careers and Circuit members are not very different in this respect. What is insidious about this institutional round is its commoditization of ethnic identity for public viewing and the treatment – in which activists often collude – of human beings as living mosaic icons. The Circuit may well have developed into an occupational culture with its own vernacular, personalities, symbols, and history. It is, however, a culture that is derided by the very rhetorics of representation which are used to legitimate the Circuit activities. People participating in the Circuit are supposed to be standing in for minority groupings. Their relations are therefore supposed to be instances of intercommunal rather than occupational relations. Accordingly, when people falter in this dance of representation, they are accused of being opportunistic and self-serving.

Academia and Identity Politics

This is hardly the only political arena in which the intractable complexities of local participation give way to glib exercises in public relations. The semi-mythical grassroots, by any classification, is not easily accessible for consultation or organized for direct political participation. Public consultations, from hearings over urban zoning to the Canadian Citizens' Forum (Spicer Commission), have therefore often ended up being rather hollow exercises, bizarre marriages of 1960s "citizen democracy" (Kennedy 1983) and 1990s conservatism. There is a significant body of research developing in the field of urban social movements which is surveying the organization and experience of local vehicles for community development and political participation. Ethnic studies also has its own copious and venerable tradition of work examining the "political construction of ethnicity" (Nagel 1986).[5] But there is a worrying gap between this large body of literature which builds upon 25 years of committed and careful scholarship in the field and the slogans of identity politics. It would be tempting to regard this as a schism between scholarly and popular readings of ethnicity, identity, and multiculturalism. However even the brief literature review with which this chapter opened indicates that this breach is integral to academic writing on this subject. Academia is crucially implicated in the politics of identity, not only in the struggles surrounding university admissions and recruitment policies but in the very way in which this "talk of difference" is theorized (Verdery 1994:51-55).

Verdery relates this involvement to the late twentieth-century reorganization of capitalism but there are also impetuses to be found closer to academic home. The first of these is the perennial tendency in ethnic studies for an analytical perspective that has frequently been more celebratory than critical. In 1978, John Higham was already complaining about the lack of a critical perspective in American ethnic studies (8). In 1994, Fredrik Barth admonished anthropologists for regularly operating "too narrowly as (self-appointed) advocates and apologists for ethnic groups in their grievances" (24). There is clearly considerable precedent for the passions and polemics of contemporary discussions of multiculturalism.

The second contributing influence comes from certain interpretations of postmodernism. By now, most of us are choking on an overly abundant literary diet of postmodernist definitional accounts so I am going to deliberately rush my version and accept, *a priori*, that it oversimplifies. Postmodernism, in its rejection of positivist universalism, has privileged positioned discourse. To quote from Aronowitz' recent analysis of the politics of identity, "one of the crucial features of the discourse is the intimate tie between knowledge and interest, the latter being understood as a 'standpoint' from which to grasp 'reality'" (1992:258). From this perspective, content and protagonist become inseparable, i.e. what is being represented is ineluctably linked with who is formulating the representation. In its anthropological incarnations, this association has often involved a conflation of culture and social identity. The inherent reductionism of this argument has been superficially muted by a stress on the marginality and hybridity of contemporary identities. How little this nuance resolves is vividly illustrated in Renato Rosaldo's (1989) critique of the cultural invisibility of upper middle-class Americans. In a trawl that hauls in a motley assortment of anthropologists as well as the retired residents of Sun City, Rosaldo finally gets down to the nub of this self-inflicted cultural blindness. The Sun Cityers refuse to acknowledge that they are overwhelmingly white, middle-class professionals.

Most of the people operating on the Montreal Circuit I've described are professionals from various minority ethnic and racial backgrounds. Not only does a narrow focus on these backgrounds tell us very little about the Circuit; it is more likely to obscure its emerging occupational dynamics. It is obvious that Rosaldo's observation raises far more questions than it answers. It is also unlikely that he really believes that such grossly construed social categories determine cultural perceptions or tell us very much about the organization of social relations or the construction of identity. This less-than-sterling moment of social analysis does, however, seem to reflect a more general tendency in recent postmodernist-influenced literature to move from contending that position *shapes* narrative or discourse to arguing that it *constitutes* the narrative or discourse, or at least should. There are times when the messenger seems to have become the only message. That this development arises from concerns expressed by such anthropologists as Faye Harrison (1991) to deal more adequately with questions of power and inequality is laudable in its intention. It does not, however, change the fact that it provides a static treatment of social relations, cultural process, and a flat reading of identity – in spite of the allusions to borderzones and fluidity – as little more than a bricolage of some very superficial categories of race, ethnicity, gender, and class.

This concern with inequality and power leads into the third contributing factor I want to sketch here: the theoretical vacuum created by the move away from Marxist theory. Obviously, this shift is part of a general rejection of grand, totalizing theories. But it also reflects a broader disorientation and retreat on the part of the political Left both within and outside academia. The factors involved are too numerous and complex to treat as a postscript to a different analysis but it is clear that the political earthquakes caused by the end of the Cold War, global capital and labour restructuring, the aftermath of Thatcherism and Reaganism, and the sacralization of state deficits have blurred traditional, political lines often past recognition. At a time when conservative and social democrat governments alike are cutting welfare programs, race, ethnicity, and gender appear to have offered a new political compass for identifying who is still on the side of the subjugated and disenfranchised. Hence the insistence that criticism of multiculturalism programs, whatever the inspiration or the source, aids and abets the "neoconservative" camp. If the multiculturalists aren't the New New Left, then who is?

The problem for those seeking a new "progressive" rallying point is that "conservatives" can also easily play at identity politics. In Canada, the Conservative government under Brian Mulroney promoted and funded much of the current multiculturalism infrastructure including the Minority Circuit I have described in this chapter. Furthermore, this form of political map-reading cannot adequately explain the *fin de siècle* upheavals which provide its impetus, while supporting analyses at times so breathtakingly reductionistic that they appear to have elevated tokenism from cynical political manoeuvring to ethical imperative.

The three factors I have outlined here – the uncritical baggage of ethnic studies, the influence of postmodernism, and the retreat from Marxist theory – have nonetheless also been key influences on the more Barthian or situationalist stream in ethnic studies. Whether it is Barth's classic essay on social boundaries which he recently claimed was one of the first applications of a postmodern view of culture (1994:12) or my own rather uncritical treatment of Armenian nationalism (Amit Talai 1989), the bulk of anthropological scholarship since the late 1960s has indeed emphasized the contingent and invented nature of ethnicity. But it has also been shaped by and has contributed to the same theoretical and

apposite — appropriate; relevant

political baggage underlying the "new essentialism" (Verdery 1994:52) of identity politics. The distinction between situationalism and essentialism is a crucial one, but the antecedents of their contemporary incarnations are far too close for complacency from any quarter. There is therefore a special onus in ethnic studies to critically engage with a political movement it has in many senses fostered.

This engagement would greatly benefit from Barth's apposite warning against confounding imagined communities and political units of action (1994:26). As we saw, the Circuit draws its political capital from precisely this kind of conflation between a select group of professionals and minority ethnic groups. But we also need to go a step further and consider why our own sociological imagination has so seldom been able to meet the challenge of Barth's caution. In spite of our awareness that terms such as community, society or nation overestimate the boundedness and underestimate the complexity of social and cultural experience, our efforts at moving beyond this popular terminology have been underwhelming. At best we have succeeded in qualifying these terms by alluding to an in-between alternative of borderzones between communities, hybrids of cultures, and transnationalism. For twenty-five years, we have acknowledged that ethnicity is a "matter of degree" associated with a wide variety of situations and expressions. Yet our most ubiquitous representation still involves discrete ethnic communities with leaders, associations, and identifiable members. It's the familiar narrative stuff with which multicultural policies and their attendant mythologies are mounted, but it hardly gives our analysis much critical edge. This chapter has not been concerned with the organization of ethnic communities, the mobilization of their membership or the representativeness of their leadership. Rather, it has tried to describe a particular consequence of the public relations of official diversity: the emergence of an institutionalized Circuit of exercises in minority consultation and representation, and the professional activists who staff them.

Notes

1. This study was made possible by a grant from the Social Science and Humanities Research Council of Canada as well as a grant from the Canadian Ministry of Multiculturalism and Citizenship.

2. Fleras and Elliott's recent book on *Multiculturalism in Canada* (1992) does attempt to explore some of the recent policy changes through the 1980s but this analysis is pitched at a fairly general, introductory level.
3. There is by now a considerable literature documenting major instances of government mistreatment of ethnic minorities, including the Chinese Head Tax (Li 1988), the Immigration Act of 1910, and the internment of Japanese citizens in World War II (Malarek 1987), to mention but a few. Furthermore, the culpability of the Canadian government in the last of these cases has now been officially acknowledged with an apology and compensation.
4. From 1986-88, I participated in the Circuit while working for an advocacy organization. While this organization was not itself an ethnic minority association, I was made responsible for developing a network of contacts with "representatives" of ethnic associations. When I left this job, I followed the activities of the Circuit at a distance through secondary sources. In 1991-92, I conducted a more systematic study of the Circuit which included in-depth interviews with 35 respondents, case studies of two coalitions, and attendance at a variety of related meetings. I was assisted in this study by Sylvie Gravel and Margie Lambert.

    Confidentiality is a tricky issue in accounts of the Circuit, since it involves public events and a number of relatively well-known figures. In addition to using aliases in place of the actual names of activists, I have also had to avoid precise references to people's organizational and community affiliations where these could easily identify them. When using direct quotations, I have left this kind of reference blank.
5. For a very small sample of additional relevant work see Amit Talai 1989; Werbner & Anwar 1991; Higham 1978; Cohen 1969; Parkin 1978; Roosens 1989; Eriksen 1992; Barth 1994; Handler 1988.

References

Abu-Laban, Yasmeen, and Daiva Stasiulis (1992). "Ethnic Pluralism under Siege: Popular and Partisan Opposition to Multiculturalism." *Canadian Public Policy* XVIII(4):365-386.

Amit Talai, Vered (1989). *Armenians in London: The Management of Social Boundaries*. Manchester: Manchester University Press.

Anderson, Alan, and James Frideres (1981). *Ethnicity in Canada: Theoretical Perspectives*. Toronto: Butterworths.

Appadurai, Arjun (1991). "Global Ethnoscapes: Notes and Queries for a Transnational Anthropology." In Richard G. Fox (ed.), *Recapturing Anthropology: Working in the Present*. Santa Fe, New Mexico: School of American Research Press. pp. 191-210.

Aronowitz, Stanley (1992). *The Politics of Identity: Class, Culture, Social Movements*. New York & London: Routledge.

Barth, Fredrik (1994). "Enduring and emerging issues in the analysis of ethnicity." In Hans Vermeulen and Cora Grovers (eds.), *The Anthropology of Ethnicity: Beyond 'Ethnic Groups and Boundaries'*. Amsterdam: Het Spinhuis Publishers, pp. 11-32.

Bibby, Reginald (1990). *Mosaic Madness: The Poverty and Potential of Life in Canada*. Toronto: Stoddart.

Bienvenue, Rita M., and Jay E. Goldstein (1985). *Ethnicity and Ethnic Relations in Canada*, 2nd ed. Toronto: Butterworths.

Bissoondath, Neil (1994). *Selling Illusions: The Cult of Multiculturalism in Canada*. Toronto: Penguin.

Bolaria, B. Singh, and Peter S. Li (1988). *Racial Oppression in Canada*, 2nd ed. Toronto: Garamond.

Cohen, Abner (1969). *Custom and Politics in Urban Africa*. Berkeley and Los Angeles: University of California Press.

Cohen, Anthony P. (1985). *The Symbolic Construction of Community*. London: Tavistock Publications.

Eriksen, Thomas Hylland (1992). *Us and Them in Modern Societies: Ethnicity and Nationalism in Mauritius, Trinidad and Beyond*. Oslo: Scandinavian University Press.

Fleras, Augie, and Jean Leonard Elliott (1992). *Multiculturalism in Canada: The Challenge of Diversity*. Scarborough, Ont.: Nelson Canada.

Hannerz, Ulf (1974). "Ethnicity and Opportunity in Urban America." In Abner Cohen (ed.), *Urban Ethnicity*. London: Tavistock Publications, pp. 27-76.

Harrison, Faye V. (1991). "Ethnography as Politics." In Faye V. Harrison (ed.), *Decolonizing Anthropology: Moving Further Toward an Anthropology for Liberation*. Washington: American Anthropological Association, pp. 88-109.

Herberg, Edward N. (1989). *Ethnic Groups in Canada: Adaptations and Transitions*. Scarborough, Ont.: Nelson Canada.

Higham, John (1978). "Introduction: The Forms of Ethnic Leadership." In John Higham (ed.), *Ethnic Leadership in America*. Baltimore and London: Johns Hopkins University Press, pp. 1-18.

Hu-Dehart, Evelyn (1994). "P.C. and the Politics of Multiculturalism in Higher Education." In Steven Gregory and Roger Sanjek (eds.), *Race*. New Brunswick, N.J.: Rutgers University Press, pp. 243-256.

Juteau, Danielle (1991). *The Sociology of Ethnic Relations in Quebec: History and Discourse*. Lectures and Papers in Ethnicity, no.2, University of Toronto.

Kennedy, Leslie (1983). *The Urban Kaleidoscope: Canadian Perspectives*. Toronto: McGraw-Hill.

Li, Peter S. (1988). *The Chinese in Canada*. Toronto: Oxford University Press.

Li, Peter S. (ed.) (1990). *Race and Ethnic Relations in Canada*. Toronto: Oxford University Press.

Malarek, Victor (1987). *Haven's Gate*. Toronto: Macmillan.

McAll, Christopher (1990). *Class, Ethnicity & Social Inequality*. Montreal: McGill-Queen's University Press.

Nagel, Joane (1986). "The Political Construction of Ethnicity." In Susan Olzak and Joane Nagel (eds.), *Competitive Ethnic Relations*. Orlando, San Diego, and New York: Academic Press, pp. 93-112.

Parkin, David (1978). *The Cultural Definition of Political Response*. New York: Academic Press.

Roberts, Lance W., and Rodney A. Clifton (1990). "Multiculturalism in Canada: A Sociological Perspective." In Peter S. Li (ed.), *Race and Ethnic Relations in Canada*. Toronto: Oxford University Press, pp. 120-147.

Roosens, Eugeen (1989). *Creating Ethnicity: The process of ethnogenesis*. London: Sage Publications.

Rosaldo, Renato (1989). *Culture and Truth: The Remaking of Social Analysis*. Boston: Beacon Press.

———. (1994). "Race and Other Inequalities: The Borderlands in Arturo Islas's *Migrant Souls*." In Steven Gregory and Roger Sanjek (eds.), *Race*. New Brunswick, N.J.: Rutgers University Press, pp. 213-225.

Takagi, Dana Y. (1994). "Post-Civil Rights Politics and Asian-American Identity: Admissions and Higher Education." In Steven Gregory and Roger Sanjek (eds.), *Race*. New Brunswick, N.J.: Rutgers University Press, pp. 229-242.

Verdery, Katherine (1994). "Ethnicity, nationalism and state-making: *Ethnic groups and boundaries*: past and future." In Hans Vermeulen and Cora Grovers (eds.), *The Anthropology of Ethnicity: Beyond 'Ethnic Groups and Boundaries'*. Amsterdam: Het Spinhuis Publishers, pp. 33-58.

Werbner, Pnina (1991). "Introduction II: Black and ethnic leaderships in Britain: A theoretical overview." In Pnina Werbner and Muhammad

Anwar (eds.), *Black and Ethnic Leaderships in Britain: The cultural dimensions of political action*. London and New York: Routledge, pp. 15-37.

Wilson, V. Seymour (1993). "The Tapestry Vision of Canadian Multiculturalism." *Canadian Journal of Political Science*, XXVI(4):645-669.

5

Mediating Identity: Kashtin, the Media, and the Oka Crisis[1]

Val Morrison[2]

In this chapter I will show how the issue of mediated identity is crucial to understanding the dual roles of popular culture and ethnicity in contemporary Western societies. The empirical focus of the paper is on the First Nations[3] musical duo, Kashtin, popular in Québec, and the media coverage surrounding them during the Oka Crisis in 1990. During the armed stand-off between Mohawks at the Kahnawake and Kanesatake Indian reservations and both provincial and federal levels of government, the music of Kashtin, who are not Mohawk, was boycotted by several influential French-language radio stations in Québec. The only direct link between Kashtin, the band, and the Oka Crisis is that both involve Natives, yet Kashtin was drawn into the heart of the media debates over Oka repeatedly and regardless of their steadfast attempts to avoid making any public statements on the issue. Moreover, we witnessed during this debate a curious about-face on the part of the Québécois media. Kashtin's status as an authentically Québécois act appeared to have been suspended and the group became Native, period. The heart of this discussion rests on establishing that the construction of identity, ethnic or otherwise, through popular cultural forms can be, and often is, largely in the hands of the media themselves. This becomes particularly problematic in the context of late 20th-century tendencies toward increased access to and visibility within the popular media, of groups hitherto largely confined to the margins of popular culture.

Kashtin: a first in Québec

Kashtin quite literally exploded onto the Québécois cultural scene in the summer of 1989 with the release of its first single, *E Uassiuian*, and soon followed up by releasing its self-entitled debut album in September. Called the success of the summer by the local music media, the presence of Kashtin has several profound implications on the development of popular music in Québec. The most obvious of these is that the members of Kashtin, unlike all previous Québécois musical stars, do not sing in French. They compose exclusively in their native language, Innu Aimun,[4] a language spoken by some 10,000 people in Northern Québec, and with few exceptions also perform publicly in this language.[5] The popularity of groups who sing in a language other than French in the province is certainly precedented, but what stands out about Kashtin is that not only does the group do well commercially, but it is also portrayed and accepted as genuinely Québécois.

The group is comprised of singer-songwriters Florent Vollant and Claude McKenzie from the Maliotenam Indian reservation near Sept-Iles on the lower north shore of the St. Lawrence river. Since its early success, Kashtin has released two more albums, the most recent of which appears on the house label of the multinational entertainment conglomerate Sony, and has toured throughout North America and in several European and Asian countries. While Kashtin has been successful in English Canada and France, notably, this analysis deals with their presence in French-speaking Québec.

That Kashtin is portrayed as authentically Québécois does not mean that the fact that both members of the group are Native is ever ignored in the province's music industry apparatus;[6] indeed, this is one of the primary focuses of discussions surrounding them, and it may be argued, one of their strong selling points. It is important, however, to point out that Kashtin has never been regarded as anything less than authentically Québécois. Moreover, Kashtin is the first act to enjoy this status while being ethnically not Québécois and performing in a language other than French. This acceptance has to do not only with the social, cultural, and political circumstances within which Kashtin emerged, but with shifts and changes in a provincial music industry which, now more than ever before, permits a diversity of musical styles and practices which are nevertheless defined as specifically Québécois. That is, developments in popular music in Québec are such that the industry apparatus has allowed not only for the existence and success of Kashtin, but for its inclusion in a musical field which until very recently was defined as exclusively French-language terrain.

Kashtin's star status on the Québécois pop culture scene is undisputed. Until the duo's success, some artists who sang in languages other than French (and this usually meant in English) could be recognized as being *from* Québec, but they were not *of* Québec. That is, they could enjoy commercial success in the province, but were not an integral part of the Québécois popular cultural scene. Kashtin's undeniable presence on this scene is attested to by several things. The fact that until the recent signing with Sony Music the group had been managed, promoted, and distributed by local independent companies certainly had an impact upon its strong presence in the province. But perhaps more tellingly, and certainly more immediately observable, they have not only been nominated for several Félix awards (the Québécois equivalent of the Canadian Juno Awards, American Grammy Awards, or the British BPI Awards), but have won a number of these, including "Best New Artists" against mainstream Québécois performers such as Villain Pengouin and Laurence Jalbert. Moreover, they have been invited to virtually all of the significant celebrations of Québécois music and culture so integral to acceptance as an important popular figure in Québec (le festival de Lanaudière; Festival d'été de Québec; les Francofolies de Montréal; and the crowning jewel for any young musical hopeful, the annual outdoor celebration of the national holiday, la fête de la St. Jean Baptiste). In the summer of 1992, they won the Espace Francophone Award for their performance at the Festival d'été de Québec. Furthermore, as evidence of their omnipresence during the year which followed the release of their debut album, they appeared either in the flesh or as the object of discussion in no less than 62 French-language televised broadcasts in Québec as well as in countless print media articles.

In order to completely understand how and why Kashtin emerged at the time that they did requires careful and complete analysis not only of the changes mentioned earlier within the music industry, but also of the social, cultural, and political climates in Québec which constantly mediate and transform various definitions of what it means to be Québécois. While such an analysis is beyond the scope of the present discussion, I do wish to point out several key developments which directly affect changing directions of Québécois popular music and which may begin to show how it is possible that in the early 1990s, groups such as Kashtin (and it is no longer the sole exception to the rule) can and do enjoy the status of authentic Québécois popular figures.

As with many local musics (Wallis and Malm 1984), the issue of authenticity is integral to an understanding of Québécois popular music. More than any other single set of cultural products, popular music, or *chanson* more specifically, is considered the sacred guardian of Québécois culture (Roy 1991). Chanson, which translates directly into English as song, is in fact much more than this in implication. The genre, which is considered to be undeniably Québécois, and which saw its peak during the 1960s in the province, resembles a combination of American coffee-house-style folk music and French chanson rive-gauche. It is a style usually performed by a sole male performer, accompanying songs to which he has composed both the music and the lyrics, either on guitar or piano. There is an emphasis on lyrics of a poetic nature, as well as on the political agenda of the performer, one which at the least has been an open celebration of the specificity of Québécois culture, and at the most an avowed and public support for Quebec's sovereignty. The "founding fathers" of this genre include icons such as Félix Leclerc (from whom the annual music awards, *les Félix*, get their name), and Claude Léveillé. Their contemporary equivalents are singers such as Daniel Bélanger, Richard Séguin, and Paul Piché, all of whom enjoy star status in the province.

While at one time the definition of chanson québécoise was restricted to the solo singer-songwriter persona, in recent years the criteria have become much less restricted. Not only are groups, electrified instruments, and female performers admitted into the fold of what constitutes chanson, but it has been argued that "mainstream pop" in the province has gained the same recognition and status as that to which chanson once had sole claim (Grenier 1993). That is, as Grenier convincingly argues, prior to the economic crisis in the music industry during the 1980s, the popular musical field in the province was neatly divided into two camps: chanson and pop-rock. These two classifications were discursively organized in a hierarchy as authentic expressions of Québécois culture vs. commercialized sell-outs inspired largely by American pop music. In the wake of the industries' rejuvenation, these two categories have been largely collapsed and the label chanson is now used "for any popular music created/made in Québec regardless of genre distinctions" (Grenier 1993:222). What this implies is that now, more than ever before, performers who sing in a variety of styles and who may or may not compose their own music and lyrics, are portrayed by the music industry apparatus as authentic symbols of the essence of being Québécois. Two other equally important developments within the local music scene which have an impact upon Kashtin's status as Québécois are relevant here. The first relates to language, and the second to a broad encompassing redefinition of ethnicity.

Implicit in all of the criteria fulfilling what constitutes authentic Québécois music is the assumption that the lyrics be composed and sung in French. As mentioned earlier, Kashtin's Innu lyrics were the first exception to this. Although the issue became one of public debate during and after the 1990 Félix Awards, where Kashtin received its first (eight) nominations, the impetus came not from the group's presence, but rather grew out of superstar Céline Dion's vociferous refusal of the award for "Anglophone Artist of the Year" during the televised ceremony. When presented with the award Dion refused it, explaining during the brief speech and later in a news conference that, among other things, everyone, including her loving fans and the members of ADISQ,[7] know that she is *not* an anglophone. She is Québécoise, and recording an album in English does not make her an anglophone. There may be several ways to look at her refusal, not the least of which is to say that it was a mere publicity stunt to ensure that her fans in Québec remained faithful.[8] Part of the fallout, however, was that the issue of what language Québécois music can be sung in had to be dealt with directly. Apparently, according to Dion in her outburst, one could be Québécois and sing in English; what one could not be at the same time as being Québécois, however, was an anglophone! The conclusive response of ADISQ was to rename the category "Best English-language Recording" in the following and subsequent years. This move accomplished two things. On the one hand, the award could be given to either an anglophone from Québec who records in English, as is often the case with the award, or a francophone who has released at least one album sung in English. On the other hand, the redefinition of the category helps demarcate the boundaries of what constitutes Québécois music. This refined definition clearly excludes both the English language (by marginalizing it as a single category among nearly 100 awards – incidentally, the same as is done at the Canadian Junos with Francophone recordings) and anglophone as an ethnic category from what constitutes Québécois ethnicity as expressed through popular music.

It is worth repeating that it was at this same ceremony that Kashtin reaped its first Félix awards within the mainstream categories which celebrate *Québécois* musical achievements, and this was regardless of the fact that they do not sing in French. When all is said and done, then, when the music industry apparatus in Québec had to spell out language criteria for what constitutes Québécois music in the 1990s, the response was that it does not necessarily have to be sung in French, but it cannot be sung in English.

Why Kashtin, Why Now?

Given the emphasis on the language of Québécois music (indeed, on language in Québécois culture generally), the success of Kashtin in the province raises several questions: Why? How? Why now? There are certainly a great number of possible answers to explain the success of Kashtin. For one thing, their music is said to cross language barriers and have an infectious beat and pleasing harmonies. This helps explain why any popular music band may succeed, but it does not answer why Québec is willing to accept, as one of its own, a duo who do not perform in the language which had hitherto been an unchallenged *a priori* criterion for popular music. In order to understand this more fully, a number of points of convergence need to be addressed. I will confine my comments here to brief thumbnail sketches which might suggest areas worthy of further detailed analysis. These comments take into account the current context of popular music in the province, some points of convergence between the Innu and Québécois cultures, and how such a convergence might facilitate the construction of the Innu, through the intermediary of Kashtin, as not only *in* Québec, but *of* Québec, *as* Québécois.

The Music Industry Context: Why Now?

During the 1980s, the international music markets saw a rise to unprecedented popularity of what has been variously called world music, ethnic music, or world beat. I will refer to this category as world music (although for a variety of reasons, the term ethnic music is particularly insightful). World music is a category of popular music which by its very definition is mass-distributed throughout the world, yet it remains associated with minority groups and/or developing countries and combines musical elements (recording technology for example) and characteristics (such as some instruments, the basic song format, etc.) of mainstream genres in the Euro-American music industry with those of various marginalized local musical cultures (Guilbault 1993). As such, world music is a popular form which combines musical styles, is usually sung in a language other than English (the traditionally dominant language of popular music in the West), and is somehow associated with minority groups (either in the West, in a developing country, or diasporically). It is important to note, however, that world music is more than a bilateral (and often unequal) combination of musical and technological elements. Much recent world music has progressed from unilateral or bilateral exchanges to become a "multi-lateral cross-fertilization between and among first and various third world musical traditions" (Pacini 1992:360).

Examples of this sort of music are many, and several people have suggested that Paul Simon's *Graceland* album was the first to mix cultural musical styles (Hunter 1991; Meintjes 1990) and thus represents a ground breaking moment with regard to world music (Hunter 1991:293). However, while Simon's album may in a sense have proved the potential popularity of world music, it is not to be confused with contemporary world music. As well as being an international star, Simon sings in English, and had already appeared on more than one major record label (Columbia and Warner Brothers) in the West. Simon's two albums may be better seen as particularly insightful examples of musical collaboration in all that this implies.

A better example of what I mean by contemporary world music is represented in the case of the Gipsy Kings, who sing in Spanish, play Spanish-style music, and who have produced three popular albums since the mid-1980s. In keeping with one of the strong tendencies in world music – that much of it originates in megalopolises – all three Gipsy Kings albums were recorded and mixed in Paris. As such, then, much world music enters the Western industry scene not as something appropriated and adjusted from another culture, but from the inside.

So world music emerged from a specific set of socio-historical circumstances which include the intensification of world communications/media networks, the eclipse of the nation-state as the site of culture *par excellence,* the end of the Cold War, and the increasing irrelevance of international borders in terms of both the movement of peoples and of monies. The music industry itself has, of course, been transformed within these more general shifts. It is no longer possible to speak of national music industries in an age when the largest French record company is owned by a German publishing firm, and CBS/Columbia is controlled by Japanese interests. By definition, popular music in the late 20th century is produced, distributed, and consumed with little regard for national borders (Frith 1988:103-4).

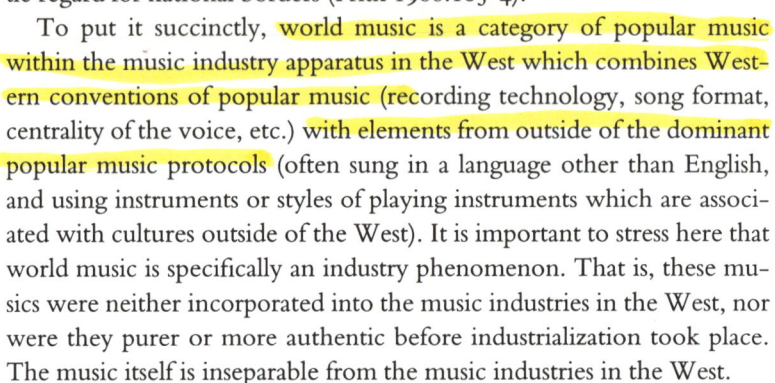

To put it succinctly, world music is a category of popular music within the music industry apparatus in the West which combines Western conventions of popular music (recording technology, song format, centrality of the voice, etc.) with elements from outside of the dominant popular music protocols (often sung in a language other than English, and using instruments or styles of playing instruments which are associated with cultures outside of the West). It is important to stress here that world music is specifically an industry phenomenon. That is, these musics were neither incorporated into the music industries in the West, nor were they purer or more authentic before industrialization took place. The music itself is inseparable from the music industries in the West.

One of the most intriguing and integral elements of world music, and the reason I earlier mentioned the appropriateness of the label *ethnic music*, is the centrality of ethnicity. That is, world music is invariably packaged and promoted as embodying the culture of the performer. Without ever explicitly saying so, the music industry apparatus constantly makes connections between the music, the public image of the group or person, and the culture from which they come. Examples of how this is the case with Kashtin include one which they integrated into their 1991-93 live performances as well as the explanatory note on their first album.

In concert, after a first set, Florent Vollant takes the stage alone with a teueikan (Innu caribou skin drum) and interprets a short traditional Innu song. Afterwards, he illustrates the instrument, and explains, in French,

> Often, they call us Montagnais, Amerindians, Aboriginals, and also savages. Where we come from,[9] there is only one word to define the First Nations, it's Innu. The Innu have only one musical instrument, the teueikan. The teueikan which is made of young birch and stretched caribou. What crosses the teueikan here (across the middle of the drum), is pieces of the feather of the night bird which we call papanashish, this creates the resonance of the teueikan. Where we come from, those who

possess the traditional music also possess communion with nature and divinatory power. The teueikan has perhaps five thousand years of history – it is what has allowed us to survive. It is what allows us to sing Ekumpua.

At this point, Vollant begins beating the drum anew and continues,

Ekumpua, a song to remind you that the Innu were the first inhabitants of America and today they are often still in search of a place for themselves.[10]

Here, Vollant switches to Innu and repeats what we assume to be the final paragraph above, in Innu, and is joined on stage by McKenzie and the rest of the band for Ekumpua, a powerful electric song driven by a strong blues flavour.

There are several intriguing elements present in this example. The implicit assumption which makes a statement like the one cited possible is that a pop music concert is an appropriate venue for a lesson in Innu culture and history. In the final section, the audience is told that the song they are to perform is to remind them of the context for contemporary First Nations social situations. Since the audience in this case, and in most cases when Kasthin performs live outside of the network of Native communities, is largely non-Innu, the meaning of the lyrics of the song are lost to them. Indeed, this monologue could have preceded any Kashtin song and would have remained, for the audience, appropriate. Yet here, we are told what function Ekumpua is to serve. This kind of guided tour of world music songs is not unusual, however. It is ever-present in the concerts, as well as on the CDs and cassettes of various world music groups. It is in part why I argue that *ethnic music* is a label not inappropriate to designate one of the integral aspects of this type of popular music. For indeed, a crucial component of these musics is the ever-present lessons in ethnicity.

In a further example, again using Kashtin but not by any means applying specifically to them, are the liner notes to their first CD, a listener's guide to another culture:

Our native culture is often perceived as a single entity, without distinction as to nations, languages and customs. This stems from a widespread misunderstanding of the "Native Peoples." There are as many cultural differences between the MOHAWKS and the INUIT as there are between the TURKS and the ENGLISH. Through its music, Kashtin seeks to tear down the walls of indifference by captivating you with the difference.

The Montagnais language (Innu Aionun) has no equivalent for the word "music." To us, music is everywhere; it vibrates through every living thing. Our forefathers sought oneness with nature through sound. They used the TEUEIKAN (the Innu caribou-skin drum) as a means of communicating with nature. Our definition of "traditional music" is reminiscent of a time when the knowledge and mastery of the various sounds of nature were the keys to the power of survival.

To Kashtin, music still holds the same power, transcending the lyrics, to pass on the traditional spirit. By traditional spirit, we mean the values our people live by, such as tolerance, sharing, generosity and respect for nature.

Kashtin wishes to use the power of sound both for your listening pleasure and to promote the survival and dissemination of Innuat values. In these troubled times, values such as these may well be what our planet needs.... (Kashtin, *Kashtin.* Trans-Canada: PPFL AC-2009).

It is clear here that part of what Kashtin, and the industry which promotes them, are selling is more than music: it is values, it is history, it is culture. It is, in their words, "the dissemination of Innuat values." I will return to this example and to its implications in a further section. To continue with the presence and importance of Kashtin specifically, and world music generally, I will briefly outline the primary network for world music in Québec.

The rising popularity of world music has been mediated in Québec through the international network that is the Francophonie, which consists of a network of nations and populations with a large proportion of French-speakers. Revolving largely around France, the Francophonie includes member nations from North America, Africa, the Caribbean, Europe, and Asia. It is important to note that while the goal of this network is to create a forum for French-speaking nations, French is often not the first language for many of the countries. In terms of the music which circulates here, "many artists on this scene sing in languages other than French (Spanish, numerous African languages, and Creole to name a few)" (Grenier 1994). One of the consequences of the rise in importance of the Francophonie on the popular music scene has been the establishments of festivals which unite artists from around the network. In Québec, the principal such event is the annual *Francofolies de Montréal*, a week-long series of concerts and events organized and run by the same people as the Montreal International Jazz Festival, *Spectrascène*. Other events which rally around the Francophonie and provide a forum for world music in the province include the *Festival d'été de Québec* and the *Coup de coeur francophone*. These events, organized around an appeal to commonality, to a diasporic Francophone identity, have provided a forum for a wide diversity of musical styles and practices, and every year their popularity has grown.[11] Kashtin, as noted earlier, has been ever-present at these events and, moreover, was the first big-name act from Québec to perform at these festivals in a language other than French. Their presence thus provides an example, in the context of the Francophonie, of the heterogeneous musical culture within official French-speaking Québec, a sort of homegrown world beat.

Innu and Québécois Culture: Why Kashtin?

In examining Kashtin's acceptance as an authentically Québécois act, several points can be made. First, although they are members of a First Nation, Kashtin are from Québec. Moreover, the reservation they are from, Maliotenam, is situated in one of Québec's most lauded tourist regions, the picturesque lower north shore of the St. Lawrence River. Indeed, the Québec tourism board uses Kashtin as a vehicle to promote tourism in that area: to a soundtrack of Kashtin singing one of their hits in the province, a promotional video pans the scenic area; while a voice-over discusses the beauty of the area, we see Claude McKenzie and Florent Vollant talking on the time-eroded rocks of Havre-St-Pierre. These shores, the voice-over continues, inspire Kashtin to give us such songs as *Tshinanu*, and the piece moves to them, performing the song, on the rocks. In the same vein, the opening of the Museum of Civilization in Québec City housed an exhibition of Native culture to which Kashtin was invited to sing *Ishkuess*, a hit from their second album, amidst some of the exhibits. Here we see two clear examples of how Kashtin is used to represent both the beauty and long history of Québec, and there is no question that they are a part of this story.[12]

The use of language as a metaphor for authenticity in Québec's musical scene also allows for the inclusion of Kashtin. Although they do not sing in French, the Innu have the distinction among First Nations groups in Canada of having French as their primary second language; both members of Kashtin are completely fluent in the language. This allows them to appear in countless television interviews during which they converse in French. Kashtin, then, appears to have arisen in a context ripe for their success. Not only could they provide Québec with an indigenous world music, something that had become a precious commodity on the international music scene, but they could, because of a variety of historical, cultural, and social circumstances, be authentic members of a Québec in the process of redefining what it means to be Québécois.[13]

Twentieth-Century Popular Music and the Mediation of Identity

Much of the argument I have made thus far rests on the media portrayal of Kashtin as authentically Québécois. In order for this position to be sustained, it is necessary to understand that these comments are not extraneous or epiphenomenal to Kashtin. Possibly the most often quoted sentence in contemporary popular music studies is one made by Simon Frith in his discussion of the industrialization of music:

> The industrialization of music cannot be understood as something which happens *to* music, since it describes a process in which music itself is made – a process, that is, which fuses (and confuses) capital, technical and musical arguments. (Frith 1988:12)

This statement tackles a position in popular music studies which views certain music and particular acts as more authentic, or real, than others. Chiefly, this view holds that once a genre or group of performers is incorporated into the music industry, their alleged political significance is appropriated and rendered benign (cf. Grossberg 1984; Hebdige 1979). Frith argues instead that no 20th-century popular music exists outside of the industrial process. I would argue, therefore, in agreement with this, that it is both theoretically and analytically unfruitful and completely partial to view Kashtin, or indeed any popular cultural phenomenon, as something which existed prior to their mediation through the music industry apparatus.

It is thus essential that we not reduce Kashtin to either their live appearances, to their CDs, or to the individuals who form the group. As Québec has come to know it, Kashtin is a fusion (and confusion) of the various embodiments of their presence, no one more real or important than any other. They are a phenomenon of 20th-century popular music, in the sense implied in the quotation from Frith above. The public's access to Kashtin is mediated by what I have called the music industry apparatus, and a key component of this are the pervasive and various commentaries surrounding them. Louise Meintjes (1990) calls these "metacommentaries," referring to those statements made in the popular media which are inseparable from the person or thing they describe and which are a key ingredient in the construction of the phenomenon. In the case of Kashtin, and world music generally, part of what is being constructed and portrayed is ethnicity and identity. This fact is particularly problematic when the music industry apparatus is outside of the culture being constructed, and leads to a wide range of considerations. Moreover, a considerable degree of the power which portrays Kashtin as Québécois is in the hands of the media which sustain this position. In other words, the Québécois identity accorded them in this context is a precarious one. While it is certainly part of the reason for their superstar status in the province, as the discussion below will illustrate, Kashtin has little direct control over this, and the status of Québécois can be revoked by the very people who have built it up.

It is important to point out, before going on to the specific case to be analyzed, that there is no one music industry apparatus which circulates these metacommentaries. I noted earlier that Kashtin has enjoyed considerable success in France, English-speaking Canada, and more recently, the United States. They are also hugely popular and ubiquitous on the First Nations reservation circuit in Canada (their song *Tshinanu,* which means *who we are,* has in fact been referred to as a pan-Native national anthem). All of these contexts need to be considered individually when coming to an understanding of what Kashtin represents in each of these settings. There is, for example, a considerable case to be made for their role in the development of a pan-Native identity in the same sense that other work in this area has suggested such constructions (cf. Guilbault 1993; Gilroy 1991; Waterman 1990). I reiterate, then, that this analysis deals with Kashtin's very specific construction in French-speaking Québec and in the metacommentaries surrounding them in this context.

The Oka Crisis

Kashtin's status as authentically Québécois was tested for the first time during the summer of 1990 at the peak of their rise to success in the province. The 78-day armed standoff between the Mohawk natives at two Montreal-area reservations, the police, and later the armed forces marked one of the most bitter land claims conflicts between Natives and both levels (provincial and federal) of government in recent Canadian history, and is commonly referred to as the Oka Crisis.

This land claims dispute, like most in the country, dates back to the early 18th century when the land at Kanesatake was granted by the French Crown to the Seminary of St. Sulpice to house Mohawks already settled in the area as well as several newly converted Catholics. In 1945, the Crown purchased land occupied by the Mohawks from the Seminary and sold it to the adjacent Municipality of Oka, which effectively split the reservation; twelve years later, a nine-hole municipal golf course, protested in vain by some residents of Kanesatake, was constructed on the site. During the 1970s, when archaeological discoveries confirmed that the site of the golf course was occupied by Mohawks well before the 1717 grant, land claims were submitted to the federal government and these went unresolved. In 1989, the Municipality of Oka announced plans to expand the golf course to 18 holes (and onto land under dispute). Following this, well into 1990, the Mohawks at the reservation held several demonstrations to protest the construction, which they claimed would not only violate land claims, but would disturb a Mohawk burial ground. This provoked a series of public debates and a moratorium on the golf course was called. Throughout 1990 a series of conflicts both within the Kanesatake community and with the Municipality of Oka ensued, culminating finally, in March, in a "power play" by the golf club membership to exclude the Mohawks from participating in the discussion of the proposed expansion. At this point, the decision was in the hands of the membership, which voted unanimously in favour of beginning construction as soon as possible.

Finding out that they had been duped, the Mohawks immediately erected a barrier and began surveillance in an effort to halt the plans. The Municipality of Oka obtained an injunction against the barricade, and once again talks broke down. The federal government requested that construction be delayed in hopes of renewed land claims negotiations, but the mayor of Oka asked the Sûreté du Québec (the provincial police force, or SQ for short) to enforce the injunction and remove the Mohawk barriers. On July 11, a force of some 100 SQ officers unsuccessfully attacked the barriers and one officer was shot and later died in hospital. The Mohawks followed this by blocking the main provincial highway in the area, and Mohawks in Kahnawake, on the south shore of Montreal, erected barricades in solidarity, blocking the Mercier bridge, the main artery into Montreal from the southwestern suburbs. SQ barricades also blocked routes into the reservations, cutting off food and medical supplies. The Mohawk barricades, manned by a group known as Warriors, who are associated more closely with the traditional spiritual leaders than with the more recent elected band council, remained in place for 78 days and left the Montreal area in the grip of a potentially explosive conflict. Indeed, in Chateauguay, the suburb most immediately affected by the Kahnawake barricades, Natives clashed violently with white residents who were threatening retaliation. These three nights of violence were met with tear gas raids by the SQ; however, with the situation clearly beyond the Sûreté's control, with talks on all fronts ending in stalemate, and under the watchful eyes of an international team of observers, Québec premier Robert Bourassa – in a precarious move – requested that the 2,500 Canadian Armed Forces troops stationed at the outskirts take control of the conflict. The barriers were finally removed, first on the Mercier bridge, then in Oka, but the heart of the conflict remained unsolved.[14] Almost five years later, the conflict still echoes and the land claim remains unresolved, although the federal government has vowed to find a solution.

During the summer of 1990, the entire country, and not least of all Montreal, was riveted to the conflict. There was scarcely a day when it was not the topic of front-page news stories and heated debate on radio and television. Tension ran high as people vociferously berated the Mohawks, the Warriors, all Natives, both levels of government, the SQ, and finally, the army. Although there was little discussion of Kashtin during this time, primarily because they spent most of the summer touring in France, they occupied centre stage as the armed standoff began to wind down. It is here that we see the precarious nature of the mediated identity of Kashtin as Québécois. As I mentioned earlier, during the Oka crisis Kashtin's music was boycotted on several influential French-language radio stations in and around Montreal. No one seems able to say exactly when or how this occurred, and discussions about it arose only as the boycott was stopped.

The issues I want to discuss are apparent mainly in six newspaper articles, two from each of the French-language dailies in Montreal: *La Presse, Le Devoir,* and *Le Journal de Montréal.* The first of these articles appeared in each paper on September 21, 1990 in response to a television newscast on Radio-Canada on September 19. The newscast was the first time the boycott was discussed. In fact, it appears to have been the first time the members of Kashtin themselves heard of it, although the report stated that CKAC and CFGL, two of the most listened-to stations in the city, had not been playing Kashtin's music since mid-July, that is, virtually since the onset of the crisis. Indeed, the director of programming of CFGL stated that even though most of them would not admit it, he would stake his job on the bet that not one single French-language radio station in Montreal had been playing Kashtin's songs since the end of July. The stations apparently pulled the songs after complaints from listeners who said that they "had had enough of Indians." By the time the newspaper articles appeared two days later, the boycott had been lifted by most of the stations, under pressure from the exposure caused by the newscast. Aside from the announcement that the music of Kashtin had been boycotted and would now be played again, there seem to be two things going on in all three of the first set of articles. While on the one hand, all three articles implicitly condemn the boycott, on the other, they also do not explicitly question the connections between Kashtin, their music, and the Oka crisis, which remain implicit. Although the title of the article in *La Presse* is "Comme si Kashtin avait bloqué le pont Mercier," (as if Kashtin had blocked the Mercier bridge) this theme is not developed at all in the article. Both the article in *La Presse* and the one in *Le Journal de Montréal* speak of Kashtin as a Native duo, without reference to the Innu nation. Only *Le Devoir*, known as Montreal's intellectual daily, clearly spells out that while the Oka crisis involves Mohawks, McKenzie and Vollant are both Montagnais.[15]

The second set of articles, all of which appeared on October 2, follow a press conference Kashtin felt compelled to call in order to respond publicly to the whole issue and give their position on the crisis. Here, although most of the comments made by the journalists remained implicit on exactly how Kashtin is directly related to the Oka crisis, the question of Kashtin's identity was tackled explicitly by Florent Vollant, who characteristically does most of the talking for the duo. Vollant insisted that while the Mohawk nation has always been a radical one, the first to take up arms in defence of Native issues, the Innu nation is a peaceful one, avoiding war at all costs. Kashtin's members make it perfectly clear that they are behind the cause, but dissociate themselves and their nation from the violence. So for the first time since the release of their debut album, we are shown a Kashtin who are exclusively Native and Montagnais; the question of their being representatives of changing Québécois culture is curiously absent. In the months preceding the conflict they were described by various media personalities as the "evolution of *our* Québécois music" (Jean-Pierre Coallier, *Ad Lib*, 1989); as being "after all, Québécois like the rest of us" (Joel Bertomeu, *Lumières*, 1989); and "maybe not 100% Francophone, but definitely 100% Québécois, even 200% Québécois!" (René Simard, *Laser*, 1989), suddenly and without warning, they were "the idols of the Montagnais top 40" (Dufresne 1990:4), "Montagnais duo, Kashtin" (Lemay 1990:C5) and "Montagnais and proud of it" (Gauthier 1990:4).[16] In this curious about-face, the construction of Kashtin as Québécois is absent. They are Native, and this appears to be just cause to call them to the centre of the Oka Crisis and request that they speak on behalf of all First Nations.

In summary, the things which stand out for me in these articles are the implicitness with which Kashtin is directly tied to the Oka crisis; the portrayal of Kashtin as Native and Native alone, regardless of the fact that these are some of the people who before the crisis were quite happy to construct Kashtin's identity as Québécois; and finally, that Kashtin was forced to borrow (and translate) the phrase used in *Le Devoir*, whether they liked it or not, to become the spokespeople for all Natives. The claim made on the liner notes cited earlier that there are as many differences between the various First Nations as there are between the English and the Turks becomes peculiarly ironic here. The theoretical issues raised by this are inevitably linked to relations of power and to who defines mediated identity. Some of the most interesting discussions of popular music and identity focus on the construction of identities in and through often new or hybrid musics. Jocelyne Guilbault's (1993) discussion of the role played by zouk in the construction of créolité or Christopher Waterman's (1990) work on the role of popular music in Nigeria in constructing a pan-Yoruba identity are cases in point. As I mentioned earlier, in fact, I would argue that there is a strong case to be made for Kashtin's playing a role in the development of a pan-native identity. However, what is often ignored in these discussions is how this process works on the other, equally interesting but not always as positive side of the coin, which shows us how identities are constructed and peoples defined from across the boundaries, that is, by nonmembers of the group in question. This issue raises the very precarious nature of mediated identities. When cultural identities are constructed, as they often are, through popular cultural forms, the components of the identity being communicated can be, particularly in moments of crisis involving the group, at the mercy of the very media through which the identity is portrayed. Thus, while Kashtin can be portrayed and constructed in the Québécois media as a sign of the changing definitions of what it means to be Québécois, the power to control this particular mediation appears to be in the hands of the media apparatus, and not in Kashtin's. This is not to suggest that Kashtin, or indeed their audience, is completely powerless in defining who the group is and what it represents; it does, however, shed light on the processes involved in the media apparatus' construction of the group's identity.

In conclusion, and somewhat reluctantly since I would rather finish on a more positive note, I would like to refer to Philip Hayward's discussion of the very popular Australian Aboriginal band, Yothu Yindi. Hayward traces the success of the band's audio and video versions of the song "Treaty" which were both re-released in second versions after the band became successful and was granted $30,000 by the Australian government to play at a concert in New York to launch the United Nations' International Year of Indigenous Peoples. The politically explicit English lyrics were translated into an Aboriginal language spoken by a few thousand remotely located Australians, and the video representations changed from politically charged ones to what Hayward calls "dream-holiday-exotic surroundings." Hayward comments that he is not criticizing the band itself, but rather "the white hegemonic discourses which have created their cultural identity and thus context of reception" (Hayward 1993:39). He argues that as long as Yothu Yindi is seen as "safe, exotic and somewhere else," they can be constructed by the Australian media as authentically Australian. It may be the case, then, that Kashtin, whose music has always been sung in a language not understood by the majority of Québécois, and whose videos are typically shot on the Maliotenam reservation on the tourist-attractive lower north shore, are constructed as Québécois exactly because they too are "safe, exotic and somewhere else." For as I hope to have shown by looking at the exception to this portrayal, when Native issues were at the forefront of political turmoil, Kashtin's definition as Québécois was, temporarily at least, quickly revoked.

Notes

1. A preliminary version of this paper was presented at the International Association for the Study of Popular Music (IASPM) — Canada, "Popular Music and Identity" conference held at Concordia University in Montreal, March, 1994.
2. The author gratefully acknowledges Carleton University, Ontario Graduate Studies (OGS), and Fonds pour la Formation de Chercheurs et l'Aide à la Recherche (FCAR) for their financial support. I would also like to thank Line Grenier for comments and suggestions.
3. The terms First Nations and Native are used interchangeably in this text to refer to Aboriginal groups residing in Canada.
4. Innu Aimun is one of several dialects related to the Cree language and classified as belonging to the Algonquian linguistic family spoken by the Innu nation of Northern Québec and Labrador. In Québec as well as in English Canada, the Innu and their language are commonly referred to as Montagnais (meaning from, or of, the mountains).
5. In concert, Kashtin performs a Beatles medley in English and their second album contained a cover version of Micmac singer Willie Dunn's "Son of the Sun."
6. I use the term *apparatus* here to refer to the wide range of industries and support media directly and indirectly involved in the circulation of popular music in Québec (i.e. record labels, artists unions and trade organizations, but also star tabloids, newspapers, television programs involved in commenting on popular music, etc.).
7. Association du Disque et de l'Industrie du Spectacle et de la Vidéo du Québec, the lone music trade organization in the province which hosts and votes on the Félix Awards.
8. Céline Dion's next album was *Dion Chante Plamondon*, released soon after this fiasco. The publicity surrounding this album, which featured her interpretations of the most famous ghost lyricist in Québec, Luc Plamondon, was unprecedented in the province and led to the first-day sales breaking all existing records.
9. I have used the translation "where we come from" for the French "chez nous," which literally means "in our home," but the expression is used to evoke all of the imagery of home: community ties, warmth, familiarity, belonging, etc.

10. This monologue is recaptured in a televised version of Kashtin's performance at the annual Montréal music festival, *les Francofolies de Montréal*. The translation is mine.
11. The *Francofolies de Montréal*, for example, began in 1990 as a relatively modest festival held in the cool days of December in various clubs and live venues throughout the city; it has since grown to the point where, for the first time in 1994, it was held in August, on the newly revamped site of the jazz festival.
12. For a more detailed discussion of the points of convergence between the Innu and Québécois cultures mobilized in the construction of Kashtin by the popular media in Québec, see Grenier and Morrison, 1995.
13. While the discussion in this paper has been confined largely to the popular music scene in Québec, there is considerable evidence that the changes in defining what it means to be Québécois reverberate in other areas as well. To be very brief here, francophone Québec has, until recently, been composed primarily of people of direct French descent [referred to as *pure laine* (dyed in the wool) or *de souche* (from the source)], mainly because immigrants to the province historically have either been anglophone, or have adopted English as their second language. In the late 1970s, in accordance with the power of the symbol of the French language as the key to the cultural survival of Québec, official government legislation attempted to circumvent this by making French the official language of Québec, one of the many consequences of which was to effectively force new immigrants to attend French school and become fluent. This, combined with new immigration sources where many arrivals already speak French, has meant that the link between language and ethnicity is much less clear cut, i.e. where once speaking French virtually confirmed a direct line of ancestors to France, this is no longer the case. Somewhat later than the rest of Canada, then, Québec is still coping with the presence of diverse ethnic groups, all of whom speak the majority language. Because of the perceived dire need to attract French-speaking immigration (Québec has a well-below-average birth rate) and to continue to preserve Québécois culture through the primary symbol of language, attempts to define and refine what Québécois means are ongoing.
14. Most of this section is summarized from Frideres 1993:368-384.
15. At this point in Kashtin's career, the term Montagnais is still widely used over Innu. Interestingly, by 1994, after the release of their third album, the term is rarely used in the media and in fact, many of those who interview the band make a point of trying to say at least a few words in Innu.

16. All of these quotations are my translations from the original French.

References

Cauchon, Paul (1990). "Deux Montagnais et la politique: Le duo Kashtin défend la cause mais se demarque de la violence." *Le Devoir*, October 2, p.B3.

Dufresne, Jean (1990). "Il était une fois un petit 45 tours..." *Le Journal de Montréal*, September 21, p.4.

Frideres, James (1993). *Native Peoples in Canada: Contemporary Conflicts.* 4th ed. Scarborough: Prentice-Hall.

Frith, Simon (1988). "The Industrialization of Music." In Simon Frith (ed.), *Music for Pleasure.* New York: Routledge, pp.11-23.

———. "Video Pop: Picking up the Pieces." In Simon Frith, (ed.) *Facing the Music: A Patheon Guide to Popular Culture.* New York: Pantheon Books, pp.88-130.

Gauthier, Suzanne (1990). "Kashtin: la musique plutôt que les armes." *Le Journal de Montréal*, October 2, p.4.

Gilroy, Paul (1991). *'There Ain't No Black in the Union Jack': The Cultural Politics of Race and Nation.* Chicago: University of Chicago Press.

Grenier, Line (1994). "Is There Anybody Out There: The Québécois Popular Music Industry in Search of Audiences." Paper presented at *Media, Culture and Free Trade. NAFTA's Impact on Cultural Industries in Canada, Mexico, and the United States.* Austin, Tex., March.

———. (1993). "The Aftermath of a Crisis: Quebec Music Industries in the 1980s." *Popular Music* 12(3):209-228.

Grenier, Line, and Val Morrison (1995). "Le terrain socio-musical populaire au Québec ... et dire qu'on ne comprend pas toujours les paroles ..." *Etudes Littéraires* 27(3):75-98.

Grossberg, Lawrence (1984). "Another Boring Day in Paradise: Rock and Roll and the Empowerment of Everyday Life." *Popular Music* 4:225-258.

Guibault, Jocelyne (1993). *Zouk: World Music in the West Indies.* Chicago: University of Chicago Press.

Hayward, Philip (1993). "Safe, Exotic and Somewhere Else: Yothu Yindi, Treaty and the Mediation of Aboriginality." *Perfect Beat* 1(2):33-42.

Hebdige, Dick (1979). *Subculture: The Meaning of Style.* London: Methuen.

Hunter, Mead (1991). "Interculturalism and American Music." In B. Marranca and G. Dasgupta (eds.), *Interculturalism & Performance.* New York: PAJ Publications.

Lemay, Daniel (1990). "Comme si Kashtin avait bloqué le pont Mercier." *La Presse*, September 21, p.C5.
Lepage, Jocelyne (1990). "Les crises passent, la musique reste." *La Presse*, October 2, p.B5.
Meintjes, Louise (1990). "Paul Simon's Graceland, South Africa and the Mediation of Musical Meaning." *Ethnomusicology* (Winter):37-73.
Pacini, Deborah Hernandez (1992). "Bachata: from the Margins to the Mainstream." *Popular Music* 11(3):359-364.
Roy, Bruno (1991). *Pouvoir chanter*. Montréal: VLB Éditeur.
Trudel, Clément (1990). "Kashtin réintègre les ondes." *Le Devoir*, September 21, p.1.
Wallis, Roger, and Krister Malm (1984). *Big Sounds From Small Peoples: The Music Industry in Small Countries*. New York: Pendragon Press.
Waterman, Christopher (1990). "Our Tradition is a Very Modern Tradition: Popular Music and the Construction of a Pan-Yoruban Identity." *Ethnomusicology* 34(3):367-379.

Discography

Gipsy Kings (1987). *Gipsy Kings*. Columbia: WCK 90919.
Kashtin (1991). *Innu*. Groupe Concept Musique: PPFLC-2011.
___. (1989) *Kashtin*. Groupe Concept Musique: PPFL4-2009.
Simon, Paul (1986) *Graceland*. Warner Brothers: 92 54474.

6

Canada's Visible Minorities: Identity and Representation

Anthony Synnott and David Howes

This paper reviews the origins and development of the concept "visible minority" in Canada, reveals some critical limitations to its formulation and utility, and offers some directions for empirical sociological research to clarify the significance and role of visibility in the construction of minority ethnic identities.

The concept "visible minority" was apparently coined in the early 1970s with a descriptive and egalitarian purpose in mind: to avoid some of the pejorative connotations of such terms as "non-whites" and "coloureds," and to stress the common problem faced by all visible minorities, namely, white racism and the colour prejudices of the white majority. The phrase is now widely used in Canadian public discourse, and the concept has been enshrined in affirmative action, employment equity, and multiculturalism legislation, including the Employment Equity Act (1986), the Federal Contractors Program (1986), the Public Service Employment Equity Program (1986), the Multiculturalism Act (1986), and the Public Service Reform Act (1993). In this legislation visible minorities are defined as persons who are non-white in colour or non-Caucasian in race, other than Aboriginal people. These minorities are divided into ten groups: Blacks, Chinese, Filipino, other Pacific Islanders, Indo-Pakistani, Japanese, Korean, Southeast Asians, West Asians and Arabs, and Latin Americans.

Our argument in this paper is that when one takes the trouble to try to relate the concept of "visible minority" back to the social reality it is supposed to designate, it quickly starts to fall apart. This finding suggests that the concept was not well formulated in the first place, and raises serious questions about the legislation which employs it. Rather than promoting equity, this legislation may be seen as further entrenching difference by "racializing" divisions which, as we show, have always had more to do with social class and cultural beliefs than with skin colour or "visibility." While this paper is concerned primarily with the deconstruction of a "naturalizing" concept, it is also concerned with social reform, and to this end, it concludes with a statement of how government policy toward "visible minorities" needs to be altered to take account of the social realities we disclose here.

Profile

Let us begin by reviewing the situation of visible minorities in Canada. In 1991 visible minorities constituted 9.1% of the Canadian population, an increase of 44% from the 6.3% reported in 1986 (Canadian Human Rights Commission, 1994:65). Among the adult population (aged 15 or over), more than three-quarters (78%) were immigrants, about 15% were born in Canada and about 7% were non-permanent residents. Visible minorities were highly concentrated in the cities and accounted for 24% of the adult population in Toronto, 23% in Vancouver, and 10% in Montreal, with different ethnic or national groups variously concentrated in different cities. Toronto was home especially to Blacks (50%), Koreans (50%), South Asians (48%), Filipinos (42%), and Japanese (31%); Vancouver to Pacific Islanders (49%), Chinese (39%), and Japanese (27%) (Kelly 1995:4-5).

Visible minorities are diverse not only in respect to their residencies but also in respect to their place of birth and the duration of their lives in Canada. For instance, most members of all the visible minorities, except the Japanese, were born outside Canada. In addition, most visible minorities (nearly two-thirds) have come to Canada since 1972, and over one-third since 1982. Yet the demographics vary, ranging from over one half of Latin American and South East Asian adults who have arrived since 1982 to only 6% of Japanese and 15% of Pacific Islanders.

All these variables have implications for employment, type of employment, education, and therefore income levels. Unemployment rates (age-standardized) were slightly higher for visible minorities than for "other adults" (as the rest of the population is referred to by census analysts): 13% to 10%. But within the visible minority group itself, there is a wide range in the level of unemployment, as is indicated in Table 1.

TABLE I

Unemployment Rates of Visible Minorities
Age Standardized
Canada 1991

JAPANESE	6%
PACIFIC ISLANDERS	7%
FILIPINOS	7%
KOREANS	8%
CHINESE	10%
BLACKS	15%
SOUTH ASIANS	14%
WEST ASIANS AND ARABS	17%
SOUTH EAST ASIANS	17%
LATIN AMERICANS	20%

Source: Kelly, 1995:6

Note that the South East Asians and Latin Americans, with the highest unemployment rates, are also the most recent immigrants to Canada of all the visible minorities, and that the Japanese and the Pacific Islanders have the lowest proportion of recent immigrants in their numbers. It is unfortunate that the category of "other adults" was not analyzed further by ethnic or national origin to permit comparisons between Canadians of various origins, colours, and identities.

Education levels also varied in the 1991 study. In general, visible minorities had a higher proportion of adults with university degrees than other Canadians (18% compared to 11%), and they also had a lower proportion of adults with less than high school levels (33%) compared to other Canadian adults (39%). Filipinos, Koreans, Japanese, and West Asians and Arabs were most likely to have a university degree, while Blacks, South East Asians, Latin Americans, and Pacific Islanders were least likely to have degrees (Kelly 1995:5-6). The result of all these, and no doubt other, variables is a considerable variation in visible minorities occupational distribution. The age-standardized proportion of visible minorities in managerial and professional occupations is presented in Table 2.

TABLE 2

Visible Minorities in Managerial and Professional Occupations
Age Standardized
Canada, 1991

JAPANESE	36%
KOREANS	27%
WEST ASIANS AND ARABS	27%
CHINESE	24%
SOUTH ASIANS	21%
BLACKS	20%
FILIPINOS	15%
PACIFIC ISLANDERS	14%
NORTH EAST ASIANS	14%
LATIN AMERICANS	13%

Source: Kelly, 1995:7

Compared to other Canadians, visible minorities were equally likely to be in professional occupations (13%, age-standardized data), and slightly less likely to be in managerial occupations (8% compared to 10%). Indeed, visible minorities men were *more* likely to be professional than were other Canadian males (14% to 11%) (Kelly 1995:7).

Visible minorities are one of the four population groups which have been targeted by the federal government as disadvantaged due to "their labour force participation and unemployment rates, their income levels, and their persistent occupational segregation" (Moreau 1991a:26; cf. 1991b). The other three groups are women, Aboriginal people, and people with disabilities. But, as Karen Kelly (1995) has noted, the visible minorities are "a diverse group," and some are much more advantaged or disadvantaged than others; and some may in fact be more *advantaged* than other Canadians.

Critique

The argument of this paper is that the concept of visible minority is profoundly problematic. Some of these problems were noted in 1984 in the *Report of the Commission on Equality in Employment*, a commission chaired by Rosalie Abella. For example, the Commission stated: "Some non-Whites face more serious employment barriers than others," and went on to observe: "To combine all non-Whites together as visible minorities ... without making distinctions to assist those in particular need, may deflect attention from where the problems are greatest" (1984:46). Having said that, however, the Commission proceeded apace, and never returned to the question of whether or not "visible minority" is well founded as a social category, or effective as a legislative tool for redressing inequalities. Since the time of the Abella Commission we have acquired much more data on the distribution of visible minorities in the Canadian social structure, more information on Canadian attitudes to visible minorities from survey data, and some information from visible minorities on their evaluations of the situation. This information needs to be examined carefully to determine how well the concept of visible minority, and the uses to which it is being put by government, coheres with social reality. We can begin by considering some of the conceptual difficulties inherent in its use.

First, not all ethnic minorities are visible, particularly linguistic minorities and religious minorities. Are these religious and linguistic minorities somehow less important than the visible minorities? Is colour a more significant variable than language? or faith? Who says so? How much more significant? And how is this difference determined and evaluated? Second, if the concept goes too far in separating some minority groups from others, it also does not go far enough. Many other minorities *not* included in the concept are also visible; the most glaringly obvious are the very old and the very young: the *chronological* minorities. Both groups comprise a disproportionate number of the poor in Canada; there are therefore sound economic reasons for including them in the category "visible minority," but they are not in fact so included. Why not?

Third, visibility is not an equally significant criterion of self-identification for all ethno-cultural minorities. Some may consider language, faith, or history, for instance, as a more important emblem of identity than visibility. Indeed the ten groups specified in the legislation have nothing in common *except* their "visibility"; and this itself is a variable whose particular significance for each group has yet to be empirically verified. What does visibility *mean* to people? For example, does it mean the same to lighter-skinned Arabs as it does to black-skinned Jamaicans? Does it mean the same to all Chinese? What does it mean to Whites, who may in fact be Jamaican too? Fourth, are all these ten ethnic (or, more precisely, national origin) groups equally visible? No: some are more visible than others, that is, in the blunt terms of public discourse, some are darker than others. Should we not, therefore, have categories by shade? To have, for example, "visible minorities," "more visible minorities" and "still more visible minorities" is obviously absurd – but then so, it would seem, is the original category. That all visible minorities face the same problems of racism is simply an assumption, one unsupported by any concrete data. Indeed, anecdotal evidence and survey data suggest that some visible minorities face much more racism than do others: Blacks and "Pakistanis," for instance, appear to be most subject to prejudice, followed by Chinese and Japanese, and Latin Americans and Arabs (Buckner 1993).

Fifth, despite the wealth of research on the status of women and Aboriginal people in Canada, there is very little on the visible minorities, and none on the meaning of visibility for these minorities. The 1984 Report of the Special Committee on Visible Minorities in Canadian Society (the Daudlin Report), entitled *Equality Now*, and "manned," literally, by seven white male MPs, is the only federal initiative to consider visible minorities. The Commission on Equality in Employment (mentioned previously), which established the groundwork for the later equity legislation, also considered visible minorities in 1984, but only as one group among four targeted for remedial and affirmative action.

Finally, the entire process of lumping "multicoloured" humanity together under one rubric, and then producing apparently sophisticated statistics on employment, income, education and so on for the "average visible minority person" is surely problematic. What is the average Black or Chinese or Filipino or Arab? It is far better to disentangle the various groups from one another and analyze the socio-economic situation of each one separately, than it is to treat them all as manifestations of a single (spurious) category. Besides, the colours spread out along the light spectrum in a hundred shades and hues from whites and creams, through beiges and yellows, to mahogany and black, with occasional blushes of scarlet or flushes of purple to brighten the paler shades of white. Pigments vary, so does the meaning of this pigmentation to self and to others, and so do the values and social structures of these many-coloured communities. Yet Canadian legislation promotes a single, simple, dichotomous distinction: visible/invisible.

A further problem is this: the legislation generally defines visibility in terms of non-white in colour *and* national origin. This opens up the intriguing possibility of options. For example, some people are of mixed race, and the possibility, therefore, presumably exists for them to choose with whom to identify and how to define themselves. In a related vein, we know mixed-race Canadians who can pass as Whites or as visible minorities and Italians who are more visible than Arabs, but who do not count as visible minorities. And we know one Canadian, visibly white so far as we can see, who identifies herself as a "visible minority" because she originally came from one of the specified regions. Thus, in some cases, it is not a region which determines visibility, nor is it colour, but rather individual *choice*. "Whites" are "visible minorities" if they so decide. And visible minorities are *not* visible minorities if they decide not to be. This ethnicity is a resource, as is colour. Identity is not so much a matter of pigmentation as of politics (Miles 1989, Goldberg 1993: 80-84).

Ethnic Stratification

But what is the true nature of the inequality which lies at the root of our problem here? In this section we look at both the economic and the ideological components of ethnic inequality.

In his classic study of social stratification in Canada, John Porter (1956) described Canada as "the vertical mosaic"; indeed, ethnicity is one of the factors which determines economic inequality. Let us therefore examine the ethnic stratification system as presented in Table 3. The most pertinent feature of this table is that visible and "invisible" ethnic groups overlap. There is no clear line of demarcation between the two. Some visible minorities, notably the Arabs and the South Asians (a term which Census Canada defines as including Bengalis, Punjabis, East Indians, Pakistanis and others) earn *higher* average incomes than some

TABLE 3

Average Income by Ethnic Origin and Sex, 1989

ETHNIC ORIGINS (SINGLE & MULTIPLE ORIGINS)	MALES	FEMALES
NORTHERN EUROPEANS	$24,447	$13,025
ARABS	$24,172	$12,086
BRITISH	$24,160	$12,926
WESTERN EUROPEANS	$23,765	$12,546
EASTERN EUROPEANS	$23,480	$13,181
SOUTH ASIANS	$23,113	$12,256
SOUTH EUROPEANS	$21,861	$11,995
FRENCH	$21,440	$11,930
WEST ASIANS	$21,421	$11,793
EAST AND SOUTHEAST ASIANS	$20,567	$13,387
CARIBBEANS	$19,373	$12,783
BLACKS	$18,362	$12,899
PACIFIC ISLANDERS	$18,357	$11,844
LATIN, CENTRAL, SOUTH AMERICANS	$17,953	$10,423
ABORIGINALS	$15,760	$9,828

Source: Characteristics of Select Ethnic Categories, Showing Single and Multiple Origins by Sex for Canada, 1986 Census — 20% Sample D. Dimensions: Profile of Ethnic Groups. Ottawa: *Statistics Canada*, February 1989, Cat. No. 93-154.

Whites, notably those of southern European (Greece, Italy, Portugal, etc.) and of French ethnic origins. The notion that all visible minorities are equally oppressed, impoverished, marginalized, and victimized by a ubiquitous Canadian racism, and that they are all equally unequal, is thus overly simple, and indeed would appear to be quite false. Canada does not have a dichotomous racial stratification system with all Whites above, and all non-Whites, now recorded as visible minorities, below. This is not to say that there is no racism in Canada — far from it — but it is to insist that the role of visibility in the economic structure has to be analyzed more closely, and not simply assumed.

More attention and resources surely need to be directed toward the most unequal on this list: the Aboriginals, as well as Central and South Americans (although many of these, of Spanish or Portuguese, or Italian or German origin may not be "really" visible), and Blacks and Pacific Islanders. Yet we must also focus our attention on those groups which have higher positions on the vertical mosaic, the Arabs and the South Asians. What factors account for their success and their apparent mobility?[1] Is it their religions? attitudes? entrance status with respect to wealth or education levels? More research needs to be done on this question.

Two other groups are also particularly interesting, but they have disappeared, having been amalgamated into broader categories in the 1986 mini-census data: the Japanese and the Jews. In the 1971 Census, which reported the mean average incomes of Canadian ethnic groups, the highest income groups were the Jews and the Japanese with average incomes $3,544 and $948 respectively above the Canadian average of $6,005 (Driedger 1989:311). Yet by 1986 the Japanese were included in the relatively low-income East Asian category; and the Jews were not specifically recognized either. It is important to note that both groups had outstripped the British *and* the French so-called "charter" groups in 1971, despite racism and anti-Semitism. One wonders how far they have climbed the vertical mosaic since then, and how they achieved this, especially considering that both the Jews and the Japanese have historically faced immense prejudice and discrimination in Canada. It is likely that attitudes and policies have changed over the years, but the critical question is this: what factors can explain the high mobility rate of these two groups?

It is becoming clear that visible minorities have nothing in common with each other, except their visibility to the majority. Yet the Canadian majority (if there is such a thing) seems to distinguish very clearly among visible minority groups.[2] Canadians do rank the visible *and* invisible minorities in a clear hierarchy of esteem, but such research as there is suggests that culture, not colour, is the prevailing determinant of attitudes. In a series of surveys probing Canadian attitudes towards six ethnic minorities (Blacks, Chinese, Italians, Jews, Pakistanis, and Poles), Environics reported that over 80% of Canadians are (or appear to be) relatively unprejudiced. More to the point, prejudice seems to be unrelated to visibility. Asked whether members of these minorities have too much power in Canada, and whether they would vote for members of these groups, Canadians (including members of these same groups, of course) reported a rank order of "too much power" as follows: Pakistanis (16.2%), Jews (14.6%), Chinese (11.5%), Blacks (9.0%), Italians (8.7%) and Poles (4.0%). Also the proportion of Canadians who "would not vote" for the said minorities was as follows: Pakistanis (16.3%), then far below, Chinese (8.6%), Jews (8.1%), Poles and Blacks tied (6.9%) and Italians (6.0%) (Buckner 1993:4, 5).

The most striking aspect of the Environics survey is the relative insignificance of visibility and colour in this hierarchy of prejudice. The most visible group, the Blacks, are intermediate to low as targets of prejudice, while a supposedly invisible group, the Jews, is ranked much more negatively than Blacks on the power questions. True, the Pakistanis, a visible minority, are the most disliked of these six groups according to this survey; but the point is that there is no unequivocal coincidence of visibility and negativity or of "invisibility" and positivity. The categories overlap – and therefore the concept of visibility/invisibility has limited utility for the understanding of racism. Evidently visibility is not everything, and to suggest that it is – still more, to institutionalize it – is perhaps to compound the problem rather than to alleviate it.³

Minorities and Identity

So far we have profiled the so-called visible minorities, criticized the criterion of visibility as inappropriate for a number of reasons – principally because it homogenizes specificities, ignoring differences in power, status, history, culture, and even visibility – and we have also shown that the ethnic stratification system (both economic and ideological) is far more complex than the simple dichotomy visibility/invisibility would suggest. Now we want to take a further look at how so-called visible minorities perceive themselves. As we shall see, they may well construct their identities on grounds which have little or nothing to do with skin colour, but a lot to do with names, languages, and above all, social class.

Names: The "Indians" of North America were so named by Columbus in the mistaken belief that he had found India. Since then Canadian bureaucracies, with some help from academics, have applied more and more labels, terms, and legal definitions to the Indians: Aboriginals and Native Peoples and Indigenous Peoples; and invented distinctions within definitions, for "Indians" may be status or non-status or Métis, treaty or non-treaty, on-reserve or off-reserve, enfranchised or Bill C-31 reinstated, and so on. These distinctions have been imposed by the

Other, the (invisible) majority. The naming rights have been removed from the subject population. Significantly, today, although the old names still live on, the Indians have re-named themselves the *First Nations*.

Similarly, Blacks in North America have been labelled "Negroes," "coloureds," "non-Whites," and in Canada at least, "visible minorities." They themselves may prefer Afro-American or African Canadian – a definition by national origin congruent with Italian American, Jamaican Canadian and so on. Thus they would be categorized in the same way as, say, Europeans. Self-naming is the first stage, surely, of empowerment and "de-marginalization" – that is, movement away from the margins.

The label "visible minority" may be applied to ten per cent of the Canadian population, but in a significant example of un-naming, it does not always stick. Paul Grayson surveyed Chinese students at York University in Toronto and found that 50% did not consider themselves to be members of a visible minority. Whether they did or not depended, not on their visibility, but on whether their friends were mostly visible minorities or not! Furthermore, when they were asked to identify which groups were visible minorities, while they did mention Indians, Koreans, Chinese, Japanese and others, they also included many populations which might usually be defined as Whites, including Greeks, Italians, Russians, Ukrainians, and others. Colour is therefore only one of many variables that are considered in reaching a verdict about visible minority status. And visibility itself may be defined more widely than just by colour: the poor are often visible, particularly the homeless. As one student put it: "Even, say, the poor. These people are visible minorities."

Power is indeed a central element in the definitional process. One student remarks: "... they call people this way [i.e. visible minority] ... when they find that people don't have power. Today I'm receiving an education, I can speak the language. I don't consider myself a visible minority." Grayson concludes that "the meaning of 'visible minority' is problematic" and he suggests that "the term should be used with caution" (1994:1-2).

Language: Labelling the Other as a "visible minority" is also problematic for linguistic reasons. Such labelling overlooks the importance of language in the construction of ethnic identity, an importance which is particularly obvious in Canada where the struggle of francophones to preserve and develop their language across the country and in Quebec has continued ever since the Conquest. More recently, anglophones in Quebec have been struggling to maintain their language rights. And ironically these two groups are not even categorized as visible nor even as minorities, but as charter groups!

The experience of the First Nations in Canada has been especially traumatic, since they have had to endure a systematic attack on their language, religion, and history – all aspects of culture which are bound up with and constitute identity. The experience of Dolphus Shae, a Dene, illustrates this point vividly:

> Before I went to school the only English I knew was "hello," and when I got there we were told that if we spoke Indian they would whip us until our hands were blue on both sides. And also we were told that Indian religion was superstitious and pagan. It made you feel inferior to the Whites. (Berger 1977:90)

Every marker of otherness appears to have been denigrated in the residential schools. Richard Nerysoo recalled similar experiences:

> When I went to school in Fort McPherson I can remember being taught that the Indians were savages. We were violent, cruel and uncivilized. I remember reading history books that glorified the white man who slaughtered whole nations of Indian people. No one called the white man savages, they were heroes who explored new horizons or conquered new frontiers ... That kind of thinking is still going on today. (Berger 1977:91)

Gloria Anzaldúa, a Mexican American, insists on the supreme importance of her language for her sense of identity – a sense that might have been learned the hard way from her youth:

> I remember being caught speaking Spanish at recess – that was good for three licks on the knuckles with a sharp ruler. I remember being sent to the corner of the classroom for "talking back" to the Anglo teacher when all I was trying to do was to tell her how to pronounce my name. "If you want to be American, speak 'American.' If you don't like it, go back to Mexico where you belong." (1990:203)

Anzaldúa details the consequences: "Shame. Low estimation of self. In childhood we are told that our language is wrong. Repeated attacks on our native tongue diminish our sense of self. The attacks continue throughout our lives" (1990:207). Now, she insists, "Ethnic identity is twin skin to linguistic identity – *I am my language*" (1990:207, emphasis added). But identity is internalized not only through language, but also and especially through music, "food and certain smells," as Anzaldúa relates:

> There are more subtle ways that we internalize identification, especially in the forms of images and emotions. For me food and certain smells are tied to my identity, to my homeland. Woodsmoke curling up to an immense blue sky, woodsmoke perfuming my grandmother's clothes, her skin. The stench of cow manure and the yellow patches on the ground.... (1990:209)[4]

In the end she sums it up: "Being Mexican is a state of soul – not one of mind, nor one of citizenship" (1990:209-10). The binary notion of visible/invisible is too weak to capture this "state of soul." As should also be apparent, identity is absorbed through many other sensory modalities besides the visual.

Colour: The phrase "visible minority" foregrounds skin colour as the primary determinant of group identification. Attaching such primacy to the visual characteristics of persons, and in particular their skin colour, is a trait which is by no means unique to North American society. The cultural significances of visual markers has many sources and in this context it is not surprising that the Canadian government has prioritized it over other markers. However, other cultures include other physical features, such as hair, and non-physical features, such as wealth, and they also evaluate features differently. Let us take the last of these issues first. Richard Rodriguez, a Mexican American, remembers how his relatives scorned pale, white skin:

> A *gringo*'s skin resembled *masa* – baker's dough – someone remarked. Everyone laughed. Voices chuckled over the fact that the *gringos* spent so many hours in summer sunning themselves. ("They need to get sun because they look like *los muertos*.")

If whites could "see" themselves as others see them, perhaps they would see others differently too: the white aesthetic is an aesthetic of "the dead" in the eyes of many "others."

Rodriguez' other reminiscences include how his dark skin was a source of immense concern to his mother. As he came in from the sun in Sacramento she would scold him:

> You look like a negrito ... You know how important looks are in this country. With *los gringos* looks are all that they judge on. But you! Look at you! You're so careless! ... You won't be satisfied till you end up looking like *los pobros* who work in the fields, *los braceros*." (1990:265)

As this implies, Mexican Americans are conscious of using other grounds than appearance as the basis on which they judge people, and they perceive this custom to be in contrast to the ways of *los gringos*, for whom appearance is everything. For Mexican Americans appearance is important, – but not for the same reasons as it is for Anglos. Rodriguez describes the "shame and sexual inferiority I was to feel in later years because of my dark complexion. I was to grow up an ugly child. Or one who thought himself ugly (*Feo*.)" (1990:271). All this changed, however, when as a student at Stanford University he took a summer job in construction in the sun, with other Mexicans, *los pobros,* working nearby. There, in the sun, getting darker all the time, he learned:

> My skin in itself means nothing. I stress the point because I know there are people who would label me "disadvantaged" [or visible minority] because of my color. They make the same mistake I made as a boy when I thought a disadvantaged life was circumscribed by particular occupations ... But I was not one of *los pobros*. What made me different from them was an attitude of *mind*, my imagination of myself. (1990:278)

Same colour but different mind equals different "race." This is a beautiful deconstruction of race: race is an attitudinal orientation and a socioeconomic fact in Rodriguez' experience, and his mother's, not a biological fact. The colours in his own family ranged from light to dark – the final shade is a matter of Mendelian chance. For him, race is class. Darkness is not a condition of the skin so much as of poverty, and a dark man who is rich is no longer dark. Moreover, Rodriguez notes ironically: "it appears nowadays a mark of leisure and wealth to have a complexion like mine" (1990:265). So the badge of poverty is reconstructed as the "mark of leisure and wealth."

The meanings of colour are socially constructed in individual accounts of identity. The "visible minority" concept, however, appears to take one (of many) phenotypical features and makes this the defining feature of the group, regardless of whether the members of the group like it or not or whether the definition is accurate; this perpetuates the invidious distinctions which democracies are trying to overcome through social equity initiatives. The term "racializes" groups – that is, it creates "biological realities" out of social distinctions, and thus not only makes the dividing lines of society more difficult to cross, but also gives them a false base in a putative physiology, and ultimately contributes to the misunderstanding of colour.

Our objectives as scholars must be to try and encourage people to stop acting on the basis of the *visual* stereotypes that they/we entertain, to contest the racialization of social realities, and to attend to the social specificity and uniqueness of each "community" in line with some of the ways in which they see themselves.

Racism, Sexism, and Visualism

Cornel West (1990:32) has written of how "white normative gazes" traditionally inhibited the freedom of expression of African Americans. Feminist writers have criticized the tyranny which "the male gaze" has exerted over the life opportunities or self-realization of women. It is instructive to consider the feminist critique of how the male gaze objectifies, essentializes, and in the process dominates female bodies, for there are many similarities here to the way "white normative gazes" operate to marginalize visible minorities. The one difference that should be borne in mind is that gender lines cut across those of class in North America, whereas ethnic divisions tend more to coincide with them.

In her *Vindication of the Rights of Woman* Mary Wollstonecraft was an early critic of the way the male definition of women in terms of their bodies – their "looks" – interfered with their life chances (1792/1985:131,146). Germaine Greer, a pioneer of the second wave of the women's movement, protested even more vociferously in *The Female Eunuch*. In the following she attacks the way women are coerced to conform to an impossible visual ideal – that of "the doll."

> The gynolatry of our civilization is written large upon its face, upon hoardings, cinema screens, television, newspapers, magazines, tins, pack-

ets, cartons, bottles, all consecrated to the reigning deity, the female fetish. Her dominion must not be thought to entail the rule of women, for she is not a woman. Her glossy lips and matte complexion, her unfocused eyes and flawless fingers, her extraordinary hair all floating and shining, curling and gleaming, reveal the inhuman triumph of cosmetics, lighting, focusing and printing, cropping and composition. She sleeps unruffled, her lips red and juicy and closed, her eyes as crisp and black as if newly painted, and her false lashes immaculately curled. Even when she washes her face with a new and creamier toilet soap her expression is as tranquil and vacant and her paint as flawless as ever. If ever she should appear tousled and troubled, her features are miraculously smoothed to their proper veneer by a new washing powder or a bouillon cube. For she is a doll. She is an idol. (1971:60)

Greer goes on to express her rage at all the ways in which the female fetish had curtailed her existence, or in other words, the ways in which the image took precedence over her lived sensuality:

I'm sick of the masquerade. I'm sick of pretending eternal youth. I'm sick of belying my own intelligence, my own will, my own sex. I'm sick of peering at the world through false eyelashes, so everything I see is mixed with a shadow of bought hairs; I'm sick of weighting my head with a dead mane, unable to move my neck freely, terrified of rain, of wind, of dancing too vigorously in case I sweat into my lacquered curls. I'm sick of the Powder Room. (1971:61)

There is evidently a very close connection between the primacy of vision and visual images in contemporary culture, and the oppression of women. The gaze is a powerful tool for controlling others' behaviour, as Camille Paglia brings out in the following passage:

Western culture has a roving eye. Male sex is hunting and scanning: boys hang yelping from honking cars, acting like jerks over strolling girls; men lunching on girders go through the primitive book of wolf whistles and animal clucks. Everywhere, the beautiful woman is scrutinized and harassed. She is the ultimate symbol of human desire. (1991:32)

The way the male gaze works is by directing attention away from itself onto the body of the female. This concealment of the point of origin of the gaze is the precondition of its power: man the spectator is set up in opposition to woman as visual object. The invisibility of the former, the unidirectionality of the gaze, and the total visibility of the latter, is the matrix which guarantees the reproduction of asymmetries. Women do look, of course; and many women, and men, enjoy being admired. But feminists insist that the male gaze, analogous to the Whites' "look," is oppressive and exploitative.

We can extend our analysis of the visual logic of gender relations to the interpretation of ethnic relations. The phrase "visible minority" perpetuates white supremacy by deflecting attention from the centre. The centre is elusive, silent, and strangely invisible, yet "exerts a real, undeniable power over the whole social framework of our culture" (Ferguson 1990:9). We need to focus our attention on the centre so we can begin to discern the logic by which all the marginal positions in society, like those occupied by "visible minorities," or women, the poor, and so on, are generated. Audre Lord has named the centre: it is "white, thin, male, young, heterosexual, Christian and financially secure" (Ferguson 1990:9). The combination of these characteristics specifies a status which is completely unique, and at the same time embodies what Lord calls "the mythic norm," which contains within itself all the tacit standards "from which specific others can then be declared to deviate," including such others as those who are grouped under the rubric "visible minority."

Once the specificity of the centre – that is, of the dominant group which "claims universality without ever defining itself" (Ferguson 1990:12) – is exposed, as Lord has exposed it, the norms which it stands for lose their credibility. For it becomes apparent that there is no necessary reason why any of the specific features which define it (the centre) should be privileged over any others – why thinness should be valued over fatness, maleness over femaleness, youth over age, and so on. Following Lord's exposé, all of the power which accrued to the centre as a consequence of its normativity, its function of supplying *the* standard, evaporates instantly, and we are brought to the realization that the real problem lies not with the visible minority being discriminated against, but with the white male being discriminated *for.* But the last word on visibility goes to the great abolitionist, Frederick Douglass, who wrote, over 100 years ago:

> There is no disguising the fact that the American people are much interested and mystified about the mere matter of color as connected with manhood ... When an unknown man is spoken of in their presence, the first question that arises in the average American mind concerning him and which must be answered is, Of what color is he? And he rises or falls in estimation by the answer given. It is not whether he is a good man or a bad man. That does not seem of primary importance. (1892/1962:512)

Our discussion has revealed there to be a strong connection between visualism, racism and sexism, that is, between the privileging of sight over the other senses, the privileging of whiteness over other skin pigmentations, and the privileging of men over women. Given this conjunction, the question arises of whether racism (or sexism) can ever be overcome so long as visualism remains entrenched, and whether racism is not best combatted through attacking visualism. Interestingly, this is precisely the strategy many of Cornel West's "cultural workers" (meaning intellectuals of minority ethnic backgrounds) have adopted. They seek to change the prevailing metaphors of public discourse from the visual register to the oral-aural register in a move that is calculated both to crack the tyranny of the visual and to valorize the oral roots of Black and Hispanic cultures (Hibbitts 1994:328-41). In place of "the gaze," these activists favour more acoustic models of social interaction, such as "listening" and "dialogue." A dialogue always involves a relation *between* subjects, unlike the gaze which tends constantly to objectify the other, and a dialogue is interactive, unlike the gaze which always distances (Levin 1993). Aurality may thus be invoked to undermine visuality, and to empower those cultures which have tended to be marginalized on account of their orality.

Whether putting an end to the tyranny of vision could unseat the tyranny of race in any ultimate sense remains, of course, open to debate. In his analysis of anti-Semitism after the end of World War II, Sartre suggested that "If the Jew did not exist, the anti-Semite would invent him" (1946/1969:13), adding that "it is not the Jewish character that provokes anti-Semitism, but rather ... it is the anti-Semite who creates the Jew" (1946/1969:143). Here Sartre reworks Voltaire's insight on God, but his point that racism plays many individual (and societal) roles is well taken. The abolition of visualism will not result in the abolition of racism, though it would undermine perhaps the foremost ground of racial prejudice. Racism is ultimately about power and the legitimation of power differentials, as well as the legitimation of actions and attitudes necessary or useful to maintain (or to challenge) a given racial or ethnic power system. Nonetheless, by talking about race in terms of colour, government may actually institutionalize biological reductionism and effectively recognize racism. Racial difference on grounds of colour then becomes a legal category rather than a social one.

Visibility does not necessarily refer only to skin colour. The Nazis made the Jews visible partly by their propaganda cartoons and their stereotyping, but also, since caricature has its limits in terms of accuracy, by the yellow Star of David. Thus an invisible minority was made visible, racialized and biologized. The star, however, and the visibility were negative symbols of what Adolf Hitler and the Nazis defined as evil and anti-culture. This visibility was a code for the Jewish culture and identity which, defined as inferior, was in turn equated with racial and biological enmity. Hence the Holocaust. The first point, however, was to identify the "enemy" – to make it *visible*.

For there are many *types* of minorities: religious, linguistic, ethnic, legal, chronological, and the aesthetically, physically, and mentally stigmatized or handicapped, in the sense that Erving Goffman (1963) used the term. Each minority has, as a minority, its unique problems with the majority society by definition; if not, it does not constitute a sociological minority. Of course the definitional process may be controversial; but only *visible* minorities – we can hardly stress the point enough – face the problem of racial and biological definition, and consequently the battery of recent works defining them, or some of them, as racially or biologically inferior (cf. Rushton 1994; Herrnstein and Murray 1994).

Conclusion and Recommendations

In 1995 the newly elected Premier of Ontario has promised to eliminate the provincial equity program. And in the United States affirmative action programs are under attack from a divided public opinion as well as the Supreme Court. No doubt there are many explanations for these policy and attitudinal changes, from the so-called "angry white male backlash" to the desire for less (and better) government, from deficit reduction concerns to beliefs that these programs have not worked anyway, and are themselves discriminatory. This paper, we will insist, does not take a position on equity. Of course, almost everyone is in favour of equity; it is the means to achieve it which arouses most of the controversy. Rather, this paper has had the more limited task of evaluating the concept of "visible minority."

While the concept of visible minorities is seriously flawed for many reasons, as we have tried to show the effort to equalize opportunities for all Canadians by targeting specific groups is surely admirable and has received widespread political support. It is hardly necessary to add that to criticize the concept, we hope constructively, is not the same as to criticize the goal of equity itself. On the contrary, it is precisely because the concept seems so flawed that it may end up thwarting the achievement of the goals it was intended to implement. The flaws in the concept, which is the tool of change, do have to be attended to in order to maximize the intent of the reforms and to minimize the confusion and the backlash. On the one hand there is widespread agreement that we need equity legislation and affirmative action to promote minorities and the marginalized. On the other hand, in Canada at least, the visible minorities are so various that not all "need" such legislation, not all want it, and some resent the whole apparatus as not only derisive but also as infantilizing. Others – probably most – are enthusiastic supporters of the legislation.

If the term, however problematic, serves its purposes of increasing ethnic and racial equality, then no doubt it can and should be maintained. Nonetheless the limitations and inadequacies of the concept are considerable. In sum, what is wrong with the concept?

1. It homogenizes the singular, the specific, and the unique.

2. It sacralizes sight and vision.

3. It ignores the significance of language, history, religion and culture, sounds, tastes and smells which also create identification.

4. It is an imposition by the majority, by "the One," by the centre (whichever metaphor you prefer) on "the Other."

5. It "racializes" many types of ethnic identification.

6. It "biologizes" the social in the construction of social reality.

In response to these problems, we recommend four policy initiatives:

1. An in-depth investigation of the twin concepts of visibility and ethnicity, particularly in relation to the types and degrees of experience of prejudice and discrimination must be undertaken. In a society which values multiculturalism it is ironic that we have had no royal commissions on racism.

2. A more focused policy on visible minorities than the indiscriminate approach of the equity legislation must be developed. The Japanese, for example, with higher average incomes than even the charter ethnic groups, have far less need of such a policy than the Aboriginal people, Blacks, Chinese and Indo-Pakistanis. Policy must be directed to where it is most needed.

3. Up-to-date statistics must be collected, on visible *and* invisible minorities, for income, occupation, and employment, to measure both the economic stratification system and differential ethnic mobility rates. Such information is a precondition for any assessment of the effectiveness of the equity programs, and for the focusing of policy.

4. Finally, while we recognize that equity legislation may be an important instrument in the equalization of opportunities for visible minorities and for disenfranchised groups generally, it may not be sufficient. We must attend not only to colour but to socio-economic status.

Notes

1. We say "apparent mobility" because there is no database and the census terminology seems to change from year to year, making longitudinal comparative analysis difficult or impossible.
2. There are no demographic ethnic majorities in Canada. The largest ethnic group in Canada is the British, who comprise 41% of the population; but arguably this group is itself composed principally of the English, Northern Irish, Scottish and Welsh as distinct ethnic groups.

3. The concept of visibility is of course a metaphor for colour and race, and especially for disadvantages by these criteria. Paradoxically, Ralph Ellison used the opposite metaphor of visibility to make the same point: "I am an invisible man" he wrote as the first sentence of his famous indictment of white racism in *Invisible Man* (1947).
4. If people identify positively with some aromas, they may also *be* identified negatively with the same, or other, aromas, i.e. by olfactory rather than visual criteria. An unemployed male in Birmingham, England, stated: "I just don't like Pakis. They stink. Pakis really reek. You can tell one on the street a mile away" (Cashmore, 1987:86). The role of odour in ethnic and race relations is discussed further in Classen, Howes and Synnott, 1993:165-9; also Classen, 1993:79-105; and Synnott, 1993:182-205).

References

Abella, Rosalie (1984). *Report of the Commission on Equality in Employment*. Ottawa. Cat. No. MP43-157.

Anzaldúa, Gloria (1990). "How to Tame a Wild Tongue." In Russell Ferguson *et al.* (eds), *Out There*. New York: The New Museum of Contemporary Art, pp. 203-11.

Berger, John (1972). *Ways of Seeing*. London: B.B.C.

Berger, Thomas (1977). *Northern Frontier, Northern Homeland. The Report of the MacKenzie Valley Pipeline Inquiry*. Vol. 1. Ottawa. Cat. No. CP 32-25.

Buckner, Taylor (1993). "Minorities on Minorities: How Canada's Ethnic Minorities View Selected Canadian Minority Groups." Working Paper Series No. 3. Centre for Community and Ethnic Studies. Dept. of Sociology and Anthropology, Concordia University, Montreal.

Canada (1984). *Equality Now!* Report of the Special Committee on Visible Minorities in Canadian Society. The Daudlin Report. Ottawa: House of Commons.

Canadian Human Rights Commission (1994). *Annual Report 1993*. Minister of Supply and Services. Cat. No. HR1.

Cashmore, E.E. (1987). *The Logic of Racism*. London: Allen and Unwin.

Classen, Constance (1994). *Worlds of Sense: Exploring the Senses in History and Across Cultures*. London: Routledge.

Classen, Constance, David Howes, and Anthony Synnott (1993). *Aroma: The Cultural History of Smell*. London: Routledge.

Douglass, Frederick, 1892/1962. *The Life and Times of Frederick Douglass.* London: Collier-Macmillan.
Driedger, Leo (1989). *The Ethnic Factor.* Toronto: McGraw-Hill Ryerson.
Ellison, Ralph (1947). *Invisible Man,* New York: Modern Library.
Ferguson, Russell, (1990). In Russell Ferguson *et al.* (eds), *Out There.* New York: The Museum of Contemporary Art.
Goffman, Erving (1963). *Stigma.* Englewood Cliffs, N.J.: Prentice-Hall.
Goldberg, David Theo (1993). *Racist Culture,* Oxford: Blackwell.
Grayson, J. Paul (1994). "'Visible Minority' Problematic for Students of Chinese Origin." *Newsletter.* York University: Institute for Social Research. Vol. 9, No. 3. Fall:1-2.
Greer, Germaine (1971). *The Female Eunuch.* London: Paladin.
Hibbitts, Bernard (1994). "Making Sense of Metaphors: Visuality, Aurality, and the Reconfiguration of American Legal Discourse." *Cardozo Law Review,* 16(2):229-356.
Kelly, Karen (1995). "Visible Minorities: A Diverse Group". *Canadian Social Trends* 37(summer):2-8
La Presse 10.1.94
Levin, David Michael (1993). Introduction. In David Michael Levin (ed.), *Modernity and the Hegemony of Vision.* Berkeley: University of California Press, pp. 1-29
Maclean's 27.12. 1993.
___. 19.6, 1995.
Miles, Robert (1989). *Racism.* London: Routledge.
Moreau, Joanne (1991a). "Employment Equity." *Canadian Social Trends.* Ottawa: Statistics Canada. Autumn:26-28.
___. (1991b). "Changing Faces: Visible Minorities in Toronto." *Canadian Social Trends.* Ottawa: Statistics Canada. Winter:26-8.
Multiculturalism and Citizenship Canada (1991). *Multiculturalism: What is it Really About?* Ottawa:Ci 96-63/1991.
Newsweek 3.4, 1995.
Paglia, Camille (1991). *Sexual Personae.* New York: Vintage Books.
Rodriguez, Richard (1990). "Complexion." In Russell Ferguson *et al.* (eds), *Out There.* New York: The New Museum of Contemporary Art, pp. 265-78.
Rushton, Phillippe (1994). *Race, Evolution and Behavior Transaction.* New Brunswick, N.J.: Transaction Publishers.
Sartre, Jean-Paul (1946/1969). *Anti-Semite and Jew.* Trans. George J. Becker. New York: Schokken Books.

Synnott, Anthony (1993). *The Body Social: Symbolism, Self and Society.* London: Routledge.

West, Cornel (1990). "The New Cultural Politics of Difference." In Russell Ferguson *et al.* (eds), *Out There.* New York: The New Museum of Contemporary Art, pp. 19-36.

Wollstonecraft, Mary (1792/1985). *Vindication of the Rights of Woman.* Harmondsworth: Penguin Books.

7
The Beauty of Valuing Black Cultures

Alrick Cambridge

Many black cultural critics are silent about the very thought of making explicit the principles by which they value black artistic creations and expressive cultures. Instead, what we are likely to find in their work is a continual play upon certain metaphorical figurations. For example, we find the quoted category "race," and the presumption that its symbolism is all important, yet not much analysis of the causal force of racial categorization (racism) itself; meanwhile we find the categories of *ambivalence, hybridity, and representation*, all of which in their repetitive and uncritical use are denuded of meaningful content. Sometimes the latter category of representation is confusingly employed so as to play both upon the act of political petitioning and upon visual depiction; and then the resulting ambiguity is celebrated as the most valuable thing about its significance.[1] Yet objects that are cheapened by over-use, and abused into the bargain, lose their value – and so do analytic categories. This truth, however, seems unimportant to our critics: for when they repetitively use the aforementioned categories, and with less and less content, it is in fact because they prize them above other values, namely norms of respect, reciprocity, shame, approval, disapproval, honour, dignity, and obligation, values about which they are silent.

For all that, it does not follow that because these writers are in fact silent about principles of valuing, that their critiques are lacking in judgements of value. No: their critiques imply that they do value certain things above others, which are then accorded more weight than those which are ignored. The truth is this: although our critics do value certain things, they do not always make explicit the principles by which they do so; and when on their behalf we make these implied principles explicit, we immediately perceive that they are principles to which we could not accede. If we defend no explicit principles for fear of "the absolutism of the *Pure*" and the Absolute, then chances are that we will become brokers of the "mélange, the hotchpotch" – "a bit of this and a bit of that"; and finally we might embrace anarchy. Yet in what Kobena Mercer[2] calls his "compelling defence" of *The Satanic Verses*, in *Imaginary Homelands*, Salman Rushdie claims that this lack of any determinate principles is the way by which revolutions enter the world.

> *The Satanic Verses* celebrates hybridity, impurity, intermingling, the transformation that comes of the new and unexpected combinations of human beings, cultures, ideas, politics, movies, songs. It rejoices in mongrelization and fears the absolutism of the Pure. *Mélange, hotchpotch, a bit of this and a bit of that is how newness enters the world, and I have tried to embrace it. The Satanic Verses* is for change by fusion, change by conjoining. It is a love-song to our mongrel selves. (p.394, my emphasis)

As I show soon, Rushdie and I glory in human diversity. But I have two polemical challenges to make against him here. My first is that I find particularly offensive the word "mongrelization," even though I am no speciesist.[3] My second is that the emphasized lines constitute a pean of nihilism, and moreover the accumulative effect of the whole statement amounts to a sceptical lack of any explicitly stated foundational principles by which to value anything. Yet it appears with lavish praise and endorsements by Kobena Mercer in the introduction to his book *Welcome to the Jungle* (p.28); and he there displays a marquee of superstar black cultural critics, including himself, who similarly celebrate and publicize the Rushdie line: Homi Bhabha, Paul Gilroy, Stuart Hall, Henry Louis Gates Jr.,[4] among others.

In this chapter, therefore, I argue for the importance of having explicit principles by which to judge black expressive cultures. The thoughts expressed here are to be seen in the light of a sketch or study for a more developed consideration of these interrelated matters. For example, the constraints of space in this chapter do not allow a full discussion of the theories of Cancian and Rex, or of the hyperbolic criticism of black expressive cultures of Gilroy and others; and much research still needs to be done in order to provide descriptions and explanations of the dynamics of Afro-Caribbean black and Asian cultures. My belief is that only when we make explicit our principles for valuing things can we make sound judgements about them, raise bold defences of the things we value, and discharge our critical responsibilities efficaciously to our community.

Defining Blackness as a Membership Norm

Let me start by stating how the category "black" is to be understood here. "Black" describes the constituency of those who have suffered anti-black racial discrimination and who accordingly employ it as a term of political self-description and cultural counter-assertion. So much is true of groupings of Asian and Afro-Caribbean constituencies who assert their blackness against whatever is anti-black. In contrast, "black" is applied also by those (including institutions) who hand out this kind of discrimination to anyone whose skin colour and distinctive bodily features can be described in that way; for among the signs taken for racial belonging, darker skin in particular is the sign of greatest social distancing. In this sense the extension of the term to include populations of Asian and African traditions is apposite. Yet the term also represents a reaffirmation of what was denied in the racist sign and categorization of black people – humanity, culture, and above all the political capacity to make history. Accordingly the category "black" indicates several attitudes all at once: anti-black racism *and* the fact of political and cultural assertion against it; and it draws attention both to the existence of racist categorizations and to the antiracist counter-assertions against the harmful discriminatory consequences they engender. The category of blackness is a membership norm, as we shall see later in this chapter; also, in what follows the category of group may be understood as any self-defining collectivity, and as such will employ rules of membership.

Weighting the Cultural Dimensions of Black Diaspora

Much of Afro-Caribbean black and Asian interest in human liberation is joined to a similar interest in the emancipation of our parental homelands. But this is because that similar interest is rooted in facts about being an Afro-Caribbean black or an Asian, and facts about our diaspora and colonial oppression. All these facts will inevitably inform our culture consciousness, and might also create the presumption that Afro-Caribbean black and Asian cultures are undoubtedly *only* diasporan, namely that they are unqualifiably *all* Asian and/or *all* African or Afro-Caribbean, and nothing more besides. In fact, our cultures are diasporan, but not in any narrowly defined way. Methodologically, and in principle, whatever cultural dimensions are defined as diasporan must already include facts about European norms of humanity and oppression – namely bondage, colonialism and racist exclusions – and also facts about the imposition of the English language and educational and political systems. This implies that Afro-Caribbean and Asian expressive cultures, even though created oppositionally to European conceptions of humanity, are nonetheless related, and by traditions that are as much African, Asian, and Caribbean, as they are British and European.

We can argue about the salience of one tradition over another, about which strand of a tradition is or is not more relevantly pertinent to the forming of Afro-Caribbean (and Asian) cultures, and debates of this sort are one lively feature of our current culture wars. But the *relatedness* of our cultures to European traditions cannot be denied. The problem then must be how to weight the European and other factors of our diasporan cultures. An example of this debate is Paul Gilroy's claim that he has a transatlantic identity, informed by a double consciousness of European and African traditions. But Gilroy weights these two traditions badly. Europe is positively emphasized, and he makes its traditions more robust and dominant by comparison to the African traditions, which he devalues in various ways. In contrast, Winston James highlights the African dimensions of Afro-Caribbean diasporan cultures; and so also do Ken Pryce and Cecil Gutzmore.[5] A more judicious way of weighting the cultural dimensions of black cultures is to admit that our Afro-Caribbean diasporan cultures are the outcomes of many infinite reversals, and that these have resulted in our cultures being hybrid in character. The writer Wilson Harris exhibits commitment to that thought in his 1967 lecture called *Tradition, the Writer and Society*, where he employs the reconstructive metaphor of the "melting pot" to place it at the centre of our Afro-Caribbean cultures. The "presence of a strange and subtle goal, melting pot, call it what you like," Harris says, "is the mainstream (though unacknowledged) tradition in the Americas" (1973:32). Harris's view of the Americas is continental in scope, and so incorporates, besides the Amerindian, African, Iberian, and subcontinental Indian cultures, the cultures of the English-speaking West Indies as well; and so far as I am aware he has never abandoned that thought at the heart of his work.

Most of the body of people living outside their traditional African homelands in the West, I maintain, are mixed or Creole populations. Hence in this chapter *hybrid* and *diaspora* are interchangeably used, because a diasporan African-Jamaican is a hybrid or Creole individual and so is an East Indian-Trinidadian or an East Indian-Guyanese; or for that matter an African-American or African-Cuban. And if there be anything of substance to ethnic categorization, or ethnicity, it is perhaps the allegiance to a parental nationality that these hyphenated terms of belonging indicate.[6]

At any rate, the first Afro-Caribbean migrants, whom I shall hereafter call the first migrants, valued the British diasporan character of their cultures, and these formed the framework within which they understood their identities, as is evidenced by the many verbal reports to that effect, uncovered by Ken Pryce (1979) in *Endless Pressure*. Yet, as Pryce also discloses, when confronting white Britons, first migrants, in their oppositional culture politics, tended to assert the African dimensions more often than not, against British oppression and the violence of racism. "It is a manifestation of the complexity and problematic nature of the relations West Indians share with white dominant society," Ken Pryce wrote, that

> though in the normal course of affairs the West Indian might appear superficially 'British,' in times of crisis and stress he may find it politically strategic and psychologically satisfying to emphasize the black or African component in his background in order to differentiate himself from the 'enemy' as a first step to building a viable political culture that has purpose and meaning. (p.138)

That attitude was not unusual. For if we compare this equivocal view of the relative weight of Africa and Europe to other accounts of pan-African advocates, we get a similar ambivalence. We only need, for example, to contrast what the pan-Africanist C.L.R. James says about his own Euro-West Indian identity with other pan-African lights to see how critical the terms of the dispute were, whether about who we are, our identification, or the components of our culture. Similar tensions over the relative weightings of the diasporan contributions of Africa and India to our Afro- (and Indo-) Caribbean cultures are to be found in the work of George Lamming, Sam Selvon, and Vida Naipaul, and these tensions could become extremely rancorous among these West Indian writers.[7]

However, to generalize an observation on Jamaica made by Mervyn Alleyne, we need to know much more about all the various groups that have contributed to our Afro-Caribbean cultural mosaic, and this will require a major work of synthesis that would trace the cultural outcomes of the different components. Once again this debate shows that the contentions over the relative weights to be accorded to the constitutive features of our diasporan cultures are likely to be interminable, and so may never be finally resolved. No negative judgement is here intended, then, when I assert that the property of ambivalence is also constitutive of our social identities and cultures, because of the latter's diasporan character; and that it *must* be a property of them, because of their constitution.

How Afro-Caribbean Peoples Use Their Cultures

The forming of an individual's cultural identity has dimensions not amenable to the categorical significance of hybridity, ambivalence, and representation. For there are norms of conduct and identity that are far more crucial to the members of black cultures — norms of valuing people and objects in terms of respect or honour because we approve of them, and the norms by which we express disapproval: in short, the norms used by ourselves and significant others to validate who we are or to withhold recognition, and similar actions of reciprocity, cooperation, and obligation. Although a satisfactory theory of the source and content[8] of these norms is hard to develop, they seem to satisfy deep emotive needs which are not touched by judgements as to whether black cultures and identities are hybrid, ambivalent, and representational in character or not; and when we come to the study of norms of valuing people and objects, then our critics have nothing whatsoever to teach us — nothing.

How might we explain why these norms have a greater grip on the mind — to paraphrase Jon Elster — and are therefore more essential to black peoples? The short answer is this: they are of greater crucial importance to black lives because they cement their collectivities, help to form their groups and individuate their identities, provide them with moral direction, help to motivate them, help to provide comfort from the pains of their everyday lives, and provide the spiritual resource of expressive self-realization. So to the foundational question — What exactly do Afro-Caribbean (and Asian) peoples use their cultures for? — we should answer: for the human needs of validating individual and group identification; for valuing honoured and respected objects; for incentive and motivation; for normative direction; for spiritual comfort; and for expressive self-realization.

Most of the aforementioned norms of culture are not acted upon in any deliberative and conscious ways, as if they were the agenda of a political manifesto. Quite to the contrary, acting upon their compelling force is unconsciousness – which is not to say they are never made conscious. Since our cultures, being diasporan, were forged in situations that related them in opposition to European conceptions of humanity – bondage, colonialism, and anticolonialism – some parts of our cultural sensibilities are highly politicized, and are therefore capable of being mobilized against anti-black targets (and also wrongly against apostates). This latter aspect raises questions about the civil constraints to be placed upon certain norms of our cultures, as developed in the conclusion of Cambridge and Feuchtwang's *Where You Belong* (1993). Thus it could be claimed with some justification that antiracism is another norm and therefore a salient purpose of our cultures. I have some sympathy for this view. But antiracism is better viewed as a *politics* or a political goal. Afro-Caribbean and Asian peoples are often forced by political circumstances to mobilize their cultures at the service of antiracist political ends. But their cultures have intrinsic values all by themselves independent of their roles in political mobilization.

Bringing Out the Beauty of Black Cultures

We need a more developed framework of norms and culture than has been presented so far in order to bring out certain features of black cultures, such as why the aforementioned norms are so important for valuing certain objects and identities vital to black peoples. That is provided by Francesca Cancian's social identity theory, as set forth in her excellent book, *What are Norms? A study of beliefs and action in a Maya Community* (1975). Applying some of her conclusions, I shall try to show why normative valuings bring out the beauty of black life, at least more appositely than do the foundationless alternatives set forth by the nihilists (those radical sceptics who are always talking about categories of hybridity, ambivalence and representation because they lack any foundational principles for evaluating black forms of life); and to contrast its positive implications with some negative ones derived from the alternative work of identity structure theorist John Rex (1995).⁹

Cancian's Social Identity Theory

Most discussion of norms suggests that they are standards for evaluating people and objects as good or bad, better or worse; and in Cancian's (1975) model this type of normative beliefs is called *ranking norms*. But they go together with two other types of norm, namely *reality assumptions* and *membership norms*, all three of which will require some characterization later. As set forth by Cancian, the theory begins with social identities denoting a collectively defined kind of person. On this account identity is a role that covers a relatively broad range of actions which includes assumptions about the possible motives or reasons for the actions of that kind of person. It is particularly difficult, however, to state the criteria for inclusion in or exclusion from the category of social identity – for example, what to lay down as the minimum amount of perceived consensus for a collective definition of a kind of person, and how powerful the motivational assumptions have to be. Nonetheless these difficulties are not insurmountable.

Norms and action

Norms are collective perceptions or beliefs about what actions or attributes will cause significant others (and oneself) to recognize and validate an identity. There are three features to highlight here:

1. Norms affect action because they are perceptions of what others (or oneself) will do or know is proper if collectively an action displeases us.

2. Norms are collective or shared in two senses: first, that people collectively conform to the norm without knowing it; and second, contrastingly, that there is agreement among those who recognize and validate the identity as to the kinds of behaviour which may be affirmed. This second sense often grows out of the first in that when we discover that we have been unaware of following a rule we will either disband the norm or share it in the second sense, with awareness and agreement.

3. Norms are located within the groups that have the right to validate the relevant identity, so long as individuals accept the right of the group to define a unique identity, rather than being incorporated within our socialized selves.[10]

The social identity theory makes no prediction to the effect that personal beliefs must be incorporated into an agent for action to take place. For besides either socialization or the identity implications of an action, the theory recognizes that there may be a correlation between beliefs and action for a variety of reasons, including manipulation, for example. Accordingly the theory does not rely on the relation between internalized beliefs and action.

Normative change, individuals, and identities

Norms are rules for being a certain kind of person, but the rules often change, and so too does the person. Indeed, it seems clear that as collective definitions of an identity, norms can vary rapidly without intensive interaction. There is also a crucial incentive side to norm change, namely that individuals are motivated to maintain unique identities when and because they become more important than other contrasting identities. When such a choice is made, commitment to the unique identity may override the norms on which it was based in the first place, and the norms may become less important. This aspect poses certain problems for the theory, but the solution appears to be that the perceived importance of different good identities depends on the extent to which these are based upon the group or significant role-model which has the authority to validate them.

Range of norms

As we have seen, there are several different kinds of norm. Ranking norms are used to evaluate the differential actions of individuals (or objects) on the basis of how well they conform to some standard or rule. They define the actions and attributes that distinguish a particular rank or status, focusing on actions that vary within the community or group. These are the basis for the everyday process of evaluating, judging, and selecting action in our communities.

There are also non-deliberative collective evaluations of actions, which Cancian calls reality assumptions. These unconscious assumptions constrain people's behaviour in certain unconscious ways. The implication of this is that rapid social changes may occur if these assumptions can be altered (and alternatively that an absence of change in their forms means that many social patterns will remain stable).

Membership norms combine characteristics of both the foregoing and constitute the standards by which an individual is included or accepted within a group (the category of blackness as stated at the beginning of this chapter is an example). They apply equally to all group members, while still allowing for different membership norms for different roles, or in different circumstances.

Thus action, in the social identity model, is a process, a patterned movement in which individuals communicate to each other that they are particular kinds of people, by the collective use of norms. One of the theory's most powerful conclusions in this regard is that individuals conform to norms when and because the norms specify how to obtain recognition and validation of significant identity, not because the actor incorporates the norms and identity into the self, as John Rex and others advocate. Thus a change in identity or role may produce an immediate and major change in the norms that are relevant to an individual.[11]

The implications of the social identity theory are radical. It puts into question alternative characterizations of black expressive cultures, such as the nihilism about principles of valuing people's actions and objects, as professed by cultural studies and postmodern theorists; it suggests that claims about internalized colonialism and racism may need to be revised (namely that a different theory may be required to understand why some black people act out these attitudes); and it challenges claims made about black people's culturally expressive behaviour as signs either of radicalism or conformity (which fail to state who may be validating the perceived behaviour or signs) and claims about the African's deculturation in the New World.

Rex's Identity Structure Theory *multi-Layered*

In *Ethnic Identity and Ethnic Mobilization in Britain*, John Rex (1995) applies the socialized actor account to black ethnicity and culture, which I call the *identity structure theory*, in keeping with Rex's own indications. Now Rex and I agree that migrant identities are historically and situationally multi-layered in complex ways. Among his powerful conclusions are, for example, that immigrant ethnic groups in modern metropolitan industrial societies have some prior basis of mobilization within their home countries, that they brought their previous identities with them to Western Europe, and that the conflicts arising out of these competing identities have by and large been contained to the benefit of the receiving nation states. In their new situation these immigrant groups developed new ways of interacting which led to the reformation of their previous ethnic identities around a stable, unassailed core.

However, there are important ways in which I disagree with Rex's account. He distinguishes ethnic identity from other types of belonging, including the observance of cultural norms and response to reciprocal interests. For Rex the essence of a purely ethnic identity is its first-person emotive "sense of sameness with one's fellow-ethnics" in contradistinction to third-person others "who do not share the same observable characteristics." Rex mentions the work of P. Weinreich as having similar results to his own, and we may therefore assume that these two accounts have enough in common to be called the Rex-Weinreich identity structure theory. Whilst the theory has some useful implications, it has also many unpromising ones. Rex suggests that the affective tie of ethnicity "*becomes 'incorporated into the self*[12] and helps to shape identity" (p.12, emphasis added). Through intensive socialization and learning (beginning with the family), the individual is "already trapped into belonging to a group" even *before* he or she develops identity (p.8). I challenge these contentions, especially for (situationally) formed black cultures in Britain; we don't need a theory of identity incorporation to explain their continuity, and both cultural and identity variation are better explained without it.

Consider what Rex aptly calls "multi-layered" social identities of Afro-Caribbean and Asian peoples. In the latter case these are formed from overlapping belongings – of families, extended kinship groups, religious groups, primordial ethnic groups, political parties, social classes and so on, he says, and are therefore already complex.

> We need to keep in mind, therefore, the fact that such identities live on and are very important for those who possess them, even when the immediate context arising from the migration to Britain as workers is one in which they face new problems... (p.34, emphasis added)

Rex's analysis of Afro-Caribbean migrants is not equally cogent, however. Between the lines he seems to be suggesting that their memories of their past faded on arrival in Britain because their cultures lacked the complexity of Asian ones and perhaps because they were socialized into their norms and identities less intensively. The untruth of this suggestion is brought out in Rex's comparison of Afro-Caribbean and Asian family forms. He contends that the Afro-Caribbean extended kinship systems are dispositionally not as stable as Asian ones, because the institutions of slavery and colonial domination supposedly "devastated" their original African structures. This resulted in the role of the father being weakened (because he was always absent from home, as a bondsman) and an increase in the importance of extended kinship. Yet the existence of two-parent families and marriage is well documented for over a century before the main migrations to Britain, and the 1982 PSI survey (of which Rex is aware) confirmed that the majority of Afro-Caribbean households with children contained two parents. Moreover, Rex and others write unfavourably about the absent Afro-Caribbean father, making the woman dependent on the network of the extended family, both for parenting and as an economic support system. Yet these patterns were not something unique only to people of African descent in the Caribbean and in Britain. There is some evidence of these patterns among Caribbean Asians, too. In *Finding the Centre* and *A House for Mr Biswas*, V.S. Naipaul gives testimony of their existence in his own Hindu family in Trinidad. Perhaps this contrary evidence is unknown to Rex.[13] At any rate, his over-reliance on the category of normative incorporation leads him to undervalue rapid normative and identity change, with disastrous empirical implications for Afro-Caribbean blacks.

Humanism and the Anthropological Presuppositions of Culture and Identity

Notice that the social identity theory discussed here gives priority to human agents, namely to black people as active creators of whatever forms of life they employ for their spiritual human needs and self-realization. Notice also that, although forms of life can and often do become objectified – and so stand over their creators in anomic and alien ways – I do not view our black cultures as social structures apart from the individuals practising their norms and validating their identities. This is because the view I take of cultures *per se* is that they are forms of life whose framework of understanding is *humanism,* in other words the framework of philosophical anthropology.[14] This is a foundational presupposition we need to own up to; and that is why I confront the problem now. Up to this point I have been describing the normative basis of black identities. But there is a related psychological side to this problem concerning what we must presuppose about ourselves as human beings, if we are to be the bearers of identities and cultures at all.

First, then, it is my view that humans could not have personal identities if we did not have selves (or inner reality), or lacked a nature; and it is the psychological relationships among ourselves, our nature, and norms and identities, which are of concern to me now. Taking our constitution as humans first of all, I defend a philosophical anthropology (and moral psychology) of human nature. The need to labour, and produce a material and spiritual life, explains why as human beings (so I believe) we have a nature; and since these needs impose themselves upon us, and we could not do without them, it follows that we must be creative in two ways at once: productively and spiritually (that is, non-materially). Every human being and every human group that has ever existed embodies these characteristics; and that's just an ontological fact about human beings, without qualification. My philosophical anthropology rests on the presupposition that what is desirable is possible, which is also my view of human emancipation and artistic and spiritual creations (Elster 1985: ch.2).

Second, I defend the idea of the encumbered historical self. We are natural organisms, but not just composed of bodily movements. What makes us human are all the spiritual components of our culture, the fact that as persons we are permeated by history, our traditions, our natural and built heritage, and our community and group belonging. In this account, human nature and our selves are variable, meaning that our constitutive material and psychological needs are permeated by history, and similarly our cognitive capacities and dispositions. Our variable selves are not just a matter of our variable identity roles; we are not merely beings without social connections, constructed like a cipher in a matrix of discourse – we are beings that are formed and reformed historically within a certain (moral and spiritual) self-interpretive group and community. These connections provide us with the range of definitions of who we are.[15] Now, the idea that we are collectively defined kinds of persons is very much dependent on our first-person perspectives of our selves. What remains after our roles and identities undergo change *is* our selves; there has to be something to change, and something remaining after there is change. Therefore I am claiming that what remains after there is a change is *our* selves, and it is this variable self through which our human nature is manifested and realized.

Third, on the preceding account our varying identity roles should not be elided with our varying selves, to which they are contingently or situationally attached. We are all that our variable selves denote, but more than the range of norms and identities by which we are recognized and validated at any one time. Thus the logic of my account is this: it advances the idea of the self and its oral incorporation of good and bad internal parental objects, which are indeed internalized, and there is interplay between this self and the norms and identities by which we are defined and validated. But as yet I can offer no account of this relationship. Rex says norms and identities are internalized; and indeed that is true of norms that are attached to the good and bad internal parental objects which underlie them.[16] That conjunctive condition is a crucial qualification of the Rex view. Cancian says norms and identities need not rely on internalization, and this is a better way of explaining variable identities. But neither author resolves the difficulties implied in the relationship between the two.

Human behaviour counts as action only when caused or motivated by intentions, desires, and opportunities, and this means rendering an action intelligible is a matter of interpreting a person's life history and the setting in which it occurred. In doing so we provide a narrative history of a certain kind about a person and her identity; if that is true it implies that a history of a certain kind is the basic genre for interpreting human action and personal identity, which holds not only for our own lives but for others too. Such narratives are descriptive of the histories we have traversed, which implies that the full definition of one's identity will usually involve both a stand on moral and spiritual matters and some reference to a validating community. This also implies that the identity a person adopts at some time in her life is indeed situational, but has threading through it an encumbered historical self, as characterized above. It is therefore essential that theories of identity are grounded in philosophical anthropology and moral psychology and that the idea of human nature as a universal feature of persons is declared as truth, on principle.

Integrity of Black Cultures

The first migrants had to rise above the troubles of everyday life in Britain: racial discrimination in jobs and housing, the colour bar in leisure and recreation, racist violence and abuse in areas of religious worship, and the pernicious forms of racist violence (symbolic and otherwise) experienced by their children in British schools. In order to rise above these troubles, the first migrants created forms of cultural life suited to serving their spiritual and emotional purposes. Today we live in different times. There is now some recognition of the harm racist exclusions do to people (especially to black people but also to white people), and campaigns to combat their destructiveness exist. Current forms of Afro-Caribbean black and Asian identity politics present new and exciting challenges; and this recent cultural agenda seems remote from the first migrants' agenda of issues. Yet this remoteness is only apparent. Today's issues of gay liberation, sexuality, gender, mixed race identities, mental health, immigration, and so on, are not remote from the continuance of racism, which is the central fact of our lives. And the alternative forms of life that first migrants were forced to create for their spiritual comfort and physical protection, such as our family systems, pentecostalist Baptist and revivalist churches, self-help groups, supplementary schools, saving systems, entertainment networks, commercial outlets, all still do persist and are the foundational support bases of our present cultural agenda.

My view is that we must value these foundational support bases – and we do so by robustly talking about their norms and celebrating their integrative (or bonding) power. And if we view Afro-Caribbean and Asian forms of life in their integrative wholes – when we enquire what black and Asian cultures do for their members – then we will be led back to a central and principled reflection upon the intrinsic characteristics of their forms and structures, and to a deeper understanding of what our cultures do for us, both as individuals and as collective inventors of our communities.

Irreverent young

One of the best ways of acquiring this understanding is to gain an insight into the present cultural agenda of our young. Consider the following examples of attitudes, ascribing different characteristics to young Afro-Caribbean men and first migrants, which have developed as models to explain defiance (or lack of it) in these two groups. The first perspective is set forth by the 1976-7 House of Commons Select Committee of Race Relations and Immigration in its report on "the West Indian Community." The committee observed that the young Afro-Caribbean population viewed themselves as "British born citizens who feel they have every right to be so recognized and have no wish to be designated West Indian" (vol. 1, p.xxv).

Several implications flow from this observation, but I concentrate on two of them here. The first is that young black people, even though not considered to be British, thought of themselves as such. In 1976 it was hard to be a black Briton without being lampooned and devalued; it was even harder to be a black English person. It was simply a contradiction or a psychological confusion to be somehow both English and black (so thought black radicals); worse still, it was both a contradiction and a sacrilege for a black to think of herself as English (so thought Enoch Powell and Powellite racists). Perhaps owing to the pressure of black rebellion, the cultural climate is changing somewhat now, and blacks who are born here can celebrate their heritage (or mixedness) of being both black and British (or even English). Moreover, they can make exceedingly empowering claims to that effect by staking out black and Asian peoples' net contributions to the cultural renewal of British national life.

The second implication flowing from the Select Committee's observation is one that we must deny – namely that young blacks have no wish to be designated "West Indian." The evidence, even then, against that observation was overwhelming, whether viewed from the psychological or from the cultural perspective. Yet there is some evidence that young black men did misguidedly and disrespectfully reject what they perceived to be their parents' culture, which brings me to consider their view as a perspective ascribing different characteristics to themselves and the older generation. According to some young black men, their parents and the older generation supposedly lacked defiance and were too deferring to whites, so they could have nothing edifying or practical to teach them, as a model of behaviour. Stephen Small exemplifies this attitude thus:

> It became clear that many young black people would not take the general acquiescence and passivity of their parents as a model, and there are many indications of a level of boldness, confidence and defiance usually missing from the older generation.[17]

In this Small captures what I believe are misguided attitudes showing disrespect on the part of young black men – but note not on the part of young black women – towards their parents and older generation, whom they thought of as both acquiescent and passive. Small's research was carried out in a London borough in the early 1980s, in a hotbed climate created in the wake of the urban black riots, and he observes that there was a feeling of a group response, determined organization, and growing discontent. Almost a decade earlier, Ken Pryce observed similar attitudes among young black men in the St. Paul's district of Bristol (1979:139). So, although misguided and irreverent, these attitudes were persistent – and we must admit to their persistence even today. But in imagining that they were the total embodiment of the defiance their parents lacked, these young black men overlooked the foundational support bases which the older generation had created to enable their quest for race equality in Britain.

Sociology without foundations and black expressive cultures

The attitudes I am criticizing here are by no means confined to young black men; they also have their counterparts in youth culture sociology. For in concentrating on the supposedly defiant qualities of young blacks and being silent about older forms of life and their social foundations – and into the bargain fetishizing these qualities as a culture of resistance[18] – youth culture sociology seems inadvertently to have endorsed the misinformed dismissiveness of young black men. This inadvertence also characterizes Ken Pryce's and Stephen Small's third-person participant-observer's silence on whether young black men are right or wrong in their attitudes toward their parents.

Now statements about the rights and wrongs of agents' behaviour imply making moral judgments; and doing so must lead us into the arena of values, of weighting competing normative claims. The idea that values or moral judgments should be an explicit element of cultural criticism seems, when we first encounter it, to be foreign to our field of study. Most recent accounts of black expressive culture, particularly postmodern and cultural studies research, forsake that approach, focusing on stereotyping and iconography, or the spatio-temporal locations of the modern city and how blacks fit into these locations.[19] But silence about such values does not equate with their absence, although it allows analysts to avoid accountability for the political and ideological premises which permeate their analyses. In a similiar foundationless manner, a number of postmodernist studies have set forth, with little challenge, various unsupported assumptions about black forms of life. For example, Paul Gilroy's (1987:199) quite false assertion of the "three core themes around which the anti-capitalist aspects of black expressive culture" coalesce forms part of his *own* intellectual project – an academic thesis about the nature of the capitalist system as a whole[20] – which is then projected on to the arena of black culture.

While this type of research is popular fare on the cultural studies circuit, it is often sterile: for the forms of a people's cultures are not to be reduced to the formula of a political manifesto. On the contrary, I argue that at the heart of a culture's core will be a cluster of social norms which a group of people will be practising more often than they will some other cluster of norms, using these norms to recognize and validate their members. The norms of a culture are social because they are shared by other people in the group, and are not just the province of one individual. Such norms are partly sustained by feelings of embarrassment, anxiety, guilt, and shame that a person suffers at the prospect of violating them (or being caught doing so). All this implies that norms are sustained by approval and disapproval; and that they have a grip on the mind because of the strong emotions their violations can trigger. These emotive aspects of norms are certainly more fundamental than the more frequently cited cognitive contents of black expressive cultures advanced by black culture critics such as Gilroy and others.[21] Thus, what the normative features of any culture show is that the rules of human behaviour have to do with feelings, with desires and expectations, with recognizing and validating identities, and with that part of human nature concerned with the needs of affective life and the emotions – not with the intellectualist project of critiquing the capitalist system as a whole.

Accounts such as the latter can be set forth as models of black expressive cultures because their advocates never practise the reflexiveness they preach. They never ask themselves the question, What must it be like to be a member of that particular form of life? (which is composed of a particular set of norms), or What does it mean to be a particular kind of person within a particular kind of culture? In short these advocates never consider questions of philosophical anthropology and moral psychology when they address questions of culture. This lack of an anthropological and normative framework is why their treatment of black expressive cultures read like political manifestos.

Unless cultural critics pay serious and explicit heed both to the values which animate black cultures and to their own values, the arena of forms of black life will remain the province of hyperbole and unsubstantiated generalizations. So in contrast to their all-encapsulating oracular models (Popper 1985),[22] I favour an analytical model which combines the ethnographic skills of social anthropology, historiography, and analytical philosophy with a deep study of substantive problems. This analytical approach is short on political rhetoric but it is infinitely more likely to produce understanding of, and place a proper value on, black expressive cultures.

Acknowledgements

This paper was inspired by Faye Trail. Claudette Williams, Len Folkes and Peter Sadler's deep knowledge of black people's culture improved it, Janey Fisher's friendship and imagination polished it, and Sze Kwan's love and encouragement and Bill Mische's labour helped me to realize it.

Notes

1. For the confusion stated here, see Kobena Mercer, *Welcome to the Jungle* p.180. This harsh criticism does not apply to the challenging work of Robert Miles (1989) and a few other writers.
2. For the quote see p.28 of *Welcome to the Jungle*.
3. Clarifying my first polemical point a little, I here state that I share no belief in the superiority of the human race over animal life, and therefore can't be accused of human racism. In my view however it is perfectly appropriate to apply the term "mongrel" or "mongrelization" to certain species of animals such as dogs, though like Sartre (who in *The Communists* and *Peace* likens anti-communists to dogs) I have nothing against dogs. It is offensive to apply such terms to categories of humans, in principle, or so I maintain. That said, all due respect to animals, who have extensive rights, which humans may not violate.
4. Perhaps in view of such works as *Signifying Monkey* (Oxford 1989) and *Coloured People* (Viking, 1995), Henry Louis Gates Jr. might be exempted from Kobena Mercer's list, as someone with values we could accede to.
5. Cecil Gutzmore's commitment to the African diaspora and African identity are developed in an unpublished critique of Paul Gilroy's *The Black Atlan-*

tic: *Modernity and Double Consciousness* (1993). See also Pryce (1979) and James (1984), ch. 10.

6. I owe this way of viewing ethnicity (or ethnic awareness) as hyphenated terms of belonging to Cruse (1987). Harry Goulbourne's *Ethnicity and Nationalism in Post-Imperial Britain* (1991) develops a challenging critique of the politics of cultural difference and ethnic awareness. This chapter would be radically different had I read this book before writing it.
7. See Lamming (1960:224). In my view Lamming is wrong about "the basic folk rhythm of the Caribbean" – but right about our attitudes to Africa. Africa could never be forgotten, whatever derision it excites within Afro-Caribbeans; but so also immigrant cultures from the subcontinent of India; the Pre-Colombian cultures; and Catholic and Protestant European cultures imported there four centuries ago.
8. See Elster (1989).
9. However, the more I read and understand John Rex's writings, the more I see him as one of our most prescient theorists of race equality in Britain today; and one who understands why having principles and valuing them is important. Hence my engagement with him here shows the deepest respect in which I hold them.
10. Obviously a theory of socialization, and Rex is aware of this, involves more than just identity internalization, as may be gathered from reading Richard Wollheim's interpretation of the Kleinian theory of the good and bad parental objects. To show that our identities are necessarily internalized would at least require both the story of oral incorporation and all concepts of defence, projection, introjection and projective identification, or so I believe, and this seems unnecessary for a theory of identity formation. See Wollheim (1974) and (1993), chs. 3-5.
11. In "Cultural Recognition and Identity" (Where You Belong, ch.4) I argued that an individual's identity depends on the recognition and identification she receives from others. Unfortunately I did not pursue this idea along Cancianian and Elsterian lines.
12. Rex is here quoting M. Gordon, *Human Nature, Class and Ethnicity* (Oxford, 1978).
13. The sociologists are not alone in their misperception of the plural complexity of Afro-Caribbean social life. Characterizing the socio-cultural aims, aspirations, and activities of the soon-to-be freed slaves during the first half of the 19th century, the historian Michael Craton (1982:119) observed: "More deeply the slaves retained and developed concepts of the family and kin quite beyond the comprehension and control of the master

class, and a concept of land tenure that was in contradiction to that of the dominant European culture." Creole slaves retained West African patterns of family forms, kinship structure, and land tenure as ancient and complex as South Asian ones. See also McAdoo (1993), Senior (1993), and Momsen (1993).

14. I owe to Paul Ricoeur the idea that ideology and the imagination can only be comprehended within a framework of humanism and thus a philosophical anthropology. See Ricoeur (1986).
15. I am indebted to the communitarian philosophers Charles Taylor and Alisdaire McIntyre for the orientation expressed in this paragraph. For an excellent study of both, see Mulhall and Swift (1992).
16. On the oral incorporative fantasy of the good and bad internal objects that the child takes into the self, see note 10.
17. In "A group of young black people,", vol. 2 of the PSI report called *Police and People in London* (1983) p.45.
18. Sadly John Rex shares this romantic view of Afro-Caribbean black cultures as a culture of resistance. An analogue of this view as it is applied to American slave societies is cogently criticized by Frederickson and Lasch (1973). See also Craton (1982).
19. See my review of Cross and Keith (1992) (Cambridge 1995) for a criticism of postmodernist treatment of black cultures and politics.
20. In *There Ain't No Black in the Union Jack* (1987), Paul Gilroy presents black music as a discursive means of conveying social and political agendas. I challenge this instrumental music-as-message account and set out an alternative view of musical value in chapter 5 of *Where you Belong* (1993). Clear signs of his revision of this earlier account of black music due to my criticism are evident in chapter 3 of his recent book, *The Black Atlantic* (1993). Yet Gilroy's apparent conceit prevented him from acknowledging my work.
21. Parts of this sentence paraphrase Elster (1989:99-100).
22. The model of oracular writing is all pervasive in the postmodernist and cultural studies literature. Yet long ago the negative consequences of this approach were criticized by Karl Popper in *The Open Society and its Enemies* (in a one volume Jubilee Edition, 1995) pp. 231-310. Radicals disdain this work, but Popper is justified. In *The Myth of the Framework – In Defence of Science and Rationality* (1994) and *In Search of A Better World* (1992) Popper correctly singles out an intellectual role-model of Paul Gilroy's, Theodor Adorno, as an "obscure" and "oracular" practitioner of the all-encompass-

ing style of social analysis. Especially see chapter 6, fittingly entitled "Against Big Words."

References

Cambridge, Alrick (1995). "Confronting the Postmodern Bull." *International Journal of Sociology and Social Policy* 14(9): 61-5.

———. (1992). "Cultural Recognition and Identity." In Cambridge and Feuchtwang (1992).

Cambridge, Alrick, and Stephan Feuchtwang (eds.) (1992). *Where You Belong*. Aldershot: Avebury.

Cancian, Francesca (1975). *What are Norms? A study of beliefs and action in a Maya community*. Cambridge: Cambridge University Press.

Craton, Michael (1982). "Slave Culture, Resistance and the Achievement of Emancipation in the British West Indies 1783-1838." In James Walvin (ed.), *Slavery and British Society 1776-1846*. London: Macmillan.

Cross, Malcolm, and Michael Keith (1992). *Racism, the City and the State*. London and New York: Routledge.

Cruse, Harold (1987). *Plural but Equal*. New York: Morrow.

Elster, Jon (1985). *Making Sense of Marx*. Cambridge: Cambridge University Press.

———. (1989). *Cement of Society: A study of social norms*. Cambridge: Cambridge University Press.

Frederickson, George, and Christopher Lasch (1973). "Resistance to Slavery." In Allen Weinstein and Frank Otto Gatell (eds.), *American Negro Slavery: A modern reader*. Oxford and New York: Oxford University Press, Pt. 2.

Gates, Henry Louis, Jr. (1989). *Signifying Monkey*. Oxford: Oxford University Press.

———. (1995). *Coloured People*. London: Viking.

Gilroy, Paul (1987). *There Ain't No Black in the Union Jack*. London: Routledge.

———. (1993). *The Black Atlantic: Modernity and double consciousness*. Boston: Harvard University Press.

Goulbourne, Harry (1991) *Ethnicity and Nationalism in Post-Imperial Britain*. Cambridge: Cambridge University Press.

Harris, Wilson (1973). *Tradition, the Writer and Society*. London: New Beacon Publications.

House of Commons Select Committee on Race Relations and Immigration (1977). *Report on the West Indian Community*. HMSO.

James, Winston, and Clive Harris (eds.)(1984). *Inside Babylon*. London: Verso.

Lamming, George (1960). *The Pleasures of Exile.* London: Michael Joseph.
McAdoo, Hariette Piper (1993). *Family Ethnicity: Strength in diversity.* London: Sage.
Mercer, Kobena (1994). *Welcome to the Jungle.* London and New York: Routledge.
Miles, Robert (1989). *Racism.* London and New York: Routledge.
Momsen, Janet (ed.)(1993). *Women and Change in the Caribbean.* London: John Currey.
Mulhall, Stephen, and Adam Swift (1992). *Liberals and Communitarians.* Oxford: Blackwell.
Popper, Karl (1992). *In Search of a Better World.* London and New York: Routledge.
———. (1994). *The Myth of the Framework: In defence of science and rationality.* London and New York: Routledge.
———. (1995). *The Open Society and its Enemies.* London and New York: Routledge, Jubilee edition.
Pryce, Ken (1979). *Endless Pressure.* London: Penguin.
Rex, John (1995). *Ethnicity, Identity and Ethnic Mobilization in Britain.* Monographs in Ethnic Relations, no. 5. ENRC.
Ricoeur, Paul (1986). *Lectures on Ideology and Utopia.* New York: Columbia.
Senior, Olive (1993). *Working Miracles: Women's lives in the English-speaking Caribbean.* London: John Currey.
Weinreich, Peter (1986). "The Operationalization of Identity Theory in Racial and Ethnic Relations." In John Rex and David Mason (eds.), *Theories of Race and Ethnic Relations.* Cambridge: Cambridge University Press.
Wollheim, Richard (1974). "The Mind and the Mind's Image of Itself." In *On Art and the Mind.* Cambridge: Cambridge University Press.
——— (1993). *The Mind and its Death.* Boston: Harvard University Press.

[Part III]

MEMORY AND HISTORIES

Introduction

Interest in the individual as a source of memory and meaning has led to the repositioning of the relationship between agency and social structure across a range of social science-related disciplines. Memory, and its place in the reconstruction of historical accounts, is now a large and significant intellectual and political enterprise (Passerini 1992). The past has never been more contingent, as the greater certainties of public historiography are contested by individual and collective memories. How events, people, and places invoking racial and ethnic identities are remembered recalls Portelli's (1993) image of a haunted house. But memory is a haunted house in which the ghosts are selected by the political agendas of the present. The papers in this section address a number of contexts: medieval German Jewry, present day reunified Germany, the state of Georgia between the 1940s and the Civil Rights Movement, and the encounters between Europeans and Amerindians at the time of the "discovery" of America. These different contexts raise important issues about what and how we remember, how we memorialize the past, and the political projects of imagined community served in collective memory.

Henri Lustiger-Thaler discusses the mnemonic negotiations prompted by the "memory encounter" surrounding the recent excavation of the Frankfurt Jewish ghetto. The excavation of the ghetto prompted a vigorous public debate about the racialization of space and a reframing both of Germany's past relationship to 14th-century Jewishness and of its present-day relationship to "otherness" within the political community. Lustiger-Thaler's paper is about what is remembered, what is forgotten, and the significance of absence. He argues that social constructs such as class, ethnicity, and race are the frameworks of remembrance. In this way he links memory with the social relationships of power regimes, and draws some interesting connections between the imagined community of the post-war German state and its relationship to "otherness." Lustiger-Thaler reminds us of the difficulties of remembering in a society which has not come to terms with its anti-Semitic past, and this has some important implications for the Jewish diaspora throughout Europe and North America.

Tracy K'Meyer explores the tensions between individual and collective memory as different kinds of historical enterprises in the reworking of the "usable past" of United States race relations and civil rights. Positioning individual memory beside shared community memory and the national collective memories of public histories, K'Meyer shows how the Christian agricultural community of Koinonia in Georgia both remembers and forgets its involvement in civil rights struggles as it celebrates its fiftieth anniversary. K'Meyer shows that individual, oral reminiscences of community members show an awareness of southern race relations and the political will to act upon that awareness. But collective community memories "forget" this political involvement and its implications. This project of forgetting fits with the public histories of the Civil Rights Movement which, in shifting from black integration to black power and hence the potency of individual (male) leaders, manages also to overlook the contributions of black women to the struggle for civil rights in the 1960s.

Robert Paine's chapter also takes up the issue of how history is written and rewritten in the light of changing moral impetuses, in this case as these have involved shifting conceptions of the initial European encounters with Amerindians. Instead of exchanging a demonized portrait of Amerindians for an equally unnuanced and simplistic caricature of 16th-century Europeans, Paine explores the debates, paradoxes, and moral oscillations provoked by explorations of the Americas. For the scholars and lawyers of Christian Europe, the existence of the Americas posed an ontological challenge to an authoritative theological canon, one which treated the world as already known and its inhabitants as descendents of one single originating couple. For the scholar, therefore, the alienness of America and Amerindians contained the seeds of heretical doubt: either the European conception of the universe had to be changed or the Other had to be reformed. The former was unthinkable to the schoolmen, if not to the more practical mariners, but it was the appropriation of the Other and its attendant political advantages which dominated the "Discovery," remaking the unknown into a "reflection of the imagined known," turning a "discovery" into a "non-discovery." In an intellectual and metaphysical sense, the Europeans never left home. The ultimate irony is that in the process of denying alterity to others, the Europeans also denied it to themselves, imprisoning themselves within existing limits of knowledge.

All of the papers in this section, in their different ways, problematize the relationship between past and present. They examine the social relationships embedded in the generation, construction, and reconstruction of histories which correspond with the political projects of the present.

References

Passerini, L. (ed.)(1992). Memory and Totalitarianism International Yearbook of Oral History and Life Stories, Vol 1. Oxford: Oxford University Press.

Portelli, A. (1993) "We're All on Tape: Voice Recording and the Electronic Afterlife." In Daniel Bertaux and Paul Thompson (eds.) *Between Generations International Yearbook of Oral History and Life Stories*, Vol II. Oxford: Oxford University Press.

8

Remembering Forgetfully

Henri Lustiger-Thaler[1]

> *Give them names, for memory's sake.*
>
> ~ JACQUES DERRIDA,
> *Memoirs of the Blind: The Self-Portrait and Other Ruins*

The lines separating remembering and forgetting have tightly woven cultural borders. One group's need to remember is often grist for another's desire to forget. It is not surprising that acts of public commemoration have as much strategically inscribed within them as they have excluded. Memory and forgetting are hence part of an embedded historical discourse that evokes as it simultaneously erases, inevitably unfolding on many different social registers and in different "memory encounters" between groups, as they attempt to articulate their sense of (dis)location within the present.

This chapter is about the border-crossings of memory and forgetting that have been culturally reproduced between native Germans, German Jews, and resettled Eastern European Jews in postwar Germany. This cultural and ethnic topography is a complex affair, its many agencies fraught with "mnemonic dangers." These have been painfully exposed in the recent preparations for the 50th anniversary of the ending of the Second World War. I will argue here that the resettled Jews of postwar Germany, the ghosts of German Jews, and native Germans are tightly bound in a *danse macabre* about constructing a basis for recollection as a social relationship within the present. The studied movements of this dance gather together unmastered memories of sameness and otherness, the secrets so brilliantly extolled in George Simmel's meditations on the mental life of the stranger.[2]

The current context within which these recollections are unfolding is even more layered with cultural complexity, through the construction of a political memory about the German nation-state at yet another critical *Null-Stunde*, Zero Hour. The 50th anniversary of the end of the Second World War is a moment of multiple memory choices about how and what to commemorate: liberation, defeat, reconciliation, the war years, or the beginning of half a century of peace. Indeed, 1995 combines all these ambivalent signifiers as collapsed cultural counterpoints, as the German nation is showered with hybrid-like commemorative moments that speak about justice in the present as a way to redraw, suture, and master the past.

Though the framing of these larger themes is important to the overall issues raised in this chapter, my immediate task is more modest in its narrative scope. I want to recount an event, a controversy, which transpired in Frankfurt am Main from 1987 to 1991. This story concerns the archaeological finding of a 13th-century Jewish Ghetto, the Judengasse (the Jews Street). The unearthing of the ruins received little attention outside Germany. They were uncovered during construction by the Frankfurt Stadtwerke (the local utilities company) in the course of expanding their Customer Relations Branch, already on the site. I use the verbs "unearthed" and "uncovered" rather than "discovered" as it was common knowledge to most informed individuals that the Stadtwerke was sitting on the historic site of Jewish German history, the ghetto. In fact, parts of the old ghetto had been uncovered, and destroyed in the process, years earlier during the building of a gas station, with little ensuing controversy from either German or Jew. The remaining ruins of the Judengasse were simply waiting for a more pregnant moment to be remembered and named.

Just so. In 1987, on a rainy May morning, bulldozers skimmed away layers of debris revealing two perfectly intact 14th-century mikvehs.[3] The Stadtwerke owned the land which contained the ruins and was determined to go forward with its planned extension, incorporating the finding into an appropriate architectural design. This precipitated weeks of demonstrations and protests by both Jewish and non-Jewish citizens of Frankfurt intent on preserving the ruins as a place in and of itself, a site of memory. The ensuing struggle came to be known as the *Börneplatz Konflict*, named after the *Börneplatz* synagogue that sat for 100 years on the western tip of the Judengasse. The grand synagogue, once the symbol of Jewish political and social emancipation in 19th-century Germany, was burned to the ground in 1938 during *Kristallnacht*, its stones moved across the city and reclaimed as a wall for a Christian cemetery.

A plaque placed by the Jewish community of Frankfurt marking the site of the *Börneplatz* synagogue became a point of rally in 1987. The protesters of the *Börneplatz Konflict* were pitted against a largely indifferent public, an intransigent City Council, and a business-as-usual utilities company. The Stadtwerke was, however, entering the contested realm of memory by maintaining the authority of its land claim, an action which would have important consequences for how the old ghetto came to be culturally contextualized, and the esthetic role the Stadtwerke was to have in that process. The incident ignited a debate about the difficult preserves of memory which resonated well beyond the parochial and municipal nature of the Frankfurt finding.

The controversy took two forms. First, there was a much needed focus upon the difficulty of remembering in a society with an unmastered relationship (*Vergangenheitsbewältigung*) to its past; second, there was a powerful emphasis upon visually representing the site of memory as an act of reconciliation with the past. The latter dimension proved more durable from a purely esthetic standpoint.[4] The site's representational content devoured other more difficult issues that were evoked in the unfolding conflict. Controversy was framed around issues of form, with proposals by artists and architects which sought to incorporate the ruins within the landscape of modern Germany through the gaze and body of the Stadtwerke.

The spontaneous protest against the Stadtwerke's plan also found a representational home in the final esthetic of the Judengasse Museum, the eventual outcome of the conflict which came to be housed within the lobby and basement of the Stadtwerke. It included a separate room which became what I will call an "anti-museum" that chronicled the demonstrations directed against the construction of the Stadtwerke/Judengasse Museum. The result was that the politics of esthetic entrapment produced a reconciled esthetic form: the new Germany gazing on constituted Otherness. This representation became the end-product of an encounter with the past, rather than the necessary springboard for sending more difficult missives into the public realm about who was being remembered and more critically by and for whom the remembering was being done.

Several things occurred here. The overt estheticization of the cultural stakes of the conflict diverted attention away from the issue of ghosts, German Jews, who form a small minority of the Jewish population in present-day Germany. But the Judengasse finding did create a "memory encounter," a hybrid-like cultural form of recognition between perpetrators, their offspring and non-Germans now resettled in Germany (Polish, Hungarian and Czech Jews, mostly former Displaced Persons, DPs). As we shall see, the Frankfurt findings reignited a pattern of mnemonic co-existence that had become entrenched in the political and cultural practices of both Germans and resettled Eastern European Jews in Germany around the legacy of absent German Jews.

This has led to a peculiar condition wherein Eastern European Jews living in Germany today, cannot be culturally apprehended without the ghost that now constitutes them. The resettled Jew emerges from this interstitial space, one that it shares with a ghost, as simulacrum, a cultural copy. This underscores a process of mnemonic replacement that inevitably creates "split fields" of recollection. This split mnemonic encounter, where forgetting and replacement become dialectically engaged, acts as a framing mechanism for the "ghostly memories" of absent German Jews, museal Jews – the wealth of their lost culture, institutions and intellectual life, the real historical subjects of the Judengasse. As I will argue later, this ultimately creates a moral basis for Germans to forget through the simulacra of resettled Jewish memory.

The Judengasse finding, and the *Börneplatz Konflict* that unfolded around it, provide a rich framework for examining how the modern German Question, and its thirst for legitimacy, is still wedded to the "Jewish Question," underscoring what Dan Diner has called their cultural sharing of a "kind of opposing commonality" or negative symbiosis.[5] These issues are infinitely more layered than the German desire to forget or the singular Jewish desire to remember. Relations between Germans and Jews, dating back to the settlements of the Middle Rhine of the 11th century, have never been simple affairs. Relations with ghosts and their accidental gatekeepers are no less bedded with cultural difficulties and mnemonic ambivalences. What Walter Benjamin once called the German Jew's "unrequited love" for Germany has taken on new and ironic meaning.

The Borders of Memory/the Frontiers of Amnesia: the postwar German state

Many elements were at work at the end of the Second World War that institutionalized Germany's complex relationship to its past. The fragmentation of postwar political life, its weak and uncertain elite structure, the Nuremburg trials' focus on the most senior Nazi officials, as well as the effects of an occupation in full force, all created a vacuum wherein the nation quietly retained its old bureaucratic, industrial, and political personnel. Nazis that participated in larger and lesser crimes moved from the Third Reich to the Second Republic with little protest from the populace. Indeed, this was widely accepted as a measure with which to maintain social order. It also conveniently excused the German state of bringing many individuals to justice, foreclosing on the possibility of pursuing genocide-related crimes.

The mass murders of Jews, Gypsies, communists, and other European peoples were rarely mentioned in any forum of public discourse within early postwar Germany. The first commemorations to the German Jewish population were placed by the occupying American Army in 1948. Yet the social amnesia of the times is not without its apologists. The philosopher Hermann Luebbe[6] has argued that the deafening silence of the Germans was necessary for the transformation of the Third Reich into the Federal Republic. Luebbe argues that the normality Germans were searching for was found in the mutual acceptance of one another's past; it was only through such acceptance that the country could rebuild its imagined community. Denazification was in this sense a less pressing project than the reconstruction of the nation, where National Socialist ideas would be, he argues, duly discredited. The essence of Luebbe's argument is to promote an understanding that the Nazi period was one of a liminal character, blurring its deeper roots in German culture.

With these mnemonic counter-arguments, Germans were drawing the lines of a moral debate which persists to this day about the responsibility of the German state to its victims. These attempts to redimension the past unfolded within a moral vacuum. Memory and forgetting could not be properly enacted as part of the reconstruction of the imagined community while the problem of claiming responsibility remained an open and festering sore. And as any astute politician of the time recognized, resolving this conundrum was key to dismantling the barriers that morally isolated Germany from the rest of Europe.

It was within this context that the cultural peculiarities of German postwar philosemitism were born. The construction of an official philosemitic discourse required a public avowal of guilt and a tempered commitment to assuming responsibility for the nation's actions, however unspecific it might be. The die was cast in 1949, through the republic's first president, Theodor Heuss. Heuss's public recognition of German culpability was ice-breaking. While it was the first official avowal of "collective responsibility" it also underscored a new political and psychological border-crossing for emerging memory-work about reconcilability, *and* it stressed the interest the German state would have in occupying a moral voice in Europe's framing of its war years. Indeed, Heuss's avowal prepared the political groundwork for the *Wiedergutmachung* (war reparations payments), which were introduced in 1953 and whose main political sponsor was the then chancellor of the republic, Konrad Adenauer.

The *Wiedergutmachung* received an icy reception from Germans of the early 1950s. Opinion polls in Germany during the deliberations, which lasted from 1951-53, showed that support was low, with only 11% of the people thinking it a good idea. As Anson Rabinbach demonstrates in his superb analysis of this period, even the minimal consensus needed to forward the initiative was fraught with political obstacles couched in anti-Semitic overtones.[7] The German population was much less philosemitic than was official German policy: the *pays réel* and the *pays légal* became entangled in an unintended dialectic.

And the German state treated the *Wiedergutmachung* much like a treaty with a former enemy, negotiating with the World Jewish Congress and the state of Israel. Yet it was certainly through the force of the *Wiedergutmachung* that the Germans held their best moral passport to post-Nazi Europe, a move masterfully manoeuvred by Adenauer and Heuss. Over the next three decades, the Jewish Question, framed by Adenauer's reparations initiative, became part of an unconscious consensus amongst Germans. Facing the past through the spectral and contained world of reparations perversely allowed a distancing from it, as a form of grudging social contract amongst Germans.

The reparations climate, the difficulty in emigration to the United States and Canada, the permanent state of war in Israel, and the ending of the Allied occupation created economic conditions wherein many Jews, still Displaced Persons and mostly from Eastern Europe, found opportunity in Germany. These groups were immediately courted by the state. They were consulted as the German state made its next bid for legitimacy in the postwar era, through subterranean and eventually official relations with the state of Israel. This placed the newly settled Jews of postwar Germany in a peculiar cultural and political situation, replacing ghosts and playing "confessors" to German "sinners" through the good offices of the philosemitic state. In this, the German body politic culturally reframed their Jewish victim by making them somewhat exotic and hyperreal in a society that had been rendered effectively *Judenrein*. Eastern European Jews, the resettled Jews of Germany, became larger than life representations, wherein their presence became key to the rekindling of German memory. As the historian Saul Friedlander suggests, resettled Jews in Germany received a negative form of power in the perverse power of absolution.[8]

Complicating this mnemonic encounter was the changed perception of the postwar Jew that emerged with the development of a Left political culture throughout the 1960s and 1970s, as anti-totalitarian politics swept up the second generation of Germans. The New Left appealed to a history of social solidarity that reached back to the pre-Nazi years, to Germany's socialist and anarchist past. This was even further consolidated with the *Ostpolitik* directed towards the state of Israel after 1967, particularly the changed perception of Israelis in Germany, as Palestinian national aspirations replaced the former's favourable status in socialist, social-democratic, and generally progressive circles.

As some commentators have suggested, the deafening silence around the issue of Jews as the victims of Germans created a collective psychoanalytical transference wherein political sentiments were given over to the "new and acknowledged victim," the Palestinian, as an unconscious effort to turn one's gaze away from the "old unacknowledged victim," the Jew. The "victim of the victim" received a wide and celebrated reception in the German New Left, one that was significantly more pronounced than in other European countries at the time. Germany was then also under the strong leadership of Helmut Schmidt, whose own anti-fascist past allowed him to abandon the strategic guilt policies of the Adenauer regime. In short, the general population never shared in the German philosopher Karl Jaspers' postwar appeal for an ethical reckoning, a "moral political revolution," as a way to rebuild the fragmented nation and imagined community.

The Construction of a Post-philosemitic German Memory

The strategic philosemitic framing of the postwar Jewish Question was bound to run its course, given the determined avoidance of the past, as a cultural practice by the German people. In the late 1980s and early 1990s the new historical consciousness around nation-state-building required an entirely different set of strategies; it needed to be built around issues in German history and memory, the political basis of which would have been impossible to construct without the previous philosemitic stage. Many of the important public controversies in Germany about the residues of the Second World War can be textually decoded in this light.

The political and intellectual climates of the *Historikerstreit* (the Historians Debate)[9] and the Bitburg episode[10] are symbolic of a radical remapping in the border-crossings of the German and Jewish Questions. From these events, the German Question emerged no longer burdened by the Nazi horror. The *Historikerstreit* and the Bitburg episodes marked the beginning of the decline of the philosemitic bonus and the ascendance of German memory. This period also marked the unleashing of old habits: the late 1980s and early 1990s were rife with attacks on Turkish *Gastarbeiters* and Jewish cemeteries. Both the memory of ghosts and the new visible outsiders became targets, illustrating how the real and symbolic Jewish Question is symbolically linked to current forms of representation of the *Ausländer*.[11]

A succinct illustration of the decline of official philosemitism, and its relationship to social amnesia and mnemonic distortion, can be found in Klaus-Michael Groll's recent book, *Wie lange haften wir für Hitler? Zum Selbstverständnis der Deutschen heute* (How long are we responsible for Hitler? Reflections on German Identity Today).[12] Groll makes the popular argument that the new Germany has rethought itself sufficiently to cast off the history of the Third Reich. For Groll, the four elements of *Vergangenheitsbewältigung* (mastery of the past) – the avowal of guilt, the acceptance of responsibility, paying off the debt, and passing the test of democracy, have all been achieved. Clearly, in Groll's post-philosemitic world, the event of the century was not Auschwitz, Treblinka or Bergen Belsen but the crime against German national unity (Stern 1990).[13]

Other discursive indicators of the post-philosemitic period are more nuanced. These can be found in the powerful memory symbols selected by the current president of Germany, Roman Herzog. Herzog commemorated the 50th anniversary of the ending of the war, on May 8,

1995, in Dresden, a city where tens of thousands of German citizens perished during the bombing by Allied forces, a city which had no visible military import. This use of symbol as innocence suggests that the Germans were not the only ones who committed war crimes. In a country as sensitive to commemorations as Germany, Herzog's site of memory, fifty years after the event, is a radical departure from the policies of the early Second Republic.[14]

The Postwar Jew as Stranded Object

Most of the Jews living in Germany today arrived after the war. To fully understand the origins of the present Jewish community in Germany is to return to the DP camps of their internment. Interview data and archival documents clearly show that the intent of survivors in the DP camps was to leave Germany as soon as possible. At the Bergen Belsen DP Camp, for example, the First Conference of Liberated Jews called for a quick exit from Germany. In the end, of the 200,000 Jews who lived in all the occupied zones from 1945 to 1950, about 17,000 remained in Germany.

Even well into the 1950s, there was a discourse that envisioned departure, waiting for the opportune moment. These turned into lengthy stays for many, who often settled in the cities that were closest to their DP camps. For instance, many postwar members of the Jewish community in Frankfurt were interned in the Zeilsheim DP camp, on the outskirts of the city. Organized Jewish life in Germany after the war consisted largely of Polish, Czech and Hungarian Jewish communities, the largest proportion of which were Polish. These groups cultivated the stance of the exile, the stranded object. It was not uncommon throughout the 1950s and 1960s for many Jewish women living in Germany to travel to the United States or Israel to have their children.

Tensions existed between the Eastern European Jews and the remaining German Jews.[15] Placed in control of important Jewish committees overlooking the legacy of German Jews, Eastern European Jews could not but show their lesser attachment to traditional sites; it was common, for example, in the 1950s and 1960s for the community to sell these to the highest bidder or to the city. One of these sites was the land on which the Judengasse was eventually uncovered. These resettled Jewish communities developed in tandem with the postwar philosemitic state. In time, they became unofficial "go-betweens" between Germany and Israel, according them a tactical usefulness, watering down the tacit disapproval they received in the larger Jewish world. For these Eastern European Jews, what began as a temporal way station became a sort of perverse cultural residence. Reclining on John Donne's poignant imagery, the bridge itself became the destination.

Times are again in flux. It is within this socio-cultural context of memory that the Judengasse ruins cautiously peered out of their hiding-place. What they saw was a city filled with the ghosts of German Jews, the museal-like stances of Eastern European Jews and their children, eyes fixed on the skyline of Manhattan or the coastline of Tel Aviv (Kugelmann, 1991).[16]

A Short History of the Judengasse

'The Aleph?' I repeated.
'Yes, the only place on earth where all places are seen from every angle, each standing clear, without any confusion or blending'.

∾ JORGE LUIS BORGES, The Aleph

Origins

The German/Jewish presence in Frankfurt am Main dates back to the middle of the 13th century.[17] Jews first settled in the same sectors of the city as native Germans. However, this cultural proximity did not last long, since with forced resettlement Jews were obliged to live in the centre of the city, near an already established Jewish cemetery. The area became known as the Judengasse, or the "Jews Street." The first signs of the ghetto have been traced back to 1462.

The spatial topography of the Judengasse grew in proportion to the development of local markets, as well as anti-Semitic policies and attacks against the Jewish community in the 15th and 16th centuries.[18] Often these occurred in tandem, as Jews were increasingly exposed to the general population, due to their role in early pariah capitalism, described in exacting detail in Max Weber's trenchant analysis of this period. By the end of the 16th century the Judengasse consisted of a 375-metre-long street with about 100 buildings. Life in the Ghetto was self-enclosed and to a large extent politically self-referential. The ghetto had an architectural feature that was a reflection of the strained relations between Jews and Christians: both ends of the street were enclosed by large wrought iron gates, which were shut in the evenings and on all Christian holidays, for fear of attack. The Judengasse served many purposes, both for the Jewish population of Frankfurt as well as its German citizens. The City of Frankfurt benefited from the taxes generated by the ghetto, due to the dense trading and money-lending activities which characterized it. This became particularly evident in the 1600s with the beginning of the Frankfurt Fair which attracted yet more merchant Jews to the city.

The negative sentiment of the population against the Jews was a constant theme in the political deliberations of the City Council throughout the 16th century. In 1570 the first hostile campaign was waged against the population of the Judengasse, led by Johans Pfeffercorn, a Jew converted to Christianity. Pfeffercorn insisted that he studied the Talmud, proclaiming that it be seized as subversive material, a claim with which the Kaiser concurred. By 1612 the climate between Jews and Christians had visibly deteriorated. Sporadic acts of violence were recorded as citizens wanted more control placed on Jewish activities, particularly in matters of money-lending. The council balked, because of the significant city revenues derived from these transactions. This led to the tragic attack on the Judengasse by the citizens of Frankfurt on August 12, 1614, known as the Fettmilchaufstand.[19]

The historical records of the *Fettmilchaufstand* note high casualties, ending with the eventual expulsion of Jews from Frankfurt. With the reestablishment of order, Jews were invited to return and promised special protection from the state. Prior to the uprising there was a tradition of according Jews visas for a three-year stay in the city. These were usually renewed automatically, or employed as pretexts to expel individual members of the community. But with the invitation to return to Frankfurt, the Jewish population was given unlimited residence in the ghetto, one of the first markers of their complex and conflict-laden assimilation within German society.

The ghetto gates thrown open

The liberation of the Judengasse came with the thunder of a French cannon. In 1796, French troops shot into the northern part of the ghetto, starting a fire that was so immense as to have political repercussions. The

Judengasse was completely destroyed, giving the Kaiser a pretext for permitting the Jews of Frankfurt to live outside the ghetto. There was also much pressure within his own coterie of Jewish advisors to do so, and the occasion was grasped as an opportunity. This ensured a wider territory for the struggle for the political rights of Jews in Germany that was to occupy the community throughout the 18th century. The tone of this struggle was captured in Bruno Bauer and Karl Marx's opposing polemics on the "Jewish Question" and the problem of political emancipation. Though no longer restricted to its confines, the Jews of Frankfurt rebuilt the Judengasse several times. Their new-found confidence throughout the 18th and 19th centuries was evident in high levels of assimilation and presence in virtually every sector of German culture, economy, and society. The symbolic culmination of this presence was the construction of an imposing temple in 1860, on the western tip of the Judengasse, the *Börneplatz* synagogue.

Fascism in Frankfurt

After Berlin, Frankfurt am Main had the largest pre-war Jewish community in Germany. So large and prolific was the community in 1929, in fact, that the National Socialists cynically referred to the city as "Jerusalem am Main." With the coming to power of the Nazis, the *Börneplatz* synagogue became a constant site of demonstration against Jewish citizens. From 1933 to 1938 the *Hitler Jugend* (the Hitler Youth) and *Bund Deutscher Maedels* (the female version of the Hitler Youth), regularly marched through the *Börneplatz* on Saturday mornings, disrupting Sabbath prayers.

By 1934, all streets bearing Jewish names, streets that had existed since the 1400s, had been changed to German. Even the name of the site, the *Börneplatz*, was changed to the *Dominikanerplatz*, after the Dominican monastery in the area. In 1935, the City Council of Frankfurt built a park in front of the synagogue, appealing to city dwellers to use it for all family occasions. The park was used for national commemorations as well. The tragic events of *Kristallnacht* ended this official policy of harassment with the final destruction of the synagogue, the last standing marker pointing to the then already absent Judengasse.

Frankfurt after the war, like many cities in Germany, became an abstract place, so destroyed was it by the Allied bombings. It is a curious addition to the story of the Judengasse that a small synagogue already unused by the community in 1933, that somehow survived *Kristallnacht* as well as the Allied bombings, was to be destroyed after the war. It was torn down in the early 1950s, in order for trucks to have access to the *Dominikaner Kloister* during the physical reconstruction of the city.

The survival of memory in the sign

In 1952 the City Council began discussions on rezoning the area. In 1954 the city allowed a flower market to be built on the site, and it was in that same year that the Stadtwerke bought the land from the Jewish committee in charge of traditional properties. The Stadtwerke built a small utilities installation and leased some of the land to a local gas station. During the construction of the gas station in 1956, contractors dug four metres into the ground, destroying nine metres of the Judengasse. The issue of the historic ruins was not raised by the Jewish community, though the findings were widely known.

Throughout the 1950s and 1960s the City Council debated the future of the *Dominikanerplatz*. The area had, since the end of the war, developed a strong neighbourhood voice that demanded a pragmatic use of the site. In 1979 the Stadtwerke put forward a plan to expand its Customer Relations facilities; however, the plan lay dormant for many years. Debate was once again stirred up with the Stadtwerke's renewed intent to pursue their building strategy, yet the Jewish community protested with support from the German Social Democratic Party, the SPD. The SPD argued that it would be inappropriate to place a building like the Stadtwerke on a site so central to Jewish memory. In July 1985, 130 professors from the University of Frankfurt co-signed a letter condemning the building proposal but the construction of the Stadtwerke nonetheless began on schedule.

It was noted in City Council records of July 7, 1985, that if authorities found the remains of the Judengasse, the city would force the Stadtwerke to halt construction and reconsider the building strategy. In 1987, during construction, two mikvehs from 1462 were found, as well as an early 18th-century house which contained them. The Jewish community asked for a moratorium on the building activity, but the reply of the Council was not sympathetic to the demand. The Stadtwerke and the City argued that if they were to build around the archaeological find, it would be at the expense of another 15,000,000 marks, a cost that would be passed onto the taxpayers of the city.

On August 27, 1987, the western wall of the Judengasse was destroyed. Thirty people protested, forcing the Minister of Cultural Affairs to act quickly to preserve a building found directly next to the destroyed wall. And more protests followed. A demonstration of 800 people wound its way though the city, ending at the *Börneplatz*, to protest the slow action of officials to protect the site. This demonstration turned into a sit-in that lasted for several days. The mayor of the city called on the Jewish community to distance itself from the occupiers, a request with which the Jewish community largely complied.[20] The police eventually removed 40 people from the site. But the protesters had made their point: the eastern side of the Judengasse was saved and the city promised to reconstruct the mikvehs.

The archaeological findings held different meanings for the many actors implicated in the controversy. For the city, the ruins were a quandary: how to acknowledge the otherness of a safely distant past (the 14th century), when its later subjects were brutally expelled from the body politic by a more recent unacknowledged past (the Second World War). The act of commemoration in this sense already had breached boundaries, as one recollection evoked signifiers from more recent times, with memory surviving in the sign. The Judengasse finding could hardly feign an archaeological folkloric existence. Its inner discursive activity pointed elsewhere.

Museum, anti-museum, and ruin

In the end, five excavated houses were incorporated into the Stadtwerke complex, housed in a museum-like structure with a separate entrance. The city gave the administration of the site over to the Frankfurt Jewish Museum. On the ground floor of the Judengasse Museum is a pictorial history of the ghetto; in the basement, within the bowels of the Stadtwerke, are the archaeological findings. The city and the Stadtwerke built a further site of memory, taking the shape of an anti-museum (a museum that argues against itself) whose sole purpose is to preserve representations of the protest surrounding the *Börneplatz Konflict*. The anti-museum is accessible only after the viewer passes through the ruins. It incorporates the protest *into* the mechanical body of the Stadtwerke, inversing signifier and signified. On entering the anti-museum the individual is confronted by an island of small stones with two constantly playing video monitors on either side of the entrance recounting the

Barbara Rose Haum

The Stadtwerke

Barbara Rose Haum

Photo Installation in the "Anti-Museum"
Translation: History is being eliminated in this park

---

heady moments of the protest. As the viewers walk around this small island of stones they are immersed in 14th-century artifacts interspersed with memorabilia and graffiti of the protest. Also incorporated into the anti-museum are photos of a hastily erected metal wall which had been painted on by individuals during the protest, an action which clearly harkened to the graffiti painted on the Berlin Wall.

The memorabilia of the 14th century and the artifacts of the protest emerge as ambivalent identifications which override the positionality of where one speaks from, particularly in a context when there is another speaker, the Eastern European Jew. The Eastern European Jew must do this in a sense from where "they are not." The space of representation of the anti-museum denounces the final use of the site occupied by the viewer. In doing this, it conflates the memory of the Judengasse with the memory of the protest, through the unauthentic voice of the Eastern European Jew as

Barbara Rose Haum

The Entrance to the Judengasse Ruins
Translation: Top of poster: Nazi Killings: We demand a memorial plaque for the Jewish, Sinti and Roma children murdered by the Nazis.
Bottom of poster: Nazis are murdering again today.

German Jew. The Judengasse became (as Homi Bhabha has poignantly remarked on the resonance of absence in commemorative sites), an *unheimlich* space for the negotiation of identity and history.[21] And appropriately, the complex opened with an exhibition entitled "The Different Stations of Forgetting." In 1992 more ruins were found in the area during routine construction work. Little was done about it; the constructed cultural memory of the event was for the moment complete.

What does the story of the Judengasse tell us about the construction of memory? Its most significant contribution is that memory is constituted through mnemonic exchanges, or "memory agencies," about the boundaries of constituted otherness. It is about the conflict-laden process of reconstituting, within the cultural memory of the present, what Toni Morrison has called "the not there," in a condition of simulacra.[22] In this regard, the "memory encounter" is a cultural relationship capable of reframing absent pasts by dividing the "time of being" between Jewish ghosts and resettled Jews, thus allowing a space for the reconstruction of German memory as a legitimate basis for nationhood.

Historical Narrativity, Genealogy, and Memory Encounters

The broader theoretical problem of articulating the uses of the past, the present and their relationship to cultural memory is a matter currently receiving attention from more and more scholars. Its treatment goes well beyond the confines of this chapter; however, I would like to make some tentative comments on the role of history as a privileged institution for the constitution of social memory, comments which may help us better understand the various ways the *Börneplatz Konflict* was framed and how the social relationship of the present is haunted and stalked by the past.

Building on the seminal insights of Maurice Halbwachs, I first contend that cultural memory is indeed "present-centred," through agencies of experiential selection.[23] Cultural memory is an interstitial space for recollection and amnesia, through the framing of the present as a relationship based on an affirming collective narrativity. The defining power of this social relationship is such that it can substitute a presence for an absence or even discover an absent voice; the marginalized, the excised. Halbwachs understood collective memory in terms of the existence of frameworks of recollection upon which individual memory relies. For Halbwachs, therefore, memory is not a tangential quality of human activity but is rather essential to the construction of present-day ideas and the integration of those ideas into ruling perceptions, ideologies, etc. We remember through social constructs such as class, ethnicity, and race as frameworks of remembrance.[24] Perhaps most importantly, for Halbwachs, memory becomes part of a system of conflicting frameworks about the present, and it becomes most evident in the passage from one societal form to another, through processes of cultural selectivity and social distortion. Halbwachs' notion of distortion can be understood as an instance of subjective reflexivity, the reconstitution of a society, community or institution, through privileging particular collective experiences drawn from the historical story line. Halbwachs' thesis is that the social interests and cultural frameworks of the present become the sociological basis for the creation of a wide range of conflicting pasts. From a mnemonic perspective, the present *is* the past.

Halbwachs' understanding of memory places considerable emphasis upon stitching together various approaches to collective interpretations as opposed to the methodologies of "historical knowing." But – and it seems entirely reasonable to ask in this context – if memory is forged in the present yet is also crucial to our construction of the past, are these interpretative frames of recollection enough to guide us safely through the strategies of historical deceivers, "who in Kundera's wonderful image, can airbrush a man out of a photograph, so that nothing is left of him but his hat" (Yerushalmi 1989)?[25] But residual knowledge about constituted otherness, or the collapsing of the other and the same, may escape Halbwachs' privileging of selective memory over history's empirical narrativity. Can the reduction of the past to the incommensurability of differing memories between others and sames destroy the very basis for remembering what can still ostensibly be called the Real?

The confrontation between history and memory as discourses sheds some light on this. Jacques Le Goff, a leading member of the Annales School,[26] explains history as a dialectical instance, wherein both remembering and forgetting are documented and made knowable.[27] History, and its method, is the privileged discourse that permits us to make sense of mnemonic knowledge. Le Goff argues that to "privilege memory excessively is to sink into the unconquerable flow of time," something that was said perhaps more starkly, and much less sympathetically, by R.G. Collingwood, who argued that memory and history are radically different mental and social processes about the organization of inferential knowledge. The most potent dimension of Halbwachs' work, the temporal and experiential component of the social imaginary and its collective memories, is what Le Goff means to subject to the rigours of an historical anthropology. Le Goff's final position points to the constituted knowledge we are left with at the end of a reasoned balancing of the historical narrative. His point of departure is about what we *have*, or how we have "sited" the constructed past as a function of accumulated and localized interpretations of knowledge. In lieu of the temporal, intersubjective, and selective dimension of remembering, Le Goff instructs us to localize systems of knowledge by writing memory *into* history, thus subjecting it to rigorous verification.[28]

All this said, however, I would like to pursue a different line of research, one that ties historical discourse to the question of authority and how it constructs "absence," an issue left untreated in both Halbswachs' and Le Goff's work. Through this I mean to recapture Halbwachs' initial insights, denuded of their penchant for selection, by directing his insights toward the problem of power. We first need to critically problematize the making of history as discourse. The original, if highly problematic, work of Michel Foucault, is of value to the issues treated here. Yet Foucault's work must be supplemented with an active subject that can recall and ask, "What *is* history?", rather than accept it as a series of discontinuous ruptures. Given the difficulties that accompany his genealogical project I can only offer, within the context of this chapter, the most tempting linkages with the problem of memory.

Foucault argues that history is a Western myth constituted on a privileged story line of subjectivity. As a form of knowledge it assumes the stance of power through the urge to domesticate the past and control it, in order to validate the history of the present. The projected intent of the historical moment, for Foucault, is assimilation to sameness, exclusion of otherness. His genealogical approach, as a search for the other, places us in a more complex position than does the historian's methodological debate with memory, over who can speak a truth: the individual left to recount his or her experience, or the official documenter as guardian of memory. Foucault informs us that history is itself as suspect as a discourse *as is the present*. He begins his critique in the context of the present, tracing its line of descent. His insights direct us to the discontinuities between the past and the present as a social construction, a position not far removed from current thinking on the difficulty of intersubjective memory. The practice of genealogy, as a history of the present and as method, thus emerges as a sort of anti-science "opposed to the effects of centralizing powers which are linked to the institution and functioning of an organized scientific discourse."[29] Foucault's intent was to signify issues which escaped public notice, inversing historical narrativity towards the experience of the other. His concern was to historicize the event of the dehistoricized.

Without entering into the volumes of critique directed at Foucault's project, I wish to signal a corrective to his critical project. I would argue that problematizing memory as a sort of "retrieved subjectivity" can have a focusing effect on the micro-discourses to which Foucault's genealogy lead. Foucault's form of historiography, or maxim of genealogy, as Richard Rorty has suggested,[30] is much less a theory than an injunction to the critical historian not to believe in the notion of history as progress or reason. If we take Rorty's open position on Foucault's methodology, we escape Foucault's own sociological functionalism about the interstitial nature of power where it becomes so pervasive and dispersed as to make resistance futile. By not claiming an agent, the interconnected system that emerges from his thought defies an advocacy position for social change, or the very purpose of recollection. Foucault's genealogical approach *as theory* does not answer the question of why one would bother to remember, or more pointedly: what is remembering a truth worth? That is the essence of the notion of "retrieved subjectivity" I mean to forward here. Memory is a form of agency, requiring the will to remember in the most complex of human exchanges.

As others have already suggested, it is important to introduce normative notions into Foucault's genealogical project to enable us to understand power regimes (or for our purposes, regimes of recollection) and how to oppose or redefine them. My sense is that the notion of "retrieved subjectivity" offers such a normative dimension by posing the question, "To whom do we attribute the triumph of meaning?" With the insight of the genealogical approach, or critical history, the other, or "the same in the other," is brought into the positionality of signifying that which has been excised or evicted. The present therefore becomes a site for retrieved subjectivity through negotiations and memory encounters, between differing groups claiming a truth. Memory in this instance becomes part of the construction of a subject (often an absent subject) through silences and their replacements within the present, as was the case with German Jews. Memory also becomes the constructed voice of otherness, or the "inbetweenness" that has become the other (the resettled Eastern European Jew).

Anecdotal Epilogues: The Stadtwerke as Memorial

The process of psychological perception involves storage at a number of levels where memory and forgetting become kindred spirits. This has been brilliantly recounted by Lawrence Langer's analysis of deep, anguished, humiliated, tainted and unheroic memory.[31] While Langer's "memory layerings" allow us to see multiple levels of recollection and how one can have a cancelling, or submerging effect, on others, it says little about the social construction of memory and forgetting between a complex of groups, the aim of the memory encounter. The process of cultural perception involves storage at no fewer levels. The story of what eventually occurred to the Judengasse ruins intertwines different experiences and pasts, creating multiple levels of storage within the present, but genealogically contained in "retrieved subjectivities" around the will to remember.

One level of storage treated summarily at the beginning of this chapter needs to be re-addressed here, that is the Judengasse as an esthetic form. The final esthetic framing of the ruins mimics in reverse an important series of sculptures which disappeared in Germany in the late 1980s: the sinking Holocaust memorials by the artists and poets Jochen Gerz and Esther Shalev-Gerz.[32] The reasoning of the Gerzes is that statues should never take the place of memory. Memorials disabuse us of the need to remember by lodging an esthetic form within a political culture that will strive to define its own truth. The Gerzes built statues which sink into the ground over a period of time, leaving the viewers with nothing other than their own silence, unfettered by the authority of the monument and its will to remember.[33]

The relationship of the reconstructed Judengasse to these forms of conceptual art is provocative in the sense that the process is mnemonically reversed. The Gerzes had the unfettered artistic agency of creating a "noisy silence" about absent, disappeared Jews by signifying a place of absence. The Judengasse, however, emerges from the ground as a ruin to be encased in the lobby of the Stadtwerke, which becomes the authoritative memorial appealing to its permanently encased subject. While the sinking statues of the Gerzes move the viewer to consider an absence, in the absence of the monument, and in the embrace and shadow of the Stadtwerke the Judengasse ruins emerge as an abject memorial.

Conclusion

On May 8, 1995, Germany entered a period of intense commemorations with the 50th anniversary of the ending of the war. Unwilling to wait for Bonn to develop an official agenda for the event, cities and towns across the country planned hundreds of public events, memorial concerts, artistic projects, etc.; many controversial commemorations took place in former concentration camps. What does the symbolic content of these events point to in the new memory encounters? In the process of distortion, who will replace whom?

As many authors have already noted, the date of the dismantling of the wall summons other times, other places, other memories. It is not an innocent date in modern German history: Wilhelm II abdicated his throne on November 9, 1918, signalling the beginning of Weimar; November 9, 1923 is the day of Hitler's failed putsch; November 9, 1938, *Kristallnacht,* was selected by the Nazis to commemorate the 1923 event, and often used the date for other terrible actions or significant proclamations. And a seemingly innocuous sighting recorded by Frank Stern[34] during the dismantling of the Berlin Wall on November 9, 1989 may hold some clues. A T-Shirt made to commemorate the falling of the Wall had scrawled on its reverse side, "*I was there, November 9th.*" The T-shirt uses the popular iconography of the 9th, subsuming the only officially memorialized one of the infamous 9ths in a new continuity between the two Germanys.

This continuity suggests that November 9, 1938 may now recede as history. As the new Germany reconstitutes its memory, November 9, 1989 assumes an authenticity that can be celebrated rather than hidden within the ruins of the nation. Memory and forgetting are in this instance kindred spirits stationed around an absence, and enacted through the contiguity of action and the search for collective narration. This vying for the same space of absence feeds upon a litany of discursive uncertainties and the indeterminacies of meaning within the cultural present. As these are fashioned into the memory encounters of the nation-state, shadows appear where distinct shades were once more evident, and the social obligation to forget masquerades as the political will to remember ... forgetfully.

Notes

1. This chapter was first presented as a paper at the International Institute of Sociology meetings, held in Trieste, Italy, July 3, 1995.
2. George Simmel, "The Stranger," in Donald Levine (ed.), *On Individuality and Social Forms: Selected Writings,* Chicago: University of Chicago Press, 1971.
3. "A mikveh is a natural water source prescribed for married women following their periods of menstruation, or after childbirth, as well as for proselytes on being accepted into Judaism." Philip Birnbaum, *Encyclopedia of Jewish Concepts,* New York: Hebrew Publishing Company, 1993.
4. Pierre Nora has spoken about this in his critical book, *Les lieux de mémoire,* Vol. 1: *La République,* Paris: Galimard, 1984.
5. Dan Diner, "Negative Symbiose: Deutsche und Juden nach Auschwitz," in *Babylon Beitraege zur juedischen Gegenwart* 9, 1986.
6. Hermann Luebbe, "Der Nationalsozialismus im Deutschen Nachkriegsbewustsein," *Historische Zeitschrift* 236:585, 1983.
7. Anson Rabinbach, "The Jewish Question in the German Question," in *New German Critique* 44, 1988, pp. 159-192.
8. Saul Friedlander, "Some Present-Day German Struggles with Memory," lecture, Jewish Museum, New York, March 31, 1986.
9. The Historians debate took place in 1986. The controversy was provoked by Ernst Nolte, in his questioning of the Holocaust as an "original" event. Nolte, as Rabinbach argues, brought to public discourse what was until then largely beer hall fare. The argument was taken up in the *Frankfurter Allgemeine Zeitung* (FAZ) by Hitler's biographer Joachim Fest and later rebutted by the philosopher Juergen Habermas. See Rabinbach, 185. See also Charles Maier, *The Unmasterable Past, and German Identity,* Cambridge, Mass.: Harvard University Press, 1988.
10. The Bitburg event was a masterful manipulation of President Ronald Reagan into visiting an SS cemetery. See Ilya Levkov, *Bitburg and Beyond: Encounters in American, German and Jewish History,* New York: Shaplovsky, 1987.
11. Making these matters yet more entangled is the current arrival of Jews from Russia. One of the key criteria of the postwar philosemitic bonus was the figure of the abstract Jew, sequestered in Berlin, Frankfurt or the TV screen through the image of Ignatz Bubis, the official spokesman of the Jewish community in Germany, himself a Polish Jew. The arrival of Russian Jews

is creating a concrete cultural reality, taxing yet further the depleted foundations of the postwar bonus.

12. Klaus-Dieter Groll, *Wie lange haften wir für Hitler? Zum Selbstverständis der Deutschen heute*, Duesseldorf: Suhrkamp, 1990.

13. Frank Stern, *The Whitewashing of the Yellow Badge: Anti-semitism and Philosemitism in Postwar Germany*, Oxford: Oxford University Press, 1991.

14. As of January, 1995, the Federal government in Bonn had not yet decided on a national policy for the commemorations, underscoring the sensitivity of the affair. Their hope is that the British Prime Minister John Major's decision to celebrate the war's ending as one of reconciliation rather than victory might be a model for their own actions. See Stephen Kinzer's "Germany's Awful Anniversary," in *The New York Times*, Jan. 15, 1995.

15. These tensions were already evident in the DP camps, with the exception of the former Bergen Belsen Concentration Camp where the two groups worked in tandem and it appears in relative harmony.

16. Cilly Kugelmann, "Tell Them in America We're Still Alive: The Jewish Community in the Federal Republic of Germany," in *New German Critique* 46, 1989, pp. 129-140.

17. The historical material for this section comes from documentary sources published by the Judengasse Museum in Frankfurt Am Main, Germany.

18. In the year 1500, there were 200 people living in 15 houses on the Judengasse. In 1560 there were 1,000 individuals inhabiting 77 houses. In the year 1600 the Ghetto numbered 2,700 people. The total population of Frankfurt in that year was 12,000.

19. The Kaiser saw the *Fettmilchaufstand* as an affront to his power, and publicly executed all the main participants involved in the revolt.

20. The Jewish community in Frankfurt had a shifting position on the matter of the Judengasse. In the end, it largely backed the city. The Greens, unaffiliated Jews, and the SPD led the protests against the construction of the Stadtwerke complex.

21. Homi Bhabha, "By bread alone: signs of violence in the mid-nineteenth century," in Homi Bhabha, *The Location of Culture*, London: Routledge, 1994.

22. Toni Morrison, *Beloved*, London: Chatto & Windus, 1987.

23. See Maurice Halbwachs in Lewis Coser (ed.), *On Collective Memory*, Chicago: The University of Chicago Press, 1992.

24. Halbwachs' conceptual term, "the social frameworks of memory," has been given new title in Ivona Irwin-Zarecke's critically acclaimed book,

Frames of Remembrance, New Brunswick, N.J.: Transaction Publishers, 1994.

25. Yosef Hayim Yerushalmi, *Zakkor,* New York: Schocken Books, 1989.
26. Maurice Halbwachs was the only sociologist invited to be on the prestigious board of the Review, headed by Fernand Braudel.
27. Jacques Le Goff, *History and Memory,* New York: Columbia University Press, 1992.
28. A middle-point between these two views can be found in the work of the sociologist Barry Schwartz. Schwartz argues that Halbwachs indeed offers a "presentist" view of the past. History in Halbwachs' perspective emerges as a series of images with no apparent connections. Schwartz insists that Halbwachs' contribution must be supplemented with a view towards historical continuity, in order to understand the full significance of memory in collective biographies. In short, a society's past, though subject to a remarkable amount of revisions and experiential distortions, still maintains a social code and common cultural cannon. Schwartz inserts a dialectic into Halbwachs' framing of cultural and social continuity, drawing him back to Durkheim's notion of the collective consciousness.
29. Michel Foucault, *Power/Knowledge: Selected Interviews and Other Writings, 1972-1977,* (ed.) Colin Gordon, New York: Pantheon, 1980, p. 84.
30. Richard Rorty, *Philosophy and the Mirror of Nature,* Princeton: Princeton University Press, 1979.
31. Lawrence L. Langer, *Holocaust Testimonies: the ruins of memory,* New Haven: Yale University Press, 1991.
32. The Gerzes' work has been well documented in James Young's book, *The Textures of Memory, Holocaust Memorials and Meaning,* Yale University Press, 1993. Young however refers to the Gerzes' work as "counter-memorials." This is a term the artists reject as their intention was not to create yet another memorial, even in a "counter-memorial" context, but to negate the formal estheticization of the monument by allowing it to disappear. Source: author's discussions with Jochen Gerz, January, 1995.
33. The Gerzes' controversial monument is currently submerged in Harburg, Germany.
34. Frank Stern, "The 'Jewish Question' in the 'German Question,' 1945-1990: Reflections in Light of November 9th, 1989," in *New German Critique* 52, 1991, pp. 155-176.

References

Bhabha, Homi (1994). "By Bread Alone: Signs of Violence in Mid-Nineteenth Century." In Homi Bhabha (ed.) *The Location of Culture.* London: Routledge.

Birnbaum, Philip (1993). *Encyclopedia of Jewish Concepts.* New York: Hebrew Publishing Company.

Diner, Dan (1986). "Negative Symbiose: Deutsche und Juden Nach Auschwitz." *Babylon Beitraege zur juedischen Gegenwart* 9, pp. 16-33.

Foucault, Michel (1980). *Power/Knowledge: Selected Writings, 1972-77.* Colin Gordons (ed.). New York: Pantheon.

Friedlander, Saul (1986). "Some Present-Day German Struggles with Memory." Lecture, Jewish Museum, New York, March 31.

Gerz, Jochen. Personal communication, January 1995.

Groll, Klaus-Michael (1990). *Wie lange haften wir für Hitler? Zum Selbstverstandis der Deutschen heute.* Duesseldorf: Suhrkamp.

Halbwachs, Maurice (1992). Trans. and with intro. by Lewis Coser (ed.), *On Collective Memory.* Chicago: University of Chicago Press.

Hayim Yerushalmi, Yosef (1989) *Zakkor.* New York: Schocken Books.

Irwin-Zarecke, Ivona (1994). *Frames of Remembrance.* New Brunswick, N.J.: Transaction Publishers.

Kinzer, Stephen (1995). "Germany's Awful Anniversary." *New York Times,* Jan. 15, p. 31.

Kugelmann, Cilly (1989). "Tell Them in America We're Still Alive: The Jewish Community in the Federal Republic of Germany." *New German Critique* 46, pp. 129-140.

Langer, Lawrence, L. (1991). *Holocaust Testimonies: the Ruins of Memory.* New Haven: Yale University Press.

Le Goff, Jacques (1992). *History and Memory.* New York: Columbia University Press.

Levkov, Ilya (1987). *Bitburg and Beyond: Encounters in American, German and Jewish History.* New York: Shaplovsky.

Luebbe, Hermann (1983). "Der Nationalsozialismus im Deutschen Nachkriegsbewustsein." *Historische Zeitschrift* 236:585.

Maier, Charles. (1988). *The Unmasterable Past, and German Identity.* Cambridge, Mass.: Harvard University Press.

Morrison, Toni (1987). *Beloved.* London: Chatto and Windus.

Nora, Pierre (1984). *Les lieux de mémoire. Vol. 1: La République.* Paris: Galimard.

Rabinbach, Anson (1988). "The Jewish Question in the German Question." *New German Critique* 44, pp. 159-192.

Rorty, Richard (1979). *Philosophy and the Mirror of Nature*. Princeton: Princeton University Press.

Simmel, George (1971). "The Stranger." In Donald Levine (ed.) *On Individuality and Social Forms*. Chicago: University of Chicago Press.

Stern, Frank (1991a). "The 'Jewish Question' in the 'German Question,' 1945-1990: Reflections in Light of November 9th, 1989." *New German Critique* 52, pp. 155-176.

___. (1991b). *The Whitewashing of the Yellow Badge: Anti-semitism and Philosemitism in Postwar Germany*. Oxford: Oxford University Press.

Yerushalmi, Yosef Hayim (1989) *Zakkor*. New York: Schocken Books.

Young, James (1993). *The Texture of Memory: Holocaust Memorials and Meaning*. New Haven: Yale University Press.

9

Shared Memory in Community:
Oral History, Community, and Race Relations

Tracy E. K'Meyer

> *Most of this is remembered history.*
>
> ∽ KAY WEINER, *Koinonia Remembered* (1992)

With these words Kay Weiner opens a book of reminiscences published for the fiftieth anniversary of Koinonia Farm, a Christian cooperative in southwest Georgia. Koinonia combined agricultural extension, rural missions, and community living in an effort to improve race relations in Sumter County, Georgia. Its fifty-year history raises issues of race and community, and provides the opportunity to consider the memory of them. Remembering happens on several levels. In personal interviews individuals recall their experiences and motivations. In conjunction with the recent fiftieth anniversary, Koinonians shaped a shared public memory. Finally, the anniversary coincided approximately with other civil rights landmarks, including the first sit-ins, the Albany movement, and the 1964 Civil Rights Act. Yet, the Koinonia story is absent from the commemoration of these events, indicating an historical amnesia about the community. By looking closely at Koinonia we can understand how memory is constructed on different levels. Moreover, taken together these memories reveal the nature of the relationship between a concern for better race relations and a concern for community.

Before proceeding I should define some terms. Community is an often-used term in current academic and popular discourse; most broadly defined it connotes a particular kind of close relationship. For the purposes of this discussion I will be using community in three ways. The first is interracial community, or a relationship between the races based on understanding and even "love." "Beloved Community" of the civil rights era evokes this idea. Second I will be discussing "Christian Community," which is a group of self-defined Christians living together, sharing, and striving to be an example of the Kingdom of God. Lastly, in this study community refers to "intentional" community, which is a group of people who choose to share geographic space, resources, and, in most successful cases, a spiritual life. Very few intentional communities in United States history have directly confronted the issue of race. Indeed, one theme in Koinonia's history is the exclusiveness of these three models of community. Another important term in this study is "shared memory," or the community's understanding of their history, including their origins, purpose, development, and group life. Shared memory gives shape to the members' lives together because they can look back and explain their actions while at the same time creating a base on which to build and a guide for the future.

The subject of all these reminiscences is Koinonia Farm, a Christian cooperative community founded in 1942 by two white Baptist ministers. The founders, Clarence Jordan and Martin England, went to southwest Georgia to minister to the material and spiritual needs of African American farm workers. Koinonians believed that a combination of economic development, cooperatives, and community building would improve race relations in the South. They would train sharecroppers in agricultural techniques to improve their productivity and economic independence. They would start co-ops with their white and black neighbours to counter the economic competition that divided people. And they would build a community where whites and blacks could live together, thereby breaking down walls of segregation.

Koinonians sought solutions to racial problems primarily in social and economic terms. They wanted to see the end of segregation and the opening of facilities to African Americans. Moreover, they wanted whites and blacks to come together and have the opportunity to know each other as equals. This desire was informed by their Christian belief in brotherhood and was manifested in their intent to share worship and to create a fellowship between blacks and whites. In the economic realm Koinonians argued for equal access to education and the end of black financial subordination. These priorities stemmed from their experiences on farms and in mission work with poor blacks. Koinonians also had a firm belief in equality before the law, but the ideals of political rights were less important in their writings and actions.

For fourteen years Koinonians worked toward their goals through agricultural extension, education, common worship and recreation, and communal life. Then in 1956 they became the target of violence, legal harassment, and an economic boycott, attacks which made them one of the "hot spots" of the South. During this time they formed a close relationship with civil rights and liberal organizations, primarily through mutual aid. Later, Koinonia acted as a base of operations and a refuge for activists in the Albany and Sumter County Movements. Although they shared a commitment to integration and a rhetoric of community, by the late 1960s Koinonians and civil rights activists had gone their separate ways. This split raises several issues about civil rights, including the meaning and proper basis of integration and the relative importance of economic, political, and social change. More important for the purposes of this chapter, the tension in the relationship between Koinonia and the movement suggests problems with the ability of community, as defined by white Christians, to bring about change in race relations.[1] This basic story, and the way it is remembered, illustrates the tension between intentional community and work for civil rights.

Individual Memory and Conflict in Community

Oral histories uncover the purpose of an intentional community. In their narratives Koinonians describe their motivations for going to the Farm. In the majority of cases people who arrived before 1950 did so out of a concern about race relations.[2] They begin their stories by explaining the roots of their awareness of racial problems, usually by telling a childhood story. Willie Pugh Ballard recalled that "At the Baptist church we learned Jesus loved all the little children of the world – red, yellow, black and white. What was happening all around me as I became aware didn't mesh with that at all."[3] Howard Johnson described a "massacre" of black sharecroppers in his home county and added that "That incident started me thinking about why some people are at the bottom of the ladder so to speak."⁴ These childhood experiences are told as the basis of the individuals' desire to do something, in Ballard's words, "to get at the root of the problem of racism in the South."⁵ They saw an opportunity to do that at Koinonia. As Johnson recalled, he joined the Farm because "There was no place [else] in the South where I could get a job which wouldn't require a compromise with segregation."⁶ In sum, these narratives describe an awakening to the problems of race relations, the determination to do something about it, and the decision to go to Koinonia to act on that determination. The structure of these interviews thereby privileges the concern about race relations and the individuals' desire to improve them.

The work that these Koinonians did in race relations was characterized by either missions and outreach or the development of a Christian fellowship. They fondly remember, particularly for the early years, their interracial friendships and activities. Marion Johnson, pointing out that any contact at that time was progress, recalls that she and her husband went to Koinonia "to meet them [African Americans] as human beings and not as a separate species; to realize they are in the human race; to witness to the way we believed Jesus Christ meant [for Christians to live]."⁷ That contact took place in the context of worship. Ballard and others tell stories of their Vacation Bible School and Friday night fellowship hours.⁸ Koinonians also met their black neighbours in agricultural work, through Monday evening classes in farming machinery and technique, and in a seed co-op organized by Harry Atkinson and Henry Dunn.⁹ What comes across in these narratives is fond memories of Koinonia making an impact on African American lives through agriculture, education, and service and of a neighbourly relationship based on church traditions of Bible School and fellowship.

Oral histories can also teach an entirely different story about Koinonia, however. Several former Koinonians contradict the idea that the Farm was devoted primarily to improving race relations. Their explanations of why they came to the Farm privilege their search for a Christian community. Con and Ora Browne, who were not from the South and had had little contact with blacks, were generally interested in social and moral issues. When Con Browne heard Jordan at Green Lake, Wisconsin, he was so struck by his vision, that afterwards one of his professors asked "can't you write about anything else but community?"¹⁰ He and his wife Ora went to Koinonia because of its philosophy of following Jesus, of sharing, nonviolence, and brotherhood. Likewise, Margaret and

Will Wittkamper were seeking "any community that believed in peace, brotherhood, and sharing."¹¹ But neither the Brownes nor Margaret Wittkamper give much attention to race relations in their narratives. In fact, all of them list racial brotherhood as only one among many interests. They also explicitly deny that race relations were ever the primary focus. "So we were there for religious purposes," Ora Browne recalled. "Not, let's say, to be just in the civil rights struggle."¹² The Brownes reaffirmed their views in a letter to me: "The emphasis on race, while an exciting and continuous strand in the community's existence, was, in my memory, not the prevailing issue with which we struggled."¹³

Even this small sample of interviews reveals significant contradictions in the memory of the purpose of Koinonia Farm. Was Koinonia a place where people worked on problems in race relations or where Christians lived in spiritual community? And what was the connection between those two goals? This conflict is further illustrated by the debate over a membership pledge and the tension in, and contested memory of, Koinonia's relationship with civil rights activists after 1957.

Between 1949 and 1951 Koinonians set up a membership process and wrote a pledge of commitment. The commitment henceforth was to the group as "the highest expression of the will of God."¹⁴ To be a member meant turning over all personal assets and yielding individual desires to the will of the whole. These developments had several consequences. Almost immediately some members left, including Willie Pugh Ballard and her husband C. Z.¹⁵ In addition, few African Americans were willing to abide by the new commitment and membership rules.¹⁶ Thereafter it became harder for Koinonia to attract blacks into the community. Finally, in the wake of these changes Koinonians devoted more and more energy to issues of inner community and spirit.

Koinonians differ in their memories of these events. To Ballard the pledge signified a change in theology and a loss of the outreach.¹⁷ Yet in recent conversations Howard Johnson insisted that the work with blacks went on uninterrupted.¹⁸ And to some extent this is true: individuals continued to visit and work with blacks, and there was an expanded youth program. But in these activities Koinonians promoted the ideals of a unified Christian community. They also spent more time trying to convince African Americans to join Koinonia on the group's existing terms and less time reaching out through shared worship and agricultural cooperation. Others saw the commitment as a confirmation of Koinonia's main direction. Howard and Marion Johnson, reflecting a shift in their own priorities, felt that it clarified the beliefs the group already shared.[19] Con and Ora Browne welcomed the increased accountability and opportunity for spiritual unity.[20] For these members, the commitment to living as a Christian community hereafter shaped their memory of Koinonia.

Another revealing conflict in the Koinonians' memories involves their relationship with civil rights activists. When the Farm came under attack for its positions on race in 1956, Koinonians developed relationships with activists and tension quickly built over how to cooperate with them. Some members worried that their identity as a community would be lost if they were considered primarily a witness for race equality. They reminded their supporters that "We are not witnessing to brotherhood alone. It [Koinonia] is a total reorientation of values – non-violence, complete sharing, and complete openness."[21] Others, however, welcomed visitors who wanted to participate in civil rights battles, and argued that Koinonia should take a leadership role in the movements for justice and non-violence.[22] In retrospect, Koinonians often made distinctions between themselves and the movement. Millard Fuller, for example, recalled Jordan expressing the belief that "Koinonia was not about better race relations," and not just about integration.[23] Yet others tell stories about their participation in meetings and marches.[24] In short, in the past and in their recollections, Koinonians have sought to define the proper balance between community living and race relations work.

Interviews can be used to understand conflicts within a community as people continue to carry their own interpretations of past issues and decisions.[25] In this case the narratives of former Koinonians demonstrate that their history is contested and that there are alternative interpretations of its past. The ambiguity over purpose in the past has enabled the community to adapt to circumstances. As conditions and needs changed, Koinonians emphasized one aspect of their identity more or less, attracting members, altering their program, and surviving. According to Barry Shenker in *Intentional Community: Ideology and Alienation in Communal Societies*, the ability to be flexible in the expression of basic philosophy is a key factor in insuring community maintenance.[26] Besides helping them to survive, this flexibility has made Koinonia and its memory a resource. The structure and philosophy of the community were used as a base from which people acted — some to develop a community, some to make a witness for racial understanding, and some to play a part in civil rights demonstrations. In other words, people went to Koinonia for their own reasons, saw in Koinonia what they needed, and lived and worked there as long as it suited their needs.²⁷ They took with them memories of Koinonia which fitted into their self-understanding and which in many cases were the source of later actions.

Collective Memory and the Meaning of Community

Koinonia's ambivalence, and the flexibility which served it over the years do not show up in the public memory of the Farm, however. Recently Koinonia celebrated its fiftieth anniversary, for which occasion the community organized several opportunities for the discussion of its past. The current Koinonia Partners asked people to send written reminiscences, then edited and published them as *Koinonia Remembered: The First Fifty Years*.²⁸ During the weekend reunion, the Partners set up a microphone and encouraged people to tell stories about their experiences.²⁹ Finally, the party ended with a sermon, delivered by Reverend Murphy Davis from the Open Door community in Atlanta.³⁰ Through these forums and over the course of the anniversary, Koinonians and their friends moulded a shared, public memory of the farm.

Several interesting themes arise out of this "remembered" history. To begin with there is little evidence of the conflict over purpose. In *Koinonia Remembered* Con Browne describes the Farm as a new kind of church or community, and gives little space to race relations other than to mention that the farm served as a refuge for civil rights activists.³¹ On the other hand, the book includes stories from people who grew up at Koinonia about their participation in the movement.³² Besides these few passages, however, the conflict between community and civil rights activism is absent. Attention focuses instead on survival, daily life in community, and Clarence Jordan. At the open-microphone sessions, "old timers" like Harry and Allene Atkinson told of early hardships such as having to build houses with scarce materials. John Veldhuizen likewise remembered how he helped to circumvent the boycott, and the threats against him when he was found out.³³ From these stories emerged a theme of survival. Other narrators recalled picnics, the smell of the fields, and lazy Saturday mornings, sharing what it was like to live in the community. Finally, Jordan played a central role in all of the reminiscences. Indeed, almost every person included something about their relationship to him or his influence on them in their comments.

Although not a major topic during the weekend celebration, Koinonia's involvement in race issues and the civil rights struggle was remembered. The stories about the boycott and hard times indirectly raised the memory of Koinonia's position on race. But the memory of Koinonia and race relations was most explicitly recalled in the sermon. Murphy Davis began by honouring Koinonia's "cloud of witnesses," the people who had gone before. She described how they were beaten, imprisoned, spit on, and harassed because, in her words, "They dared to turn their dreams into deeds." After reminding the congregation of their predecessors, Davis reviewed the "call" of the community: "to stand on the front line of the battle for racial and economic justice" and "to make a contribution to the lives of those who suffer and are oppressed."[34] With these words Davis smoothed over ambiguity and conflict about the relative importance of race relations and community. In the process, however, she also smoothed over much of what Koinonians had actually done. She was not remembering the agricultural extension, or jobs and housing partnerships, nor the failed attempts at developing cooperatives or getting African Americans to join the community. Through the sermon and other events Koinonians remembered a time when the Farm was "famous" as a symbol of integration, but not the tensions inherent in their ideas about how to improve race relations.

The public memory of Koinonia shared at the fiftieth anniversary was a result of forces shaping the book and the reunion. Individuals who had a personal stake in the way the community is remembered took a leadership role in the commemorations and invested their time in them. But people who felt distanced from Koinonia did not send reminiscences into the book. Note for example that neither Willie Ballard, who left Koinonia because she wanted to do more outreach, nor Howard Johnson, who left for a more unified community, was represented. In addition, current members, the people with the greatest stake in the community, planned the events and picked the speakers; the sermon served their interest in establishing continuity. Finally, the children of the early generation participated in the planning and presentations, weighing the balance of attention in favour of certain individuals. Jan and Lenny Jordan, for example, both had important roles in the celebration. The nature of the forums for remembering Koinonia also shaped the history. At the open-mike sessions people told stories that followed from the previous one, the result being that there were sections on "early years," "funny stories," and Jordan anecdotes, and it was unlikely that someone would volunteer to tell a story that broke significantly from the pattern.[35] The sermon was intended to be the final word, and thus the inspiration for the future. Davis' emphasis on clear goals, solid shoulders to stand on, and a call for future work served this purpose.

The fiftieth-anniversary celebration, in effect, produced a shared memory of a usable past. Conflicts within the community went almost completely unexpressed, and the changes over the years and the adaptability that probably helped Koinonia survive were not part of the story. Instead the remembered history was a story of inspiration, overcoming adversity, and commitment to ideas. In this history what kept Koinonia going in the past was the members' refusal to yield to the pressure of circumstances, keeping their "eyes on the prize." This type of remembrance serves a purpose for the community: it gives the present members a clear, unambiguous past to have pride in, but it also provides a clear mission – to work against injustice – and an assurance that obstacles can be overcome.

Historic Memory, Race, and Community

A third level of memory, besides personal and communal, is historic memory, that is, the memory of the Farm recorded by historians. Where does a community fit into the broader story? The external view can be instructive. Here the issue is why historians do not record the story of Koinonia, or as Jacquelyn Hall put it years ago, "Why don't people remember Koinonia as part of the civil rights movement?"[36] The answer, I believe, lies both in Koinonia's divergence over time from the civil rights movement, and in the manner in which historians have written about the movement.

Between 1957 and 1963, Koinonia Farm was considered an important front in the southern civil rights struggle and a vital resource for the movement. When the farm first came under attack for its interracial lifestyle and work with African Americans, national magazines like *Newsweek*, *The Christian Century*, and *The Nation* carried the story. These reports linked Koinonia with other events, such as the school integration battle in Little Rock.[37] During the attacks Koinonia received aid from people who recognized the importance of their use of "nonviolence in combating racial discrimination."[38] When violence and financial trouble threatened their very existence, the Farm's supporters urged them to hang on because they were "a demonstration, long before the segregation decisions that integration works."[39] Finally, when civil rights struggles heated up in southwestern Georgia, Koinonia played a vital role by being a refuge and base of operations. Activists, especially members of the Student Non-Violent Coordinating Committee (SNCC), lived at the Farm and held meetings and retreats there. Individuals in the local movement, like Lena Turner, honored Koinonia's role: "Koinonia had demonstrated to young Negroes of Americus something everything else in their world has denied: that whites and black can live and work and build together."[40]

Despite the contemporary recognition of Koinonia's role, the current literature on the civil rights movement includes little evidence of the community. Even the vast majority of work on white participation does not mention the Farm. In interviews key figures in the local movement do not tell about Koinonia in their primary narratives, although when prompted they have long stories about the Farm's role.[41] Occasionally the community received attention for its part in the state and in the Albany movement, most notably in Paul Bolster's 1972 dissertation on civil rights movements in Georgia.[42] In general, however, though considered a "hot spot" at the time, Koinonia has been absent from the historical memory of the movement.

One reason Koinonia is not remembered as part of the civil rights struggle is because by the end of the 1960s the community and the movement had parted company. Koinonians sought to change race relations through economic aid and cooperation, but when the *Brown v. Board of Ed* decision made integration the primary civil rights issue, the farm became one of the first scenes of concerted violence over the issue. Thereafter outsiders supported Koinonia as an integration effort. In addition, Koinonians shared the goal of building a beloved community based on racial harmony with the movement and tried to accomplish it by inviting activists to live and share with them at the Farm.[43] By the mid 1960s, however, the movement changed emphasis to voting rights and black power instead of integration and community. For Koinonians these goals depended too heavily on coercion and political power, and so they left the movement and severed ties with it. Civil rights activists had moved beyond a witness for interracial living to issues of rights and power. Koinonians, rejecting the direction of the movement, left it to focus on their own community building and economic development work, and for years after this dissociation, individuals at the Farm had no interest in preserving the memory of the community's former role. Because civil rights activists and historians also showed no interest in commemorating it, the role of the Farm in the period between 1957 and 1963 was forgotten.

The lack of interest among activists and scholars in recording Koinonia's role reflects the way the civil rights movement is treated by historians. Over the years a narrative of the civil rights movement has been established by the works of Harvard Sitkoff, Robert Weisbrot, and others as well as by the Eyes on the Prize series.[44] This narrative focuses on Martin Luther King, city protest campaigns, desegregation, and voting rights. The story "begins" with *Brown* or Montgomery and "ends" with the Voting Rights Act or the Merideth March. Recent review essays point out the emphasis given to these stories as well as federal court cases and laws, other leaders, and organizations and their rivalries.[45] Recently, however, there has been more attention to community studies and "local people." John Dittmer, for example, by examining the Mississippi story in depth, uncovers much more complexity in the movement,[46] while other historians search for the roots of the movement or the role of other groups including women and progressive whites.[47] Yet the focus remains on political and legal issues and how this new material fits into the overall narrative.

But there were other paths to better race relations which are not as often remembered. In the case of Koinonia Farm, economic development through agricultural extension and cooperatives and the attempt to build an interracial community have gone unrecorded. In addition, as historian Kathryn Nasstrom has argued, the organizing efforts of African American women around neighbourhood and poverty issues have been forgotten.[48] These efforts are not remembered, in part because historians tell stories which they deem significant in light of results: in Atlanta, for example, the success of certain black male political leaders has cast that history as the story of black political power. Because there is still no economic equality, true integration or interracial community, solutions which were sought to bring them about are discounted, regardless of what lessons they might teach. In addition, historians privilege stories which fit into our national self-image. Americans see integration as an expression of equality; attention to voting rights and political change suits our belief in the rule of law and democracy. On the other hand, approaches that may be more all-encompassing, or which require broad structural change, do not enter our historical consciousness. In short, Koinonia's strategy of building an interracial community of equals is forgotten by history because for it to be successful would have meant a prior or accompanying redistribution of economic and social power.

Scholars are beginning to devote more attention to the construction of historic memory, including the place of civil rights and race relations within it. Nasstrom, for example, demonstrates the gendered nature of the civil rights memory of Atlanta and the manner in which significant women's activism has been erased from the public story of the movement there. The Martin Luther King holiday has inspired discussion of how the memorialization of King downplays his radicalism and the efforts of other activists.[49] Dealing with a different century but still the theme of race and memory, Scot French has shown how the memory of "Nat Turner's Rebellion" was constructed in such a way to reassure white Virginians that they had race relations under control.[50] Koinonia's history and the memory of it add to this growing body of scholarship by demonstrating the place of community and civil rights in our national collective memory.[51]

The historic memory of the civil rights movement shapes contemporary attitudes about race relations and approaches to improving them. The standard narrative privileges a few brave leaders – a trend reinforced by the celebration of the Martin Luther King birthday holiday – and the protest campaigns which led to the Civil Rights and Voting Rights Acts. In doing so it leaves the impression that only the extraordinary individual can produce change. Furthermore, it teaches that the movement was successful and was finished in 1965.[52] The poverty, education, and neighbourhood organizing of African American women and the economic cooperation sponsored by Koinonia are forgotten, robbing the present generation of lessons available from these alternative and economics-based approaches to change. Finally, the efforts of Koinonians to create an interracial community is on different levels of memory at best contested and at worst forgotten altogether. This enables contemporary audiences to avoid the fact that interracial community, or real "integration," cannot depend solely on African Americans accepting white standards, and requires change in economic and political power to be successful.

The discussion of memory in community can lead the researcher down many paths. I have discussed three levels of memory and what they teach about race relations, community, and the relationship between them in history. On the level of personal memory, people recall their own experiences. Their narratives lead us to discover conflict and change within a community. Shared memory, or what a group remembers about itself, is the product of various forces and can be quite different from even the sum of personal memories. It serves the purpose of providing the community with a base for the present. And historical memory is how historians remember a community and place it into its context. The nature of historical memory on a given subject can lead to investigations of what gets remembered, why, and what that tells us about American national memory. Discussions about memory can obviously cover much ground, from individual experiences to why Americans favour certain histories of the civil rights movement at the expense of less political and potentially more radical approaches. Once we understand the different layers of memory, perhaps we can begin to explore the links between personal experience and community – even national – understanding of the past.

Besides illuminating the nature of memory on various levels, Koinonia's story sheds light on the relationship between race and community. In short, Koinonia's failure demonstrates the inability of "community" by itself to successfully address racial inequalities. The early Koinonians intended to fight racial problems through agricultural development, education, missions, and living in community. They did make a contribution to the lives of their African American neighbours and to the relations between whites and blacks in that area, but they were hampered in their efforts by two factors. Internal uncertainty about their purpose and the decision to give equal or greater weight to maintaining a unified Christian community prevented them from pursuing their own strategy fully. In addition, Koinonians underestimated the need for broader social change – especially the balancing of economic and political power – which was required before a "beloved community" could develop. Other civil rights activists, especially those in SNCC, recognized this and moved away from beloved community and into economics and black power. Koinonia is not remembered by historians because it does not fit into a story of the civil rights movement which emphasizes political rights. Furthermore, by not remembering Koinonia and its lessons contemporary audiences do not have to deal with the fact that "community" as defined by whites does not appeal to African Americans without accompanying political and economic change.

The case study of Koinonia proves the significance of oral history as a tool for uncovering the link between race relations and community.[53] It opens a window to personal motivations and allows us to understand how people defined their commitment to doing something about racial problems. Inconsistencies in narratives reveal tensions within a group, in this case Koinonia's ambivalence over their purpose and how to pursue it. More broadly, interviews hint to the issue of how community and change in race relations can be incompatible. In part, oral history does this by illuminating the perspective of rural African Americans; it was personal narratives which revealed why African Americans did not join Koinonia, for example. Finally, oral history re-establishes a history that has been forgotten by probing beneath the traditional civil rights narrative to uncover the story and the lessons of alternative approaches to change.

Notes

1. After the split Koinonia reconfigured itself into Koinonia Partners, a modified community that focused on building partnerships between whites and blacks in farming, small industries, and housing. Koinonia recently celebrated its fiftieth anniversary and is still active in ministries and cooperative life. They are currently undergoing some changes, however. Immediately after the 1992 reunion they began restructuring themselves to equalize the status of blacks and whites within the community. In addition, the effect of the floods of the summer of 1994 has not been completely assessed.
2. My primary respondents were Willie Pugh Ballard, Howard Johnson, Harry and Allene Atkinson, Con and Ora Browne, and Margaret Wittkamper, and some of their children. All of these people joined Koinonia Farm between 1944 and 1953 and lived there for at least seven years. Other members will be occasionally quoted as well.
3. Interview with Willie Pugh Ballard, Oct. 10, 1990.
4. Interview with Howard Johnson, July 20, 1992.
5. Interview with Willie Pugh Ballard, Oct. 20, 1990.
6. Interview with Howard Johnson, Nov. 24, 1990.
7. Interview with Marion Johnson, Nov. 24, 1990.
8. Interview with Willie Pugh Ballard, June 2, 1992.
9. Interviews with Con Browne, Nov. 17, 1990 and Harry Atkinson, June 5, 1992.
10. Interview with Con and Ora Browne, Nov. 17, 1990.
11. Interview with Margaret Wittkamper, Oct. 25, 1990.
12. Interview with Ora Browne, Nov. 17, 1990.

13. Con and Ora Browne to Tracy K'Meyer, Sept. 23, 1993. The Brownes have declined to be interviewed further by myself or by another researcher because they fear they are not remembering things accurately.
14. Interview with Willie Pugh Ballard, Oct. 20, 1990.
15. Interview with Willie Pugh Ballard, Oct. 20, 1990. Other couples also left, including Gene and Jack Singletary, Cliff and Ann Sanford, and Harry and Allene Atkinson. The Atkinsons eventually returned and signed the commitment.
16. Interview with Alma Jackson, July 9, 1990. In this interview Jackson explains that he was not ready to give up his freedom for the discipline and selflessness required of Koinonia.
17. Interviews with Willie Pugh Ballard, Oct. 20, 1990 and June 2, 1992.
18. Interview with Howard Johnson, July 20, 1992.
19. Interview with Howard and Marion Johnson, Nov. 24, 1990.
20. Interview with Con and Ora Browne, Nov. 17, 1990.
21. Con Browne to Jack Burdin, Sept. 5, 1957 in the Clarence Jordan/Koinonia Farm Papers, mss. 756 in the Hargrave Rare Book and Manuscript Collection of the University of Georgia Libraries, Athens, Georgia. Hereafter cited as MS 756 box#:folder#.
22. Lota Eustice to Raymond J. Magee, Nov. 22, 1957, in box 1 folder 1957C in the Clarence Jordan/Koinonia Farm Papers, mss. 2340 in the Hargrave Rare Book and Manuscript collection of the University of Georgia Libraries, Athens, Georgia. Hereafter cited as MS 2340 box#:folder#. Ross Anderson in particular argued for more participation, and eventually left Koinonia to join the peace movement. See MS 756 5:1 Ross Anderson to Rufus, Sue and All, Jan. 31, 1958, for example.
23. Interview with Millard Fuller, Dec. 13, 1990.
24. Interviews with Dorothy Swisshelm, Feb. 3, 1991, Lora Browne, Mar. 9, 1991, and Greg Wittkamper, Nov. 18, 1990.
25. Samuel Schrager, "What's Social in Oral History," *International Journal of Oral History* 4(2)(June 1983):88–89.
26. Barry Shenker, *Intentional Communities: Ideology and Alienation in Communal Societies* (London: Routledge and Kegan Paul, 1986) especially chapter 5, "Ideology."
27. I am indebted to conversations with Andrew Chancey about this and many other aspects of Koinonia's history.
28. *Koinonia Remembered: The First Fifty Years*, ed. Kay Weiner (Americus: Koinonia Partners, 1992).

29. Most of these stories went unrecorded. I recorded a few speakers and took notes on others. Koinonia Partners did not record the sessions.
30. The sermon has been reprinted as Murphy Davis, "Dreams into Deeds: Celebrating Fifty Years of Koinonia," *Sojourners*, September 1992, pp. 19-23.
31. Con Browne, "Koinonia: An Introduction," in *Koinonia Remembered*, pp. 1-2.
32. See for example Jan Jordan Zehr, "Total Focus," in *Koinonia Remembered*, p. 77.
33. Stories by John Veldhuizen available on tape in possession of author.
34. Davis, "Dreams into Deeds," p. 22.
35. This pattern is similar to the "recognition effect" described by Patrick Hagopian in "Oral Narratives: Secondary Revision and the Memory of the Vietnam War," *History Workshop* 32 (Fall 1991): 145. The recognition effect is the process by which narrators hear others tell their stories, then shape their own tale to match it. Through this process narratives get shaped and certain themes or incidents get privileged. This is part of what makes memory and narrative a social construction. For more on the construction of individual memories in a social setting see Schrager, "What's Social in Oral History."
36. Personal conversation with author.
37. "The Other Cheek is Turned in Georgia Bombing," *Christian Century*, Aug. 22, 1956, p. 965; "Embattled Fellowship Farm," *Time*, Sept. 17, 1956, p. 79; William A. Emerson, Jr., and Joseph B. Cummings, Jr., "Everyman's Land — Or a No Man's Land," *Newsweek*, Feb. 25, 1957; "Editorial," *Nation*, Sept. 22, 1956, p. 229.
38. MS 756 24:9 "Support Koinonia," *CORE-lator* (Spring/Summer 1957):4.
39. MS 2340 1:1957 Halleck Hoffman statement on Koinonia for the Board of the Fund for the Republic, 8-21-57. See below for the *Brown v. Board of Ed* segregation decision.
40. MS 756 24:10 "Americus, Place of Courage," *Southern Patriot* 23(9) (November 1965):2.
41. Interviews with Charles Sherrod, Mar. 1, 1991; Carol King, Feb. 28, 1991; and Lorena Barnum Sabbs, Mar. 3, 1991. In each case the subject told a story of their participation in the movement which did not include Koinonia, then when specifically asked went on to tell a whole second story about their participation including Koinonia's role.
42. Paul Bolster, "Civil Rights Movements in Georgia," Ph.D. dissertation, University of Georgia, 1972.

43. On King and Beloved Community see Kenneth L. Smith and Ira G. Zepp, Jr., *Search for the Beloved Community: The Thinking of Martin Luther King, Jr.*, (New York: University Press of America, 1986), in particular chapter 6, "The Vision of the Beloved Community." Sherrod discussed his vision of the Beloved Community in an interview with the author on Mar. 1, 1991.

44. Harvard Sitkoff, *The Struggle for Black Equality, 1954-1992* (New York: Hill and Wang, 1993); Robert Weisbrot, Freedom Bound: A History of America's Civil Rights Movement (New York: W. W. Norton and Company, 1990); "Eyes on the Prize," a television documentary by Blackside, Inc., 1987.

45. For recent reviews of civil rights historiography see Steven Lawson, "Freedom Then, Freedom Now: The Historiography of the Civil Rights Movement," *American Historical Review* 96(2)(April 1991): 456-471 and Adam Fairclough, "State of the Art: Historians and the Civil Rights Movement," *Journal of American Studies* 24(3)(December 1990): 387-398. Another review of recent thinking on the civil rights movement is *New Directions in Civil Rights Studies* edited by Armstead L. Robinson and Patricia Sullivan (Charlottesville: University Press of Virginia, 1991), which is a collection of essays on the movement.

46. John Dittmer, *Local People: The Struggle for Civil Rights In Mississippi* (Urbana: University of Illinois Press, 1994).

47. The collection *Women in the Civil Rights Movement: Trailblazers and Torchbearers*, ed. Vicki Crawford *et al.*, (Bloomington: Indiana University Press, 1990) is a good sample of work on women in the movement. Other works include Paula Giddings, *When and Where I Enter: The Impact of Black Women on Race and Sex in America* (New York: Morrow, 1984); David Garrow, ed., *The Montgomery Bus Boycott and the Women who Started it: The Memoir of Jo Ann Robinson* (Knoxville: University of Tennessee Press, 1987); and biographies such as Cynthia Brown, ed., *Ready from Within: Septima Clark and the Civil Rights Movement* (Navarro, CA: Wild Trees Press, 1986). The literature on southern liberals has grown and includes Thomas Krueger, *And Promises to Keep: The Southern Conference for Human Welfare, 1938-1948* (Nashville: Vanderbilt University Press, 1967); Linda Reed, Simple Decency and Common Sense: The Southern Conference Movement, 1938-1963 (Bloomington: Indiana University Press, 1991); and Morton Sosna, In Search of the Silent South: Southern Liberals and the Race Issue (New York: Columbia University Press, 1977). A recent book which tries to put white participation in perspective and looks at the contributions of moder-

ates is David Chappell, *Inside Agitators: White Southerners in the Civil Rights Movement* (Baltimore: Johns Hopkins University Press, 1994).

48. Kathryn Nasstrom, "'The Women Have a Tremendous Part to Play': Remembering Atlanta's African American Women and the Voter Registration Drive of 1946," paper delivered at the Organization of American Historians annual meeting, April 16, 1994.

49. See Clayborne Carson, "Martin Luther King, Jr.: Charismatic Leadership in a Mass Struggle"; James H. Cone, "Martin Luther King, Jr., and the Third World"; and Vincent Gordon Harding, "Beyond Amnesia: Martin Luther King, Jr., and the Future of America," in *Journal of American History* 74 (Sept. 1987): 448-476.

50. Scot A. French, "Plotting 'Nat Turner's Rebellion': A Slave Girl's Testimony in Social Memory, 1831-Present," paper presented at the Southern Historical Association annual meeting, Nov. 10, 1994.

51. According to Alon Confino in "Collective Memory," *Encyclopedia of Social History*, ed. Peter N. Stearns (New York: Garland Publishing, Inc., 1994), collective memory is "what a social group, be it family, class or nation, remembers of its past." This concept has received more and more attention from historians as a way to talk about how Americans remember their past. Oral historians in particular are interested in how individuals construct their history in a social setting and how personal narratives reflect both personal and public memory. See, for example, Schrager, "What's Social in Oral History"; Elizabeth Tonkin, *Narrating Our Pasts: The Social Construction of Oral History* (Cambridge: Cambridge University Press, 1992); Michael Frisch, "The Memory of History," in *Shared Authority: Essays on the Craft and Meaning of Oral and Public History* (Albany: State University of New York Press, 1990); and "Memory and American History," ed. David Thelen, a special issue of the *Journal of American History* 75(4)(March). The work of Nasstrom, French and others, as well as my work on Koinonia, elaborates the idea of memory and history as it particularly applies to the memory of race relations.

52. This point is also made in a review essay on oral histories of the civil rights movement, Kim Lacy Rogers, "Oral History and the History of the Civil Rights Movement," *Journal of American History* 75 (Sept. 1988): 567-76.

53. On the importance of oral history in studying civil rights more broadly see Rogers, "Oral History and the History of the Civil Rights Movement." In this article Rogers argues that oral history can help scholars understand the local genesis of the movement, the radicalism of grassroots activists, and the changes in individual political and social consciousness.

References

Manuscript Collections

Clarence Jordan Papers, mss. no. 756, Hargrett Rare Book and Manuscript Library at the University of Georgia Libraries, Athens, Georgia.
Clarence Jordan Papers, mss. no. 2340, Hargrett Rare Book and Manuscript Library at the University of Georgia Libraries, Athens, Georgia.
Clarence Jordan Papers, mss. no. 2341, Hargrett Rare Book and Manuscript Library at the University of Georgia Libraries, Athens, Georgia.
Koinonia Partners Archives at Koinonia Partners, Americus, Georgia.
Vertical File at the Hargrett Rare Book and Manuscript Library at the University of Georgia Libraries, Athens, Georgia.

Interviews

Sue Angry, July 17, 1992 and Dec. 22, 1990
Harry and Allene Atkinson, May 21, 1990 and June 5, 1992.
Willie Mae Pugh Ballard, Oct. 20, 1990 and June 2, 1992.
Con and Ora Browne, Nov. 17, 1990.
Lora Browne, Mar. 9, 1991.
Millard Fuller, Dec. 13, 1990.
Alma Jackson, July 9, 1990.
Chester Jackson, Nov. 4, 1990 and April 26, 1992.
Howard Johnson, July 20, 1992.
Howard and Marion Johnson, Nov. 24, 1990.
Jan Jordan, May 1, 1991.
Jim Jordan, June 15, 1992.
Lenny Jordan, May 24, 1992.
Carol King, Feb. 28, 1991.
Carranza Morgan, Mar. 1, 1991.
Lorena Barnum Sabbs with Thelma Barnum, Mar. 3, 1991.
Charles Sherrod, Mar. 1, 1991.
Gene Singletary, July 10, 1990 and Oct. 25, 1990.
Dorothy Swisshelm, Feb. 3, 1991.
John and Joan Veldhuizen, May 4, 1991.
Greg Wittkamper, Nov. 18, 1990.
Margaret Wittkamper, Oct. 25, 1990.

Books and Articles

Bolster, Paul (1972). "Civil Rights Movements in Georgia." PhD Dissertation, University of Georgia.

Brown, Cynthia (ed.) (1986). *Ready from Within: Septima Clark and the Civil Rights Movement.* Navarro, CA: Wild Trees Press.

Chappell, David (1994). *Inside Agitators: White Southerners in the Civil Rights Movement.* Baltimore: Johns Hopkins University Press.

Confino, Alon (1994). "Collective Memory." *Encyclopedia of Social History*, Peter N. Stearns (ed.), New York: Garland Publishing, pp. 149-150.

Crawford, Vicki, et al., (eds.) (1990). *Women in the Civil Rights Movement: Trailblazers and Torchbearers.* Bloomington: Indiana University Press.

Davis, Murphy (1992). "Dreams into Deeds: Celebrating Fifty Years of Koinonia." *Sojourners*, Sept., pp. 19-23.

Diltmer, John (1994) *Local People: The Struggle for Civil Rights in Mississippi.* Urbana, Illinois: University of Illinois Press.

"Editorial" (1956). *Nation*, Sept. 22, p. 229.

"Embattled Fellowship Farm" (1956). *Time*, Sept. 17, p. 79.

Emerson, William A., and Joseph B. Cummings, Jr. (1957). "Everyman's Land – Or a No Man's Land." *Newsweek*, Feb. 25, p. 37.

Fairclough, Adam (1990). "State of the Art: Historians and the Civil Rights Movement." *Journal of American Studies* 24 (December):387-398.

French, Scot A. (1994). "Plotting 'Nat Turner's Rebellion': A Slave Girl's Testimony in Social Memory, 1831-Present." Paper presented at the Southern Historical Association annual meeting, Nov. 10.

Frisch, Michael (1990). "The Memory of History." In *Shared Authority: Essays on the Craft and Meaning of Oral and Public History.* Albany: State University of New York Press.

Garrow, David (ed.) (1987). *The Montgomery Bus Boycott and the Women who Started it: The Memoir of Jo Ann Robinson.* Knoxville: University of Tennessee Press.

Giddings, Paula (1984). *When and Where I Enter: The Impact of Black Women on Race and Sex in America.* New York: Morrow.

Hagopian, Patrick (1991). "Oral Narratives: Secondary Revision and the Memory of the Vietnam War." *History Workshop* 32 (Fall):134-148.

Harding, Vincent Gordon (1987). "Beyond Amnesia: Martin Luther King, Jr., and the Future of America." *Journal of American History* 74 (September):448-476; included in special issue along with Clayborne Carson, "Martin Luther King, Jr.: Charismatic Leadership in a Mass

Struggle," and James H. Cone, "Martin Luther King, Jr., and the Third World."

Krueger, Thomas (1967). *And Promises to Keep: The Southern Conference for Human Welfare, 1938-1948*. Nashville: Vanderbilt University Press.

Lawson, Steven (1991). "Freedom Then, Freedom Now: The Historiography of the Civil Rights Movement." *American Historical Review* 96(2):456-471255.

Nasstrom, Kathryn (1994). "'The Women Have a Tremendous Part to Play': Remembering Atlanta's African American Women and the Voter Registration Drive of 1946." Paper presented at the Organization of American Historians annual meeting, April 16.

Reed, Linda (1991). *Simple Decency and Common Sense: The Southern Conference Movement, 1938-1963*. Bloomington: Indiana University Press.

Robinson, Armstead L., and Sullivan, Patricia (1991) *New Directions in Civil Rights Studies*. Charlottesville: University Press of Virginia.

Rogers, Kim Lacy (1988). "Oral History and the History of the Civil Rights Movement." *Journal of American History* 75(September):567-76.

Schrager, Samuel (1983). "What's Social in Oral History." *International Journal of Oral History* 4(June): 76-98.

Shenker, Barry (1986). *Intentional Communities: Ideology and Alienation in Communal Societies*. London: Routledge and Kegan Paul.

Sitkoff, Harvard (1993). *The Struggle for Black Equality, 1954-1992*. New York: Hill and Wang.

Smith, Kenneth L., and Ira G. Zepp, Jr. (1986). *Search for the Beloved Community: The Thinking of Martin Luther King, Jr.* New York: University Press of America.

Sosna, Morton (1977). *In Search of the Silent South: Southern Liberals and the Race Issue*. New York: Columbia University Press.

"The Other Cheek is Turned in Georgia Bombing" (1956). *Christian Century*, Aug. 22, p. 965.

Thelen, David, (ed.) (1989). "Memory and American History," a special issue of the *Journal of American History* 75, March.

Tonkin, Elizabeth (1992). *Narrating Our Pasts: The Social Construction of Oral History*. Cambridge: Cambridge University Press.

Weiner, Kay (ed.) (1992). *Koinonia Remembered: The First Fifty Years* (Americus: Koinonia Partners).

Weisbrot, Robert (1990). *Freedom Bound: A History of America's Civil Rights Movement*. New York: W. W. Norton and Company.

Other

Con and Ora Browne to Tracy K'Meyer, Sept. 23, 1993
"Eyes on the Prize," a television documentary by Blackside, Inc., 1987.
Tape of conversations at Koinonia Partners Reunion, April 1992. In possession of author.

10

Dilemmas of Discovery: Europeans and "America"

Robert Paine

> Europeans knew something, however vaguely and inaccurately, about Africa and Asia. But about America and its inhabitants they knew nothing. It was this which differentiated sixteenth-century Europeans to America from that of the fifteenth-century Portuguese to Africa. (Elliott 1992:8)

The focus of this essay is on the European following the Discovery. Nonetheless, this leads us back to the ontology of the Other in which Europeans cast Amerindians. I also hope to put into context the *lack of* excitement which the Discovery occasioned in Europe, even though it was, in so many ways, without historical precedent. Throughout, and especially, I try to illuminate and explicate the sense of dilemma which the Discovery of America and contact with the aboriginal inhabitants presented to late Medieval/early Renaissance European thought. Essentially, what I offer is a report on some recent scholarly writings that are, I believe, of the highest calibre and, certainly, of considerable anthropological relevance.[1]

Another World?

> They laid low, without distinction, every enemy encountered. Everywhere there was frightful carnage, everywhere lay heaps of severed heads.... [They] forced their way ... to the center of the city and wrought unspeakable slaughter as they advanced. (Sardar et al. 1993:36-37)

That happens not to be an account of Spaniards in the New World, but of twelfth-century crusaders when they reached Jerusalem and written by William, Archbishop of Tyre. I choose it for the way it presages and belongs to an understanding of what was to happen (and why) in the New World. In the post-Crusade centuries, the Christian "triumphant self-image" (Sardar et al. 1993:38) was shaken by Islamic expansion into southeastern Europe and the Iberian peninsula. A response of Christianity was to project its "own inner demons – [its] fears, anxieties and disowned self" on Islam (Sardar et al. 1993:38,88).[2] Eventually, Muslim hegemony over Spain was broken, bit by bit: the *Reconquista*. Muslims were "enslaved, and sold, [and] the concept of 'purity of blood' was used to humiliate and destroy thousands" (Maxwell 1993:44). Then in 1492 in Spain, the last Muslim bastion fell, the Jews (short of instant "conversion" to Christianity) were summarily expelled, and the day after that edict was issued, Columbus set sail:

> Within a year of the fall of Granada, Spain had acquired a new conquista, the vacuum was seamlessly filled, and conquistadors were preparing to set off for *otro mundo*, another world. (Sardar et al. 1993:40-41)[3]

But there was a profound reason for "America" *not* being another world – in the sense, at least, of being a "new" one. In 1492, it was accepted that the world was a sphere, but also, that the known inhabited earth of Europe, Africa, and Asia was an island: *Orbis Terrarum*. This belief was fundamental to another: that humankind was descended from one single originating couple, and the teachings of Christ and His Apostles had reached the very ends of the inhabited earth (even if they did meet with temporary rejection in places). Thus Columbus's landfall had to be the eastern coast of Asia of *Orbis Terrarum*.[4] However, other transoceanic voyages that soon followed revealed the *geographical* error (Figure 1). But this did not mean that the notion (founded, as it was, on doctrinal first principles) of one inhabited *Orbis Terrarum* was itself in error.

I

Continuous line: Shores explored by Columbus.
Broken line: Shores unsuspected by Columbus.

II

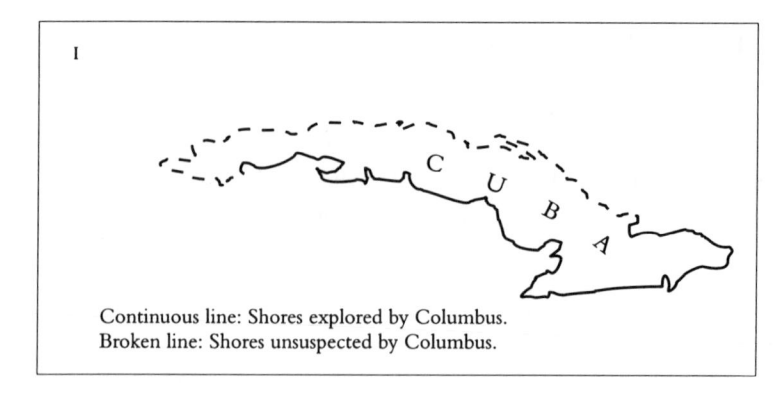

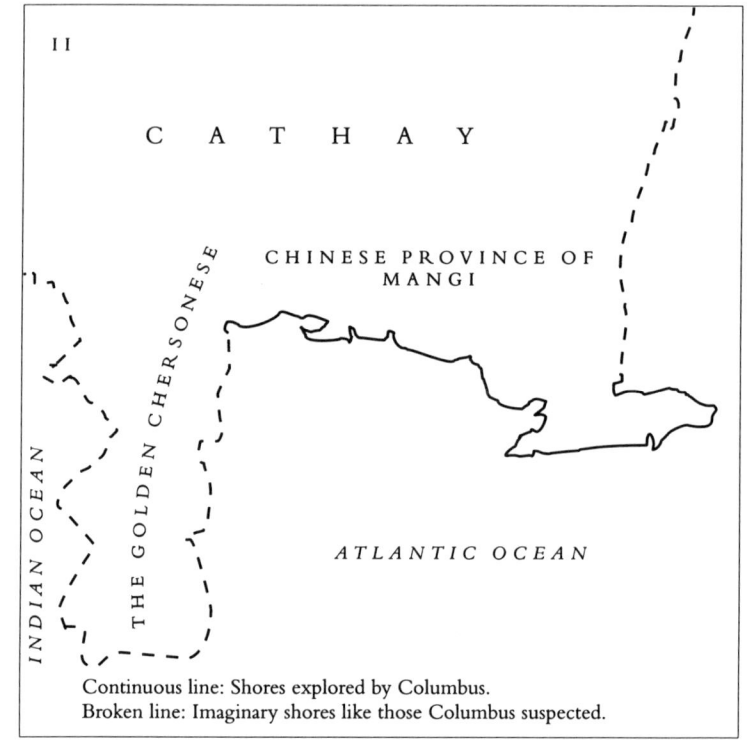

CATHAY

CHINESE PROVINCE OF MANGI

THE GOLDEN CHERSONESE

INDIAN OCEAN

ATLANTIC OCEAN

Continuous line: Shores explored by Columbus.
Broken line: Imaginary shores like those Columbus suspected.

Sketch maps of southern Cuba to illustrate Columbus' ideas on his second voyage.
Taken from: Edmundo O'Gorman, *The Invention of America*, 1961.
Bloomington, Indiana: Indiana University Press.

Along with "discovery" went the exercise of an authoritative canon of theological doctrine: "all that could be known had to be made compatible with [the] recognized canon of sacred and ancient authors. [The theory of knowledge] claimed that the external world and all human life was legible, *secundum scriptura*" (Pagden 1993:12). A fourth continent, America, had to be added to the *Orbis Terrarum*, but it had to be ontologically "the same" as the other three. Suggestions of "another island," an *orbis alterius*, were heretical.[5]

But what of the native of this fourth continent who is already there? Care had to be taken not to depart from the premise of *secundum scriptura*. Edmundo O'Gorman approaches the question allegorically, speaking of four men when before there had been three:

> suddenly, a fourth man appears of whom nothing is known. He is recognized as an individual of the human species.... This is not sufficient, however, to identify the newly-arrived individual as a person.... [T]here is only the possibility of some day *becoming* a real man whose life has significance according to European standards. (O'Gorman 1961:134-35, emphasis added; cf. Pagden 1993:7)

Hence the American Other. This Other, "pagan rather than heretic" and thus unlike Moslem and Jew, "is dwelling entirely in the hollow of absence" (McGrane 1989:10) – *that* is the unique quality of the Amerindian Other at contact.[6] Yet it is exactly this state of "absence" which the early Europeans in America "see" that is problematic for them at times. For example, in Columbus's *Journal*, along with the "they are without" references to the savages are the "they are very handsome" and even the "they are the best people in the world" allusions (cited in Todorov 1984:35-36). Of course "the evidence" changes as the contexts of "contact" change (see Hulme 1992: chapters 1 & 2). One consequence is radical oscillation in Europeans' perceptions (and moral judgments) of "the natives"; the theme of bestiality,[7] for example, alternates with that of primeval innocence,[8] and that of "Arawak" (innocence) with that of "Carib" (bestiality).[9]

The Amerindian: brother and barbarian

> Wherein, then, do these Americans dwell? In the Garden of Eden or in Satan's Wilderness? (Macedo 1992:12 [adapted])

There was eschatological urgency to finding an answer, for only through conversion of all humanity to Christianity "would man finally be able to achieve his *telos* and earn release from his earthly labours" (Pagden 1982a:19). In this sense, then, pagans such as the Amerindians held hostage the spiritual welfare of Christian Europe, and this allows for Pagden's otherwise unexpected argument that theologians and lawyers and the missionaries of that time took their task as "not to describe a remote 'otherness,' but to arrive at an evaluation of Indian behaviour which would eliminate that 'otherness'" (Pagden 1982a:5; cf. Ryan 1981:536). However, the pagan Indians were also held to be "barbarians," and as such, they were without *logos*.[10]

The dilemma thus posed, the university theologians and lawyers – the "schoolmen" of Salamanca and Paris with Francisco de Vitoria (1492-1546) pre-eminent among them – searched for an answer in the Aristotelian theory of "natural slavery" (Pagden 1982a: chapter 3). In the words of one of them:

> As the Philosopher says in the third and fourth chapters of the first book of the *Politics*, it is clear that some men are by nature slaves, others by nature free; and in some men it is determined that there is such a thing [i.e. a disposition to slavery] and that they should benefit from it. (Cited in Pagden 1982a:38)

Such a bald reading of Aristotle was unacceptable, however. First, "[if we accept it,] there must be some fault with God [but that's unthinkable]" (Las Casas in Pagden 1982a:50). Second, if *by nature* the Indians are but slaves, then the way to their Christian conversion – and the eventual fulfilment of the human *telos* – is barred.[11] A way out of this impasse was found through resort to the Aristotelian notion of both moral and rational growth through "habituation" or *ethismos*.

Thus the ontology of the Amerindian – in the minds of the schoolmen – changed.[12] Much of the "enslaved" condition of the Indian, following Vitoria, was "not because they lived in some alternative world but because they had failed to understand this world as it really is" (Pagden 1982a:74). Witness, for instance, their failure to appreciate the *vitae communicatione*, the natural channels of communication between groups: natural law dictated that such channels be kept open; indeed, the Indians' refusal to "receive" the Spaniards violated this dictate and, argued Vitoria, gave the Spaniards a just title for conquest (Pagden 1982a:77).

Witness, too, their (imputed) food habits: one could eat too "low" (insects) and the Indians did; one could also eat too "high" (cannibalism: "Man is clearly not a food for man" [Vitoria]) and the Indians did that as well (Pagden 1982a:86). It is their "poor and barbarous education" (Vitoria) that is at fault, and in that they are like peasants. But neither peasant nor Indian is *innately* inferior: with habituation he can throw off his moral and intellectual disabilities and interpret the world correctly. Until that happens, though, the Indian, for his own good, should remain under tutelage. This moves the question of Indian behaviour to being a matter of culture, albeit with still a strong (Aristotelian) psychological postulate – from being a "natural slave" the Indian was now a "natural child" (Pagden 1982a:106).

This grappling of the schoolmen with the problem of placing the Amerindians in the overall scheme of things, throws into relief two issues of particular relevance to us. The first is the tension over "sameness," which is played out between the perceived barbarity of the pagan Amerindians and the Christian doctrine of the unity of human creation and redemption. The second returns us to the sacred textual authority of the given structure of creation and the enormity of any step that might appear to change it – by introducing a new part into the whole, for example. Both issues were taken care of through the notion of a period of human infancy: "They, these 'savages', are not like us as we are now, the argument went, they are like us as we once were" (Pagden 1993:117).

In terms of European political interests, even this modified stance on Amerindian "nature" was advantageous: "the Indians ... exist ... incompletely until they have been mastered" (Pagden 1982a:48). But what when the "habituated" Indian *has* learned the ways of civil (Christian) society? The answer of the schoolmen of Salamanca was as straightforward as it was politically "prejudicial and scandalous":

> when [the Indians] no longer require any tutor the king of Spain ought to leave them in their first and proper liberty. (Pagden 1982a:107, citing Bartolme de Carranza)[13]

Divergent Universes: moral and physical

> Between civility and incivility a familiar and inoffensive tie of kinship had to be discovered and confirmed. (Hodgen 1964:387)

Amerindians had to be "naturalized," to be drawn into the European conception of order. In effect, what was proposed was a "hierarchy of being" with notions of gradation and eventual "graduation"; for the time being, though, "the Indians" would be a *similitudines homines* (Hodgen 1964:415-416).[14] In fact, the prevalent Eurocentric "ethnology" (as Hodgen dubs it) held – as did Prospero of Caliban – that all who were not one of us were "filth ... and most brutish."[15]

Yet the Middle Ages were far from being a period of "isolation and introversion." Indeed, the contrary was nearer the truth: merchants dealt with "tribal buyers and sellers from the far west of Scotland to the far east of China"; missionaries and pilgrims, even army garrisons, would have prolonged contact with non-Europeans (Hodgen 1964:78). Nevertheless, much of the medieval mind was mired in the legendary of the "monstrous and wondrous" issuing forth from "a literature fashioned by the encyclopedists and the Mandevilles, full of pseudo-anthropological lore bearing little relation to any groups of human beings living or dead" (Hodgen 1964:87). Nor should this lore be mistaken as the ethnological legacy of Herodotus: "Having lost touch with the classics, medieval scholarship purveyed a preposterous and fabulous sediment of what had once been a comparatively realistic antique ethnography" (Hodgen 1964:34).

But why? One important clue, following Hodgen again, is the sanctioned limits to curiosity: "scientific inquiry" prior to the Renaissance "was profoundly distrusted" – in canonical circles – "as meddlesome and impertinent. It was spoken of as *turpis curiositas*" (Hodgen 1964:207). Thus early Medieval travelers, for all their venturesomeness, took "their world picture for granted, they neither criticized it nor felt the need to relate their experience to it" (Hale 1967:334). In short, there was "little interest in alien ways, little reaction to cultural diversities" (Hodgen 1964:86). In the knowledge that all that could be known about the world had to be made compatible with the recognized canon, "their minds and thoughts were elsewhere." To a noteworthy degree, then, the world of the European, even at the time of the Discovery, "still sought its future in the past" (Hodgen 1964:114).

It seems that Renaissance "curiosity" – with *correction* as its corollary – emerged first, and relatively unproblematically, among the practical mariners and navigators exploring new reaches of *Orbis Terrarum*; rather than among the cloistered scholars upon whom the weight of "the canon" fell more heavily. A new authority began to accrue to experience. Already in 1488, Diaz, in his voyage to the Cape of Good Hope, reported crossing the "torrid zone" which supposedly sealed off *Orbis Terrarum* from the Antipodes. And by the time of Magellan, mariners may scoff at the ancients' talk of monstrous figures: such "are false and fabulous," reports an early sixteenth-century text (McGrane 1989:8). Nevertheless, Raleigh, otherwise scholarly and sceptical, accepted (in writing of the discovery of Guyana) reports of monstrous beings and of Amazons.[16] True, there was scholarly correction and adumbration of the known as it had been known, but not rejection. Raleigh, this time in his *History of the World* (1614), addressing the question of how the Americas were populated, attempts biblical genealogical exegesis: Noahides; dispersal of the Jews. Grotius (1625) foresaw "a great danger to piety" if such ideas are thrown out: reliance on the ancients *is* faltering, and there is the fearful spectre of the polygenesis of the human race – only the Bible remains (Grafton 1992:149, 151, 208, 210; cf. Ryan 1981).

Indeed, the scholarly community is afflicted with contradictions, ambiguities, and paradoxes in the wake of the Discovery. There is tension between information and knowledge. Thus Anthony Grafton, in *New Worlds, Ancient Texts* (1992), writes of the sixteenth-century Sebastian Munster:[17]

> As a cartographer, he fully recognized the independent existence of the Americas: a new continent in the West, not part of the East. As a narrator, he denied it, and perpetuated the original confusion of Columbus and others about the identity of the Americas and the Indies. (101)

For the sixteenth-century mariner and explorer, however, it was quite otherwise: "not only opening up new territory and new routes, he was constantly adjusting his inheritance of guesses about what the world looked like in the light of what he found" (Hale 1976:334).[18]

Remarkable here is not the ambiguity of the encyclopedist in the uncertainty of his intellectual world, but the confidence of the mariner, adjusting his inheritance of guesses: "For centuries European sailors had seen only the edges of an oceanic world; in a mere two decades, they were able to discern its totality" (Maxwell 1993:39).[19] The change went far beyond the physical. "To the Middle Ages," Hale suggests, "the Ocean Sea was rather like the upper atmosphere before the invention of oxygen masks and pressurized aircraft, a fatal zone delineating the physical limits of existence" (1967:336). Now there was the expectation that "space ... could be appropriated in imagination according to mathematical principles" (Harvey 1990:246), and, thanks to the importation of the Ptolemaic map from Alexandria to Florence around 1400, "[t]he most far-flung places ... [thus] fixed in relation to one another by unchanging coordinates" (Harvey 1990:245, citing Edgerton 1976).

However, acceptance of the Copernican heliocentric model (published in 1543), for example, was hesitant, begrudging – and slow, not only because of the undoing of much of both ancient and medieval thought but also because of their enduring influence. As with Munster so (in a manner) with Copernicus: on the one hand, "[t]he astrology and cosmology of Ptolemy and the physics of Aristotle would have to be rebuilt from their foundations if he [Copernicus] was right" (Grafton 1992:112); on the other, Copernicus still used "classical concepts and models" and his "model of the planetary system was as conservative ... as it was radical in its placement of the sun" (Grafton 1992:115).

Appropriating America: moral geography

> Since antiquity European culture has been founded on the concept of the *oikos*, the *domus*, the household.... [Then] *communitas christianae* [became] the heir to the Greek *oikumene*, the community of man, [and] exclusion from that community implied a species of non-existence. (Pagden 1993:2,7)

Thus, Pagden concludes, "European moral geography offered the image of a carefully circumscribed world" (7). And suddenly, America! Separated by the "Ocean Sea" (in contrast to Asia and Africa) from that *oikumene* circumscribing the moral domain, possibly even the human domain itself, there was a shocking uniqueness about both the landmass and its natives:

> ... America was still, in John Locke's celebrated phrase, 'in the beginning' of the whole world.... America was new in both senses of the word: new in relation to geological and human time, and new in relationship to us, the human observers. (Pagden 1993:117)

Yet it had to be brought into the *oikumene*.

First and foremost, then, "America" was a challenge to the European imagination. Recalling the axiom that "the real is as imagined as the imaginary" (Geertz 1980:136), I restate it in its more familiar form: the imagined may be as "real" as the real. With the sixteenth-century Portuguese specifically in mind, Macedo writes:

> expectation precede[d] knowledge, interpretation [was] superimposed on observation, and analogy neutralize[d] difference.... [They] recognized what they did not know, projecting onto the things and people they encountered their own desires, fears, ideas, phantoms, superstitions – in short, their 'imaginary.'(Macedo 1992:9,8)

Thus a "discovery" is turned into a non-discovery through a process by which the unknown ends as a reflection of the imagined known (Paine 1995). In this profound sense, then, meeting Amerindians presented a challenge to the European that was not met: "human alterity [was] at once revealed and rejected" (McGrane 1989:7, citing Todorov 1984).

At best, one such as Munster "could imagine strange races only in terms of the ancient oppositions between gentleness, nudity, and the Golden Age and savagery, monstrosity, and murder" (Grafton 1992:111). At worst, "sixteenth-century cosmography nature is not natural ... but rather 'fallen,' 'demonical,' not a neutral space but a black and void backdrop ..." (McGrane 1989:16). Similarly, "there is Christianity but no 'religion.' Religion is not yet the genus of which 'Christianity' will be merely a species" (McGrane 1989:16; cf. Tillich 1963:41-43).

At the same time, though, a subtle implication of the advances in cartography was to give new power, for a while, to moral geography whereby "map precedes territory" (Harley 1992:531). So now, in a political sense, too, one knew a land before ever reaching it:

> New England, New France, or New Spain were placed on maps long *before* the settlement frontiers of New England, New France, or New Spain became active zones of European settlement. (Harley p.531; emphasis in original)

Harley appropriately dubs this as "anticipatory geography."[20] An immediate implication of particular consequence in the present context is that "[Amer]Indian geography is silenced in the maps of America.... Cartography ... served to dispossess the Indians by engulfing them with blank spaces" (Harley 1992:531; cf. Richardson 1993).[21] What Edward Said speaks about in *Orientalism* finds its echo in this early "America":

> [The European] will designate, name, point to, fix what he is talking or thinking about with a word or phrase, which then is considered to have acquired, or more simply to be, reality. (Said 1991:72)[22]

Furthermore, even as Europeans "saw" the native population as belonging to another place or another time to that of their own (European) experience, they "saw" (to a quite fanciful extent) the landscape that lay before them in familiar images. Thus the early Navigators "saw" Andalusian slopes, the Conquistadores "saw" Spanish cities, and Cortes was depicted as riding into Mexico on an elephant (Fernandez-Armesto 1993:10). A century or two down the road there is a disdainful echo in Diderot's exaggerated comment, "America never suggested to any European, wonders of its *own*" (Pagden 1993:162). In other words, the enterprises of exploration and subsequent settlement especially, are likely to draw upon conservative chords of perception with their secret analogies. These take the sting out of the strange and dangerous by implanting familiar (i.e. domesticated) signs and symbols.[23] Thus in counterpoint to the dramatized distance between settler and aboriginal (where the settler "sees" "absence": p.xx *supra*) and to the settler's sense of being outside his domain, is the nurturing of a sense of what one holds to be close despite exterior evidence to the contrary. Thence the imperative of domestication.[24]

This, it seems to me, accounts for the "illusion of sameness" and statements of "identity in terms of home" that Harley (1992) finds in early (European) American maps.[25] So even without the authority of the canon, the settler, "[making] the unknown and the nearly unimaginable familiar enough for it to become imaginable, ... did not need ... to understand very much" in order to feel cognitively secure (Pagden 1993:27,36).[26] Some intellectuals of the day took the matter still farther, declaring against travel itself. Ryan (1981:521) reports, for example, that "neither Montaigne nor any other skeptic was particularly interested in seeing the world through the eyes of the exotic:[27] That would simply be exchanging custom for custom, folly for folly." Travel or "distance" was widely held to be "the cause of estrangement from tradition and from a former Noachian condition" – "degeneration" follows (Hodgen 1964:379; see chapter 6, *passim*).[28]

I find it reasonable to connect such a disposition to the perplexing and anxious issue of human heterogeneity – physical, cultural and, ultimately, of "being." In the course of the post-Discovery century – that is to say, in the intellectual world of Montaigne rather than of Columbus – there was, it seems, a modification in the way the issue was perceived. What had been the sacrilegious spectre of polygenesis became, in some circles, a matter of cultural incommensurability.[29]

However, this was still an anxiety-provoking issue. Montaigne recognized cultural *difference*,[30] yet, aghast over the implications (which seemed only all too likely) of cultural *incommensurability*, he asked: "What truth is that, which these Mountaines bound, and is a lie in the World beyond them?" (cited in Hodgen 1964:374). It was anxiety-provoking because civil behaviour and a settled life go together – the argument ran; what hope, then, of civility in a world of cross-cultural incommensurabilities? Such uncertainty in a world apparently void of reason, Ryan argues, led even sceptics such as Montaigne to continue "to submit themselves to the rule of faith" (Ryan 1981:52).

Conclusions

> A justified, and often long overdue, sympathy for the victims of European conquerors and colonists should not of itself preclude a serious and dispassionate attempt to understand the mental world of these Early Modern Europeans." (Elliott 1992:xiii)

Much of this chapter has been about how Europeans of the Discovery epoch handled alterity, and also, how historians that write about them do. Searching for the essence of the matter I go to J.H. Elliott (1992 and 1993) and his concern with the way in which much current writing on Amerindian-European relations "tends to create a set of assumptions and expectations far removed from those of sixteenth-century Europeans themselves" (1992: xiii). One common reason for this, he suggests (1993:38), is "to satisfy the urgent demands of our own moral concerns." We construct the Other of the sixteenth-century Amerindian and the sixteenth-century European accordingly. One result is (sometimes) that the Amerindian of that time "is today made to appear more 'one of us' than the sixteenth-century Spanish friar" (1993:38). We are left to suppose that "the friar" was remarkable for his insensitivity, to put it mildly, toward the Amerindian Other.

Of course the truth is far more complex and nuanced. Europeans, secular and clerical, *were* insensitive and worse; but at the same time there *was* a fundamental reason – as demonstrated in Pagden 1982a especially – for standard-bearers of European thought in the Americas (such were the friars) wishing to conceive of the natives of the new continent as "brothers, not others" (Elliott 1993:38). Not that it happened that way, and in inquiring why, my principal guide is Tzvetan Todorov (1984).

Difference cannot exist without the notion of likeness, and vice versa; but only weakly imagined in the sixteenth century was an ontology that allowed difference to be integrated into the norm of social life and cultural expression. Amerindians were either to be "added to" the European civilization or eliminated. On the one hand, we have Bartolome De Las Casas, Dominican and one-time Bishop of Chiapas: "with time they will be like us."[31] On the other, there is another Bishop of Chiapas: "[t]hese people do not know how to judge the gravity of their sins other than by the rigours of the penalties with which they are punished" (cited in McGrane 1989:25). For Todorov, Las Casas's was the "greater prejudice" for it meant "identifying the other purely and simply with one's own 'ego ideal'" (Todorov 1984:165; cf. Greenblatt 1992:137-38).

One may well say of the Discovery that its mission was "to chart sameness."[32] In effect, the European remained the sole subject in this transcontinental, transcultural meeting and did not have to call into question his own categories (Todorov 1984:240-41; Harris 1982:4-5). Such a state of affairs was crossed with paradox and irony (as we recognize today). In becoming "known" in this way, the Amerindian "brother-and-barbarian" effectively remained unknown. The very notion of brother-and-barbarian, furthermore, bespoke of internal *incoherence in a grand colonial enterprise*[33] whose agenda was "to encircle, to contain, [to convert,] and ultimately to possess" (Pagden 1993:27). Then there is the piquant irony concerning the Discoverer himself. As Fernandez-Armesto (1992:193) puts it, Columbus "abjure[d] his achievement in discovering a new continent because he could not face failure in the attempt to reach an old one." On several counts, Columbus neither would nor could include in his being the new "intellectual globe" (Grafton) heralded by the Discovery.

One hundred years on, Francis Bacon could – or would.[34] In *Great Instauration*, his manifesto of 1620, he argues for new methods of investigation and, equally important, new canons of interpretation whereby "Fruits and works are as it were sponsors and sureties for the truth of philosophers." In short: experience and empirical evidence over canonical text; scholars must pay attention to the findings of practical men. As for the knowledge and wisdom of the ancients, past efforts had been directed to verifying them, not correcting and extending them; the mistake had been to assume that the generations that followed them were "younger" whereas *they* were older (in knowledge) (Grafton 1992:197 ff.).

However, "emerging inventive energies" did not sweep all before them; in fact, "time-honoured religious beliefs set constraints to discussion" (Butzer 1992:544). The equating of civilized life with Christian belief endured. The Amerindian was to be brought into the Christian/civilized fold. And for those who resist? "Who can deny that the use of gunpowder against pagans is the burning of incense to our Lord," says Oviedo, an early governor of the settlement at Hispaniola (Todorov 1984:151). We saw that even this repeats a pattern belonging to European affairs. There was, then, despite the professions of a common identity to all humanity, a line which when perceived to be crossed signified "the incomprehensibility of difference" (Macedo 1992:8).

The final emphasis for this essay is that a denial of alterity to others is also a self-denial of that precious sense. Therein resided the European dilemma. With the denial of alterity by the supposedly civilized to the supposedly *un*civilized, alterity and self-knowledge were confined within the theory of knowledge of the Christian canon. Few found a route leading to an alterity which allows self-knowledge to arise out of the observation of differences.[35]

Postscript

The past, as presented in this chapter, sometimes echoes in the present day. In 1991, the Supreme Court of British Columbia brought down a judgment in the *Delgamuukw et al. v. R* case (McEachern 1991) rejecting land claims of the Gitsksan and Wet'suwet'en peoples against the crown. The judgment is a "landmark" one for its return to (and retention of) colonial precepts regarding aboriginal peoples and their (absence of) land rights. The significance of the case lies especially in the critical attention it has aroused among anthropologists and also within the legal profession. See, for example, the essays in *BC Studies* (1992), the proceedings of a conference with aboriginal spokespersons and academics of several disciplines (Cassidy 1992), and an anthropology doctoral dissertation (Culhane 1994). The case is under appeal.

Notes

1. First and last, it is to these authors – the anthropologist's "informants" in this case – that I am especially indebted. I hope I haven't garbled them. A number of colleagues were good enough to read and discuss the several drafts this has been through, and I call out their names in the companion piece with which it was entangled (Paine 1995). One of them, however, must also be named here: Stuart Pierson, historian of science. I have done my best to heed his searching comments; I know, full well, he will still find things amiss, but the paper is much improved thanks to his interventions.
2. Pope Pius II in his *Historia* execrated the Turks, for example, as "Gens truculenta et ignominiosa," as a people that dogs bite on sight, as having revolting sexual and gustatory habits (Flint 1992:57,61,186). Nor should it escape notice that the projection of "demons" and "disowned self" tore apart the Christian world itself; Grafton points up the significance: "It was an unhappy coincidence for New World peoples that the period of exploration coincided with that of the sixteenth-century religious wars, always cast as battles between orthodoxy and heresy, and the particularly virulent eruption of witch-hunting in the seventeenth century" (Grafton 1992:92).
3. No small part of Columbus's motivation in seeking the sea-route to "the Indies" (a route that would also be safe, or safer, from Islamic threats) was to bring back the expected gold in order to finance the crusade that would recapture Jerusalem for Christendom. For an overview of the period see Wolf 1982, especially chapter 2 ("The World in 1400") and chapter 5 ("Iberians in America"); also Blaut 1993.
4. The "new" about Columbus's journey was its route (though even that was not strictly true: viz. the Norse sea-crossings and possibly others'): "I should not go by land to the eastward, by which it was the custom to go, but by way of the west, by which down to this day we do not know certainly anyone has passed" (the *Journal*, cited in Flint 1992:183).
5. For fuller treatment of the issues of this paragraph, see Paine 1995.
6. The "utterly alien" quality constructed out of "the negation of our normality" as stressed by Fothergill (1992:38) is also there, but it is not unique to the Amerindian: it is also present in the case of Jews and Muslims vis-à-vis Christians.

7. Bestiality, that is, in its broadest construction as behaviour abhorrent to the civilized — viz. a variety of sexual practices, human sacrifice, and cannibalism. Regarding cannibalism, by the end of the fifteenth century the anthropophagi were a constituent feature of exotic landscapes (Pagden 1982a:81; Grafton 1992:71, 108-09) and Arens's point is well-taken: "The significant question is not why people eat human flesh, but why one group invariably assumes that others do" (Arens 1979:139; cf. Harrison 1993:11). A possible general explanation is that the notion of the Other (itself suggestive of anxiety over ontological categories) posits a need for an "anti-cultural" category, and cannibalism, as bestial/unnatural behaviour, serves this end. Schneider's (1968) problematizing of the ontology of "the natural," with special reference to sexual practices, in this century's America provides a useful backdrop for thinking about some of the metaphysical and moral problems Europeans presented themselves with in their encounters with Amerindian populations.

8. Nor is this without its problems. For example, Helder Macedo, pondering the journals of Pero Vaz de Caminha from the same period, sees here a "profound perplexity." How is Caminha (or Columbus) "to reconcile his religion, based on the idea of sin, with what he thought was the evidence that there still existed in the world a prelapsarian innocence?" (Macedo 1992:10).

9. Hulme sees the genesis of this "Carib-Arawak" distinction as a colonial one with the force of a self-fulfilling prophecy: "any Amerindian settling near a colonial town must 'be an Arawak,' Q.E.D. And likewise any hostile Amerindian must, by definition, 'be a Carib'"; worse still, *The Handbook of South American Indians* buttresses much that is in these early characterizations (Hulme 1992:65; 49).

10. "Barbarians," from the Greek *barbaroi*, literally non-Greek speakers, comes to mean "unintelligibles" (Macedo 1992:8). As "language was [held to be] the prime indicator of rationality, that what a man spoke was, to a very large degree, what a man was.... The close association in Greek thought between intelligible speech and reason made it possible to assume that those who were devoid of *logos* in the one sense were probably devoid of it in the other" (Pagden 1993:120). Indeed, such was the conclusion in the New World: beginning with Columbus, the Europeans — who could not understand the Amerindian languages! — had difficulty in acknowledging Amerindian tongues as language (Sider 1987, *passim*; McGrane 1989:17).

11. Following Aristotle, the natural slave can have no share in virtue except with reference to a "whole" person who is his "master," and there is the inescapable conclusion that "[t]he function of the natural slave is ... to *be* a slave" (Aristotle 1912: 1260a).
12. But not of African slavery: see Pagden (1982a: ch.3) on Spanish classificatory groupings of slaves and pagans.
13. Hence Carlos Fuentes' claim that "What distinguishes the Spanish colonization from the other European colonizations — the French, English, Dutch, and Portuguese — is that Spain was the only colonizing empire that debated with itself about the nature of its acts of conquest and colonization. It [was] a debate of a power with itself" (Fuentes 1991:6). An outstanding occasion was the debate between Las Casas, missionary and Amerindian patron, and de Sepulveda, theologian and legal scholar, on "The Just Causes of War against the Indians" — the Valladolid debate of 1550 (Pagden 1992b:xxviii-xxx; Cannizzo 1985, *passim*).
14. Already in the fourth century, St. Augustine had vouched for the existence of *similitudines homines* (Hodgen 1964:416).
15. This applied not just to the "Indians" of the new continent, but to the Negroes of Africa and the Celts of Scotland and Ireland and is found in Spenser's *Faerie Queene* (1590) (Hodgen 1964:364-65).
16. This was the "world" of Mandeville's (imaginary) *Travels*, and, astonishingly, Raleigh remarks: "wee finde his relations true of such thinges as heeretofore were held incredible" (Hodgen 1964:409, citing from the Hakluyt Society reprint of 1848, pp.85-86).
17. Publisher (in 1542 an edition of Ptolemy) and cartographer and writer (*Cosmographia* [1544] among other works).
18. Note the contrast with the previous citation from Hale on the medieval traveller (pp.322-3 *supra*).
19. Consider: Portuguese exploration of West African coast; settlement of Madeira 1420-25, of Azores 1427-39, conquest and settlement of Canaries 1483-1500; Bartholomew Dias reaches the Indian Ocean in 1488, Columbus the Antilles in 1492, Vasco da Gama the coast of India in 1498 — and 29 years after Columbus's first voyage Magellan circumnavigates the globe.
20. Edward Said best captures the epistemology of this sense of the anticipatory where he writes: "... if we agree that all things in history, like history itself, are made by men, then we will appreciate how possible it is for many objects or places or times to be assigned roles and given meanings that acquire objective validity only *after* the assignments are made" (Said 1991:54; original emphasis).

21. Cartography backed by *contract* — not between the colonized and colonizer of course, but between the colonizer and his sovereign. "Contracts appropriately issued by sovereigns of any nation state permitted colonists to claim native or unoccupied lands.... Through the contract, kings assumed political ownership over lands claimed in their names" (Sanchez 1991:25). And "kings" bolstered their legitimacy through the Pope of Catholic Europe. Thus "in 1493 Pope Alexander VI 'donated' to the Catholic monarchs Ferdinand and Isabella sovereignty over all the new-found lands in the Atlantic which had not already been occupied by some other Christian prince" (Pagden 1992b:xvi).

    And the "contract" would be read out — as a (fetishistic) demonstration of "legal" probity — to Amerindian communities that had now become the property of the Castilian crown. The "document known as the 'Requirement' (or *Requerimiento*) ... began with a history of the world since Adam ... moved swiftly on to the grant made by the Pope ... and the obligation of every Indian to pay homage to the agents of the Crown and to obey their orders.... The facts that the document was in Spanish, a language no Indian could then understand, and that it made no attempt to explain the complex legal and theological terms ... and that it was frequently read at night to sleeping villagers or out of earshot of the Indians were disregarded. *What mattered was the act*. Once the Europeans had discharged their duty to inform, the way was clear for pillage and enslavement" (Pagden 1992b:xxiv-xxv, emphasis added).

22. As for the choosing of names, "fundamentally, *names Christened*" (McGrane 1989:20; original emphasis). This should be understood as part of the cosmography in connection with the imperative of conversion (cf. Papal Bull of 1496). At the same time, "[f]lattery, too, had its place ...'Virginia' (after Elizabeth I, the Virgin Queen), 'Montreal' (*Mont Royal*, for King Francis I).... And self-flattery was never far behind, as 'Lake Champlain,' 'Frobisher Bay,' and 'Pennsylvania' attest" (Axtell 1992:59-60).

23. Again, Said's *Orientalism* is not a bad guide as to how the early European colonists in America (with some angst) represented to themselves their presence there: "One tends to stop judging things either as completely novel or as completely well known: a new median category emerges, a category that allows one to see new things, things seen for the first time, as versions of a previously known thing. In essence such a category is not so much a way of receiving new information as it is a method of controlling what seems to be a threat to some established view of things" (Said 1991:58-59).

24. Even "American flora and fauna were forced into classical botanical and biological categories" in the conviction, in this case, "that everything in the world conformed to a pre-ordained set of laws — the law of nature" (Pagden 1993:10).
25. An example is a map of Virginia from 1612: "what strikes the [eye] is not the wilderness but the gentility of the landscape: an open park land is portrayed, dotted with round trees like the familiar oaks and elms of southern England or lowland France. By creating an illusion of sameness, by defining identity in terms of 'home,' the map made America easier to assimilate into the European consciousness" (Harley 1992:531).
26. Sixteenth-century European fishermen's awareness/unawareness of Newfoundland, whither they went every year, is precisely on account of the uncomplicatedness of the circumstances, an illuminating case in point: Newfoundland was "as well known to thousands of fishermen in western Europe as the shores of the bays and rivers of their home counties ... Yet in another sense there is the paradox that to Europeans of the sixteenth and early seventeenth centuries Newfoundland was scarcely known at all. It was simply taken for granted" (Quinn 1982:16-17).
27. This is particularly interesting in Montaigne's case (1533-1592) given his scrupulous attention to the native voice in cultural description. He also sought first-hand reports from Europeans with "no invention to build-upon ... not Pedanticall, nor Friar-like, nor Lawyer-like" (cited in Hodgen 1964:192).
28. Diderot (1713-1784) would speak of "the active, punishing, wandering and dissipated profession *metier* of traveller" (Pagden 1993:157); he even argued that travel dims the imagination.
29. See, for example, Francis Bacon's *Advancement of Learning* (1605). It was recognized that the posited monogenetic heritage had been breached three times: by Cain and his descendants, by the sons of Noah and theirs, and once again at Babel. This offered a scriptural solution to the problem of cultural differences (Hodgen 1964:228-29).
30. "[N]othing," he wrote, "wherein the world differeth so much as in customes and lawes.... It is credible that there be naturall lawes; as may be seene in other creatures, but in us they are lost" (cited in Hodgen 1964:208-209).
31. He was far from alone in this thought. Thus Pero Vaz de Caminha: "The only thing these people [naked savages] lack to become true Christians, every one, is to understand us." But as Macedo (1992:12) informs us, "two

convicts — two criminals condemned to penal punishment — were at once entrusted with that pious task...."

32. The formulation is Nigel Rapport's who also sees the Discovery saga as illustrating the proposition that "absence," of itself, is no guarantor *against* the assumption of knowledge, and conversely, "presence" is no guarantor *of* knowledge (Personal communication: February, 1993).

33. Whose geo-political scope and pretension are suggested by the Treaty of Tordesillas of 1494 whereby Spain (that is, Castile-Aragon) and Portugal staked out their claims: "They drew a dividing line 370 leagues west of the Cape Verde Islands. Castile, believing that it now controlled a direct route to the Orient, claimed all lands west of the line — and thereby acquired the major part of the Western Hemisphere. Portugal, intent mainly on keeping the Spaniards out of the South Atlantic, took all lands to the east of the line and thus came into possession of Brazil" (Wolf 1982:131).

34. "Surely it would be disgraceful if, while the regions of the material globe — that is, of the earth, of the sea, and of the stars — have been in our times laid widely open and revealed, the intellectual globe should remain shut up within the narrow limit of old discoveries" (*Great Instauration* cited in Grafton 1992:198).

35. Trigger (1985, particularly chapters 1 and 3) touches upon a number of the issues of this essay as they were played out in later centuries, especially in nineteenth-century Canada. Berger (1991) and Richardson (1993) are also relevant texts. Memmi (1965) remains a powerful account of the psychological condition (riven with ambivalence) of "colonizer." I would also draw attention to *America in European Consciousness, 1493-1750*, edited by Karen Ordahl Kupperman: published in 1995 by the University of North Carolina Press at Chapel Hill after the completion of the present essay.

References

Arens, W. (1979). *The Man-Eating Myth: Anthropology and Anthropophagy*. New York: Oxford University Press.
Aristotle (1912). *The Politics of Aristotle*. Translated by William Ellis, Introduction by A.D. Lindsay. London: J.M Dent & Sons Ltd (Everyman's Library).
Axtell, James (1992). *Beyond 1492. Encounters in Colonial North America*. Oxford: Oxford University Press.
B.C. Studies (1992). Theme Issue, "Anthropology and History in the Courts." *B.C. Studies*, No. 95 (University of British Columbia).

Berger, Thomas R. (1991). *A Long and Terrible Shadow. White Values, Native Rights in the Americas, 1492-1992*. Vancouver/Toronto: Douglas & McIntyre.

Blaut, J.M. (1993). *The Colonizer's Model of the World. Geographical Diffusionism and Eurocentric History*. New York/London: The Guilford Press.

Butzer, Karl W. (1992). "From Columbus to Acosta: Science, geography, and the New World." In Karl W.Butzer (ed.), *The Americas Before and After 1492: Current Geographical Research*. Annals of the Association of American Geographers, 82(3):543-65.

Cannizzo, Jeanne (1985). "On the Just Causes of War: The Debate at Valladolid." Montreal: CBC Transcripts.

Cassidy, F. (ed.) (1992). *Aboriginal Title in British Columbia: Delgamuukw v. The Queen*. Lantzville & Montreal: Oolichan Books & Institute for Research on Public Policy.

Culhane, Dara (1994). *Delgamuukw and the People Without Culture. Anthropology and the Crown*. Unpublished Doctoral Dissertation, Simon Fraser University.

Edgerton, S. (1976). *The Renaissance Re-Discovery of Linear Perspective*. New York: Basic Books.

Elliott, J.H. (1970/1992). *The Old World And the New 1492-1650*. Cambridge: Cambridge University Press.

___. (1993). "The Rediscovery of America." *New York Review of Books*, June 24, pp. 36-41.

Fernandez-Armesto, Felipe (1991/1992). *Columbus*. Oxford: Oxford University Press.

___. (1993). "America First." *London Review of Books*, Jan. 7, p.10.

Flint, Valerie I.J. (1992). *The Imaginative Landscape of Christopher Columbus*. New Jersey: Princeton University Press.

Fothergill, Anthony (1992)."Of Conrad, Cannibals, and Kin" In Mick Gidley (ed.), *Representing Others: White Views of Indigenous Peoples*. Exeter: Exeter University Press, pp. 37-59.

Fuentes, Carlos (1991). "Neither Discovery Nor Encounter But the Imagining of America." *Encounters: 10* (University of New Mexico), pp. 4-7.

Geertz, Clifford (1980). *Negara. The Theatre State in Nineteenth-Century Bali*. New Jersey: Princeton University Press.

Grafton, Anthony (1992). *New Worlds, Ancient Texts. The Power of Tradition and the Shock of Discovery*. (With April Shelford & Nancy Siraisi) Cambridge, Mass.: Harvard University Press.

Greenblatt, Stephen (1991/1992). *Marvelous Possessions. The Wonder of the New World*. Chicago: University of Chicago Press.

Hale, John (1967). "A World Elsewhere: Geographical and Mental Horizons." In Dennis Hays (ed.), *The Age of the Renaissance*. New York: McGraw-Hill. pp. 300-350.

Harley, Brian (1992). "Rereading the maps of the Columbian Encounter." In Karl W. Butzer (ed.), *The Americas Before and After 1492: Current Geographical Research*. Annals of the Association of American Geographers, 82(3):522-35.

Harris, Leslie (1982). "The Owl of Minerva." In G.M. Story (ed.), *Early European Settlement and Exploitation in Atlantic Canada*. St. John's: Memorial University of Newfoundland, pp. 1-80.

Harrison, Simon (1993). "Transformations of identity in Sepik warfare." Presented at the ASA IV Decennial Conference (*The Uses of Knowledge: Global and Local Relations*). (typescript)

Harvey, David ([1980] 1990). *The Condition of Postmodernity*. Oxford: Blackwell.

Hodgen, Margaret T. (1964). *Early Anthropology in the Sixteenth and Seventeenth Centuries*. Philadelphia: University of Pennsylvania Press.

Hulme, Peter (1986/1992). "Columbus and the Cannibals" & "Caribs and Arawaks." In *Colonial Encounters: Europe & the Native Caribbean 1492-1797*. London: Routledge, pp. 13-88.

Macedo, Helder (1992). "Recognizing the Unknown: The Discoveries & the Discovered in the Age of European Overseas Exploration." *Camoes Center Quarterly* 4(1,2):8-13.

Maxwell, Kenneth (1993). "Adios Columbus!" *New York Review of Books*, Jan. 28, pp. 38-45.

McEachern, Allen (1991). *Reasons for Judgment of the Honourable Chief Justice Allen McEachern*. Vancouver: Supreme Court of British Columbia.

McGrane, Bernard (1989). *Beyond Anthropology: Society & the Other*. New York: Columbia University Press.

Memmi, Albert (1965). *The Colonizer and the Colonized*. Boston: Beacon Press.

Morison S.E. (1941). "Columbus and Polaris." *American Neptune* 1:123-37.

O'Gorman, Edmundo (1961). *The Invention of America*. Bloomington: Indiana University Press.

Pagden, Anthony (1982a). *The Fall of Natural Man: The American Indian and the Origins of Comparative Ethnology*. Cambridge: Cambridge University Press.

___. (1982b). Introduction In Bartolme de Las Casas, *A Short Account of the Destruction of the Indies*. ed. and trans., Nigel Griffin. Harmondsworth: Penguin Books, pp.xiii-xli.

———. (1993). *European Encounters with the New World: From Renaissance to Romanticism*. New Haven: Yale University Press.

Paine, Robert (1995). "Columbus and Anthropology and the Unknown." *Journal of the Royal Anthropological Institute* (New Series), 1(1): 47-65.

Phillips, William D., Jr., and Carla Rahn Phillips (1992). *The Worlds of Christopher Columbus*. Cambridge: Cambridge University Press.

Quinn, D.B. (1982). "Newfoundland in the Consciousness of Europe in the Sixteenth and Early Seventeenth Centuries." In G.M. Story (ed.), *Early European Settlement and Exploitation in Atlantic Canada*. St.John's: Memorial University of Newfoundland, pp. 9-30.

Richardson, Boyce (1993). *People of Terra Nullius. Betrayal and Rebirth in Aboriginal Canada*. Vancouver: Douglas and McIntyre.

Russell, Jeffrey Burton (1991). *Inventing the Flat Earth. Columbus and the Modern Historians*. New York: Praeger.

Ryan, Michael T. (1981). "Assimilating New Worlds in the Sixteenth and Seventeenth Centuries." *Comparative Study of Society and History* 23(4):519-38.

Said, Edward W. ([1978] 1991). "Imaginative Geography and Its Representations." In *Orientalism. Western Concepts of the Orient*. Harmondsworth: Penguin Books, pp. 49-72.

Sanchez, Joseph P. (1991). "The Ambiguity of Legitimacy: Entitlement and the Legacy of Colonialism." *Encounters: 10* (University of New Mexico), pp. 24-30,50.

Sardar, Zia, Ashis Nandy, and Merryl Wyn Davies (1993). *Barbaric Others: A Manifesto on Western Racism*. London/Boulder, Colorado: Pluto Press.

Schneider, David M. (1968). *American Kinship: A Cultural Account*. Englewood Cliffs, New Jersey: Prentice-Hall.

Sider, Gerald (1987). "When Parrots Learn to Talk, and Why They Can't: Domination, Deception, and Self-Deception in Indian-White Relations." *Comparative Studies of Society & History* 29:3-23.

Tillich, Paul (1963). *Christianity and the Encounter with World Religions*. New York: Columbia University Press.

Todorov, Tzvetan (1982/1984). *The Conquest of America: The Question of the Other*. New York: Harper & Row.

Trigger, Bruce (1985). *Natives and Newcomers. Canada's "Heroic Age" Reconsidered*. Kingston & Montreal: McGill-Queen's University Press.

Wolf, Eric (1982). *Europe and the People Without History*. Berkeley: University of California Press.

[Part IV]

NATIONALISM AND TRANSNATIONALISM

Introduction

Given the extraordinary complexity of cultural and social organization, it is hardly surprising that multi-level analysis has posed so formidable a challenge. Unfortunately, rather too often we have converted an unavoidable analytical shortfall into a competition for sociological primacy. In the field of ethnic studies, this rivalry has manifested itself in successive claims for the greater generative significance of what are in fact complementary processes. Consideration of state and more recently global impetuses have, therefore, sometimes come at the expense of individual experience and local groupings, trading one partiality for another. People, however, cannot step out of the local to participate in national and global systems. Perhaps, therefore, as Parminder Bhachu notes, the "local and the global are the same moment" (ch. 12).

The following two chapters highlight the importance and the possibility of considering the dynamics *between* multiple sites and frameworks of cultural production. Anthony Cohen's essay moves between three levels: event, locality, and nationalist movement. The event is the occasion in 1992 of a lecture by John Goodlad, the leader of the Shetland Fishermen's Association at the Gaelic College in Skye. Goodlad argued that Scottish political autonomy could open the way for successful development of large-scale commercial fishery in the Highlands and Islands in the Shetland model. The lecture prompted a detailed critique from an audience member, a development policy specialist with thirty years of experience in Shetland and the Western Isles. Cohen situates both the speech and its critique in the tension between the rhetorics of local discourse in island communities like Whalsay and nationalist rhetoric. That tension, Cohen argues, highlights a central problem for nationalist movements: nationalism is most compelling when it is meaningful in the terms of local and individual experience. The objective of such movements is, however, the diminishment of local consciousness in favour of a national identity. Politicians, Cohen argues, overestimate their abilities to subordinate or even to eliminate these local and individual interests in pursuit of nationalist projects.

In Parminder Bhachu's chapter, the production of the local is itself problematized. She notes that for a large number of people worldwide, the local may shift several times over the course of a lifetime. This is certainly the case for "twice and thrice" migrant Asian women whose families have moved successively to Africa, Europe, and in some cases further on to North America. Bhachu emphasizes the transformative role of these women whose production of identity and local diasporic spaces draws upon a wide range of sources including family migration histories and peer cultures, as well as class and regional locations in national and global economies. The role of these women as agents and catalyzers of cultural reproduction is illustrated through the shifts which have been occurring in an increasingly elaborated Sikh wedding economy. Bhachu is particularly concerned with the expansion of dowries and the shifts in consumption styles which they incorporate. These changes have resulted in a heightened role for, and increased control by, brides who have been able to use their wages to make significant contributions to their own dowry. The role of Sikh women as British wage earners has thus been translated into an elaboration of a cultural tradition that has survived over two centuries through successive migrations.

11

Owning the Nation, and the Personal Nature of Nationalism: Locality and the Rhetoric of Nationhood in Scotland[1]

Anthony P. Cohen

The language of ownership lends itself well to the expression of identity. Identity "belongs to" someone, even though it may be by public attribution rather than (or conflicting with) self-ascription.[2] Indeed, children may come to experience identity through the expression of possession. The British child talks, with emphasis, of *"my* Mum," *"my* house," *"my* school," as if these were extensions of herself. These possessive associations extend also into the arena of social membership which characterizes a more mature assertion of identity: *my* family, *my* country. This paper focuses on the last instance, the ownership of nation; and, in particular, on the problems which nationalism poses for ownership of the terms of local discourse. It does seem to be a real problem, since the terms which are politically appropriate to a specific locality and to the putative nation may be incongruent, even irreconcilable, rather than merely different. Further, the words through which someone expresses nationalism (or nationhood) may well be felt by others to intrude on their own proprietary rights. I will illustrate this difficulty by making reference to a recent argument concerning Scottish fishery development, in which assertions about the comparability of Shetland and the Western

Isles rested very tenuously on a devolutionist proposition sustained by nationalist rhetoric.

The relativities of locality and nationalism signal the even greater complexity of the possessive question, "whose nationalism?" Recent anthropological work has addressed explicitly the relationship of nation to individual in ways which make it imperative for us to look carefully at the individuals who are spokespersons for nationalism and advocates of nationhood. To put the matter simply, nationalists as individuals mediate nation*hood* through their own personal experience and aspirations, making an association between themselves and the nation which they then also impute to others.

It is this association that I wish to consider here: nationalism as an expression of the national*ist*. The -ism and its advocate are inextricably related. This is as true of the audience as it is of the advocate: the arguments for nationalism must be cogent within the experience and circumstances of the individuals who interpret it as appropriate to themselves. The nation, as constructed by the nationalist, becomes at once a compelling medium both for locating and depicting their selves. Through their ownership of their selves, people "own" the nation. Indeed, writing about Quebec, Handler sees nationalism in terms of Macpherson's notion of "possessive nationalism" (1988:152ff).

One of the problems of self-conscious national ownership – the association of individual with nation which I call "personal nationalism" (Cohen 1994b) – occurs when it becomes confused with statehood: that is, when the appeal to nationalism demands that people commit themselves to a political position, rather than just requiring them to have an affective orientation to a nebulous body of symbols. It gives people something to disagree about, rather than something around which to unite. But this makes life rather difficult for the advocate who sees political nationalism, or the statehood of the putative nation, as both the objective of policy and the solution to policy issues. It is a problem particularly when the argument for this kind of nationalism seems to fall outside the personal experience of the audience as a whole or of some of its individual members, or outside of what they believe to be the personal experience of the advocate, or which evoke propositions about the politics of nationalism which historically have been and remain extremely contentious. It is just such a case that I present here, a case in which nationalism as political program poses difficulties of political, cultural, and personal dissonance.

Scotland and Nationalism

Political nationalism as an explicit concern in Scotland preceded the demise of the autonomous Scottish state under the 1707 Act of Union with England. Although the Crowns of England and Scotland had already been united for a century since the kingship of James I/VI (England/Scotland), it was not until the 1707 Act that Scotland became subject to the Westminster parliament. The presence of a powerful southern neighbour had long made subordination by England a real threat, and the explicit determination to resist it made in the eloquent Declaration of Arbroath of 1320 was a permanent strategic consideration for independent Scotland. Following the Union, secessionist eruptions occurred at intervals, and Scotland retained its own Church, distinctive legal and educational systems, and a measure of discretion over the formulation and implementation of domestic policy.[3]

Since the middle of the nineteenth century, the issues of either full independence or a substantial devolution of powers to a Scottish parliament have rarely been off the agenda, although electoral support for them has only become significant since 1974, and even since then has been inconsistent. A referendum held in 1978 resulted in a bare majority for devolution, but failed to reach the proportion required by law. The proposal fell and so, partly in consequence, did the Labour government. However, over the last ten years, three political factors have made the independence/devolution argument the dominant issue in Scottish politics: the increasing support for the Scottish National Party (SNP); an agreement, through the forum of the Scottish Constitutional Convention, among the Labour and Liberal Democrat parties and other non-partisan bodies to pursue devolution; and a major collapse in the Scottish Tory vote, which has emphasized the essentially undemocratic nature of Scottish government. Labour and the Liberal Democrats are both now committed to the restoration of a Scottish parliament; the SNP is committed to seeking full independence within the context of the European Union. But the argument between the devolutionists and those seeking full independence is not merely a partisan quarrel; rather it reiterates historical disputes within the SNP and wider nationalist movement over the last one hundred and fifty years.

Although they diverge on issues of policy and strategy, the antagonistic tendencies would tend to find more common ground on some propositions which are central to Scottish tradition and to the expression of Scottish nationhood. Foremost among these is a diffuse commitment to democracy in a political sense and as a commitment to the rights of the individual. The term "self-government" serves well here as a means of expressing the convergence of these themes: individuals have inalienable rights to the determination and pursuit of their own options, prominent among which must be the right to give political expression to their putative nationhood.[4]

The case I discuss here relates partly to the Shetland Islands, the northern and insular extremity of Scotland, whose historical-political relationship with Scotland has been as ambivalent as that of Scotland with England. Orkney and Shetland, both outposts of Norse settlement, were sold to the Scottish Crown in 1469. The alienation of the economy and of power by the Scots feudal nobles and their followers, and the fairly swift demise of Norn as the lingua franca left a considerable cultural legacy of resentment, if not hostility, toward Scotland, exacerbated by the economic peripherality of the islands and the exploitation of their fishing grounds by other north European countries. Shetland became a labour pool for the British Royal Navy and, later, the merchant marine. Between the mid-nineteenth and mid-twentieth centuries, the population of Shetland halved through emigration to mainland Britain, Australia, New Zealand, and Canada, and through the devastation of the two World Wars. In terms of ethnic identity and orientation, the Norse tradition remained strong, celebrated in every aspect of popular culture, reinforced by close ties with Norway during the 1939-45 War, and, during the very recent past, through the involvement of Norwegian shipyards and finance in the redevelopment of Shetland's fishing fleet.

The Shetland economy only began to emerge from its endemic depression in the early 1960s, largely on the basis of the revival in fortunes of its major indigenous industry of fishing, supplemented by those of knitwear and crofting. But this revival of economic fortunes was overwhelmed by the discovery of oil in the Shetland Basin of the North Sea, and the subsequent location on Shetland of oil-related industry and facilities. During the 1970s and 1980s, Shetland developed the most modern privately-owned inshore fishing fleet in Britain, principally based on the two island communities of Burra Isle and Whalsay, the latter being the community with which I have been concerned since 1972 (Cohen 1987). Even during the mid-1970s, when the SNP enjoyed unprecedented electoral support throughout Scotland, it was weak in Shetland, partly because its policy on North Sea oil was insensitive to local claims;

but partly also because of the lingering sense that Edinburgh may be no more alien than London, and was not much less distant culturally or geographically. In the 1987 general election, the local devolutionist Orkney and Shetland Movements put up a joint candidate; since then, they have reached a rapprochement with the SNP, and the latter's support on matters of fishery policy may soften attitudes, in the fishing communities at least, to nationalism. However, Shetland seems to have remained predominantly sympathetic to the Liberal cause, with a strong, if highly localized tradition of Labour support in some crofting areas and in Lerwick, the "capital" town of the islands.

The other area I touch on here is the extreme insular west of Scotland, the Outer Hebrides and Western Isles, ethnically, linguistically and religiously distinct from Orkney and Shetland, and economically very much weaker. The Western Isles are firmly in the Scottish *Gadhealtacht*, the Gaelic-speaking communities of the west and north. The local economy has persistently failed to alleviate the high rate of unemployment, and the indigenous industries of fishing, crofting, and weaving have not significantly modernized. The Western Isles is a Labour parliamentary seat, but returned an SNP member in the 1970s.

The Case

The terms of argument about development strategy in northern North Atlantic and northern European societies seem to have remained essentially unchanged during the last thirty years. The issue was – and is – "big or small?" Industrial or intermediate technology? Wholesale transformation or marginal adaptation? Of course it is not a peculiarly northern argument, and has perhaps become even more pointed now in the wake of the economic and technological transformations of the 1980s, which have led to deindustrialization, de-skilling, unstable markets, recession, and environmentalism throughout the capitalist world. Since the Second World War, the argument in Shetland has been a matter of popular discourse, by no means limited to the professionals. The terms of the debate are unaltered – big or small? – although the scale of each alternative has certainly changed; and it is now less concerned with how to keep tradition alive, than with how tradition is articulated with economic activity and dynamism.

In the early 1960s, a group of activists, professionals, and intellectuals who crystallized around the Shetland Council of Social Service and the quarterly magazine, *New Shetlander,* were enthusiasts for the small-scale development of indigenous resources, arguing that the economic survival of a remote, depleted, and politically marginal population could not sensibly be made to depend on substantial investment from the centre, and had also to recognize the very limited extent to which investment could be generated locally. For parts of Shetland, in particular Yell and Northmavine, the imperative was to find ways of stemming outmigration. Elsewhere, in Whalsay and Burra Isle, it was to capitalize on the development of the new, versatile fishing boats which could be rigged for seine nets in the autumn and winter, and for drift nets in the spring and summer. The existence of these rather different needs indicated that the iconic fisherman– crofter was already probably becoming something of an anachronism, and that the pluralistic activities of the rural household were contracting and becoming more specialized. Thirty years later, these enthusiasts who composed the first development plans, who experimented with canning reested mutton soup, and who cast their eyes over the Faroes as a model both of economic and political development, though mostly now retired, are still active in various capacities as advocates of appropriate development, still looking sceptically on any suggestion that in Shetland and comparable localities big might be axiomatically confused with beautiful.

Of course, much has happened in the meantime. Shetland acquired an oil industry and, in consequence, the infrastructure has been radically transformed; her population has grown by some 25 per cent. The fishing fleet has grown massively both in catching power and value: the Whalsay fleet alone, valued at £250,000 in 1962, is worth more than £35 million today, a considerable asset in a community of only one thousand people. The latest addition to the fleet, a second hand purse-seiner, was purchased in 1993 for more than £4 million (see Cohen 1987). But the value of the catch by the Shetland fleet has been surpassed by that of farmed salmon which, uniquely in Scotland, are owned privately in Shetland, because of the fortuitous advantages of udal law which derive from the islands' Norse heritage. Yet throughout this transformation of the rural economy the debate has continued: big or small? Each new capital-intensive development in the fishery has caused passionate argument, both because of the debts incurred, and because of the putative threats to marine stocks posed by increased catching power. Repeated interventions by British and European governments and by the European Commission have politicized the issue of conservation, and have stimulated advocacy for the protection and enhancement of privileged local access to stocks in "Shetland waters." Organizations espousing political devolution have periodically flourished and declined. And there still hovers over all this a sense of precariousness related to the historical spectre of depopulation. Long before the first oil came ashore, for example, there was profound and proper concern about its longevity. And the arguments about depletion of the fish stocks have always been conducted with an eye on the future, on the next generation of fishermen, rather than just on next year's catch.

This being so, there has been a proper determination not to permit the arguments to be alienated by the politicians. They are still conducted in the wheelhouse, the kitchen, the pub, and on the pier. And because they are everybody's property and are based on everyone's experience, the person who presumes to raise them in public is required to do so with a proper regard for local expertise and information. Flights of rhetorical fancy will not do; too much is felt to be at stake. The uninformed public voice is commonly treated in Shetland and elsewhere in northern and western Scotland as, quite simply, irresponsible. Of course in Shetland, as elsewhere in northern Europe and the northern North Atlantic, social relations are conducted within an idiom of egalitarianism – I make no claims about the *reality* of egalitarianism – which makes suspect the motives and credentials of anyone who is willing to take the risk of expressing an opinion in public, or to assume a position of leadership. Successful leaders, those who may be regarded as exercising real influence, rather than just appearing to do so, have to pay very careful attention to the ways in which they speak publicly. If they have acquired locally a reputation for trustworthiness, it may well be less because of the objective content of what they have to say, than because their message is couched in terms which are locally recognizable as being authoritative, that is, in terms of which they are acknowledged to be the rightful owners.

It seems reasonable to assume that these local idioms have changed, more subtly than I think is sometimes supposed. But they have not disappeared. What has changed is the degree to which the context of such utterances can be regarded as local, and context clearly impinges on the claim of ownership. People have become increasingly used to seeing and hearing their local leaders on a non-local platform, yet are reluctant to change the way they listen to them. What is said may be modulated by the speaker's assumption of a different kind of idiom; but his or her local audience hears the message in their characteristic register. The obverse is true as well: a speaker may simply be insensitive to local idiom; and, as a consequence, delivers a message which is received in a quite different way, of which he or she may be blithely unaware. The nature of the rhetoric is itself becoming an issue.

My example of such dissonance highlights with a nice explicitness the demand for "responsibility" among those who presume to lead. In 1992, John Goodlad, the leader of the Shetland Fishermen's Association, delivered the annual Sabhal Mor lecture at Sabhal Mor Ostaig, the Gaelic College in Skye. His lecture was published in Shetland, was later televised elsewhere in Scotland, and has been republished in English, Gaelic, and Shetlandic. It precipitated an intriguing discussion between him and an interlocutor who was a prominent member of the 1960s enthusiasts. I do not claim that these two men are representative of any groups or bodies of opinion, although they may be. However, they are both experienced and authoritative advocates of development policy for Shetland (and elsewhere in the Scottish Highlands and Islands) who take Scotland as their political frame of reference, and whose fundamental disagreements of interpretation and view may otherwise be masked by their use of similar iconic terms.

First, what did Goodlad say? He insisted that the kind of fisheries development which had taken place in Shetland could provide a model for other areas of the Highlands and Islands. He was talking to a Western Isles and west Highlands (and largely Gaelic-speaking) audience, of course, whose local fishery had resisted capital-intensive reinvestment, but had remained small-scale and part-time, eschewing both the so-called industrial fishery and the purse net. To make this argument, he had to collapse substantially not only disparities within Shetland, but the many significant differences between Shetland and other areas of the Highlands and Islands. He pointed to the strength of culture in Shetland and among "the Gaels," symbolized by their distinctive languages, which, he argued, gave them strong senses of identity. Such identity, he suggested, was a prerequisite for economic dynamism: "After all, we can only decide where we are going if we understand where we have come from" (Goodlad 1993:13). Shetland experience shows that "there is nothing to prevent our communities (i.e. communities elsewhere in the Scottish islands) developing commercially successful fishing industries" (Goodlad 1993:15).

In collapsing Shetland and the Western Isles, he contrasts them unfavourably with the Faroese, who have used their political autonomy to take control of local waters and to give their own fishing fleet privileged access to their stocks (Goodlad 1993:17). He insists that this is the way the Highlands and Islands must go: political devolution used to stimulate large-scale economic development based on a technologically-modern, capital-intensive fishery:

> There is little room for the 'crofter-fishermen' in the modern world of fishing. Full time specialists with technology comparable to the best of the Faroese and Norwegian fleets is needed. (Goodlad 1993:19)

So, he demands, let us be damned with those weekend environmentalists trying to preserve their idyllic holiday retreats — marine stocks are substantial, certainly large enough to double the Shetland take in Shetland waters without risking long-term damage to their reproductive capacity:

> Emotionally based arguments, totally lacking in scientific validity, made by people from outwith our area now directly jeopardise our economic future. Is it not the case that the environmental lobby could pose as big a threat to our communities as the clearances did in the past? (Goodlad 1993:27)

This is a far cry from the measured judgements of the academic fisheries geographer which he had been previously. How should we listen to him? Given the constraints of time, and the fact that he was addressing an essentially lay audience, it is understandable that the speaker may have felt justified in exploiting his rhetorical licence, rather than offering a closely reasoned argument. He had three major points to make. First, that the development of a commercial fishery in the west could be accomplished as successfully as in Shetland (a contention which treats as axiomatic the success of the Shetland fishery). Second, that the objective conditions which have enabled success in the one (ranging from the ubiquity of good natural harbours, to the existence of a supportive and substantial indigenous culture) were present also in the other. And third, that a necessary condition for further development is the achievement of substantial political autonomy.

I think we may reasonably assume that these three points are interrelated in the nationalist vision which emerged between the mid-1970s and the late 1980s. As I mentioned earlier, Shetlanders seem to have been left cold at the earlier date by the manifest insensitivity of the SNP to local rights – for example, to a substantial share of oil revenues and of the catch in local waters. It was in the aftermath of the 1974 general elections, and the 1978 referendum, that the nascent Orkney and Shetland Movements gathered momentum as entities separate from the SNP. During the 1980s, some convergence of views was negotiated and, in 1987, the SNP undertook not to oppose the joint Orkney and Shetland Movements' candidate at the general election. The candidate was John Goodlad. The Movements themselves did not contest the 1992 election, throwing their weight more or less officially behind the SNP. The focus had thus changed from the parochial distinctiveness of Shetland to the integrity of Scotland as a plausible framework for policy and common action.

I was intrigued by the response to the lecture made to me by a development policy specialist who has had a close engagement both with Shetland and the Western Isles (and elsewhere in Scotland, Scandinavia, and the South Atlantic) for more than thirty years. His detailed critique of the lecture struck me initially as somewhat excessive: he seemed to be addressing the lecture as if it were an academic exegesis rather than essentially political rhetoric. However, my experience of Whalsay has convinced me that the tone of his critique is exquisitely sensitive to that of the critical scrutiny which the lecture would have received there, however it may have been treated elsewhere. Be that as it may, I treat his reaction here strictly in its own terms as the views of a person with long and expert knowledge of the Highlands and Islands and with a commitment to the integrity of Scotland as a political and policy frame of reference.

Among his points were the following. First, that while it is indisputably the case that "culture" and "identity" are significant factors in development, it is not clear whether they themselves explain economic dynamism, or are motivated by its obvious success. Second, he suggested that the success of the fishery in the Faroes could be explained by the absence of any economic alternative, in particular, by the absence of cultivable land. He chided John Goodlad for his sweeping condemnation of environmentalists; he challenged his dismissal of the Faroes as an appropriate comparator to the Western Isles and Shetland in the matter of political autonomy. But his three central substantive points of attack were these: the assumption that the fishery had to develop along capital-intensive lines; the assertion that a substantially increased local catch could be accomplished without inflicting profound damage on marine stocks; and the looseness of John Goodlad's arguments about political autonomy. I will pass over the first two to concentrate on the third, the autonomy argument.

He questioned Goodlad's call for "more say in our own affairs." What, he asked, are the aggregations? Who are "we"? Shetland? The Western Isles? The Northern and Western Isles together? The Highlands and Islands? Scotland? The most trenchant aspect of his critique called attention to the essentially rhetorical style of the lecture, implying to me his view that the flimsiness of the argument was irresponsible, given Goodlad's public prominence. He argued that Goodlad's standing and acknowledged expertise placed on him an "obligation to treat the matter more comprehensively" for the general benefit. In this regard, he felt that the imputation to the Western Isles of a "lack of dynamic" might prove to be damaging in itself.[5]

It is precisely this demand for responsibility in the public expression of opinion that seems to me to chime with the kinds of demands that Whalsay people make; indeed, it is a value to which they claim "ownership." In my experience, discussion of the fishery in Whalsay is meticulously informed. Fishermen follow international developments closely and regularly read the fisheries press. Of all Shetland's prominent political figures, I would risk the view that John Goodlad is the one who is held in the highest regard by most people in Whalsay, not just because of his prodigious work rate in Lerwick, Edinburgh, and Brussels, not just because of his record of far-sightedness in matters of policy and of organization, but also because of his unquestioned expertise on the fishery. His public statements on fishing may have been contentious, but they have always had the required properties of control, of information, and of selflessness. I do not think that the local admiration for Goodlad is unduly biased by the fact that he is half-Whalsay by descent. I suspect that the tone of the lecture would have struck many of his Whalsay admirers as out of character, in a similar way that it impressed his critic as, literally, irresponsible; it was outside what may have been regarded as his title to ownership. In the mouth of a politician, it might have seemed unremarkable, but the idiom of political rhetoric tends not to be well received in Whalsay. It is suspect; and I think the same is probably true of other areas which have been impressed historically by their own precariousness.

Goodlad has continued to insist on his view of the necessary course of development, seeing a movement towards large-scale technology as the irresistible tide of history. At the 1993 meeting of the Scottish Rural Forum, he repeated his view that the Western Isles and Shetland must be at the cutting edge of innovation, or they would fall behind with dire consequences. One of the most contentious aspects of his lecture was the proposition that Shetland might serve as a paradigm for the Western Isles, which glosses over the substantial cultural and socio-economic differences which obtain between the two island groups. For obvious reasons, he also neglected to mention the social risks and costs which were entailed in the decision of Shetland fishermen to reinvest during the late 1970s and early 1980s, notwithstanding the financial success of the fishery and the tradition of borrowing to invest which had become established, at least in Whalsay, since the 1960s. In order to qualify for bank loans (which were themselves a precondition of grants) skippers and their co-owners had to raise substantial deposits. In many cases, this was done by putting very considerable pressure on their close kinsmen. I have notes recording the complaints, resentment, and anxieties of fathers, grandfathers, brothers, and even unrelated friends and neighbours to what most of them felt to be irresistible pressure to make loans in circumstances in which they genuinely feared financial disaster. Goodlad's interlocutor correctly drew attention to the fallacy of assuming that Whalsay could provide a model for *anywhere* else, let alone the relatively disadvantaged Western Isles.

He also insisted on two other central objections: first, that it is far from axiomatic that "big and high-earning" is preferable to "small but content"; and second, that increasing substantially the local catch must place the stock at grave risk. He cited as an example the destruction of the Atlantic-Scandinavian herring stock between the Faroes and Iceland. There seem to me to be two matters of general interest in this argument. The first, to which I have already drawn attention, is the substantive dispute about development strategy. The second, and less tangible, concerns the public presentation of contentious statements on which the future of communities may be deemed to hang. The critic did not suggest to me that Goodlad's opinions were irresponsible (although he left no doubt about his view that some of them were profoundly flawed); rather, that it was in the manner of their expression that he failed in his "obligation." This amounts to saying that what passes elsewhere as acceptable political discourse will *not* do here in the marginal, vulnerable, but politically sophisticated and literate communities of the Scottish periphery.

It seems to me that it was the *style* of the lecture – exceptionable, even perhaps unnoticeable elsewhere – which triggered the critique and which, I believe, would have raised the hackles of fishermen and others in Whalsay with whom I have discussed related matters over more than twenty years. It suggested a looseness which was typical of "politics," and not, therefore, of island discourse. In Whalsay, this position would not be taken out of a feeling of intellectual superiority, but out of a fear of what might be at stake. It is the precariousness and peripherality of remote communities, not their intellectual pretensions, which make them expect more of their leaders. John Goodlad, I have suggested, had a different kind of agenda: first, to be provocative; second, and far more important, to show how increased political autonomy, far from being an esoteric constitutional issue, could bear directly on the most pressing issues of everyday life. But the imputation to him of "irresponsibility" followed from a view of his lecture as flimsy rhetoric. For *his* purposes, only rhetoric, and, specifically, *nationalist* rhetoric, would do.

I use the word "rhetoric" descriptively rather than judgmentally: I do not think that he was engaged in a gratuitous attempt to manipulate or to impress; and, indeed, his critic does not accuse him of this. He does suggest, though, that his argument was loose in ways which are not characteristic either of his *local* discourse or of his audience. I would not suggest anything other than that the man was saying what he thought; and that, if there was an argumentational looseness in his presentation, it derived from his wish to relate to one another his three central propositions: that increasing the local proportion of the catch would not harm stocks; that Shetland and the Western Isles are broadly similar; and – the *coup de grâce* – that to increase Shetland's success, and to extend it to other regions of Scotland, require substantial political autonomy.

Elegant and intriguing analyses of political speech are often inclined to neglect the prosaic possibilities that people do sometimes mean what they say; or, as Robert Dahl (1962) suggested thirty years ago, that speakers become committed to what they say; or, as David Parkin (1984) suggests, that people may speak in the ways that they do because they regard them as culturally appropriate. John Goodlad was out of his usual context. It may be that he saw himself as giving an essentially political speech, and adopted the idiom which he thought appropriate to his audience and to the occasion. Had the lecture been given in Shetland, he might not have spoken in quite these terms. I think what lies between him and his critic is only partly a matter of opinion; the other difference which divides them was his choice of rhetorical mode. Of course, the criticism of him goes beyond substantive differences of opinion. It extends to a question of "responsibility," to the assertion that he had failed in his "obligation" by his choice of rhetorical mode. This aspect at least of the critique must itself be regarded as a rhetoric, the rhetoric of *local* discourse.

But the implication of the critique – and this is certainly the view that I would expect to find in Whalsay – is that a departure from local discourse is irresponsible. Moving from the local is moving from the specific to the generalized, from the empirical to the abstracted, from the experiential to the theoretical, and such moves entail the falsification of a concrete reality. There is an important lesson here for nationalists. Nationalism may be compelling if it can be mediated by personal and local experience, but it risks becoming implausible when it tries to alienate and appropriate that experience and to extend it to people from whom one has always claimed significant difference – that is, when it impugns the saliency of valued boundaries. To return to the themes of personal and Scottish nationalism, it impugns people's democratic right to make the nation for themselves. But of course the logic of nationalism is precisely to privilege national boundaries over those to which people more frequently orientate themselves. That was the speaker's problem.

Clearly, the case I have introduced here concerns only two people, of opposed views, both unusual men who I would hesitate to depict as typical of any tendency or of anyone other than themselves. However, their dispute does illustrate a real problem for nationalism which is to develop a discourse with which people in diverse parts of the society can feel comfortable, a difficulty which is exacerbated when that society, like Scotland, has well-developed traditions of local distinctiveness and of individuality which may be emphasized or glossed over as people believe the circumstances demand. Politicians may believe that they can do it because they do not perceive the difficulty: they claim to know what people think, and spend time and effort trying to put words into our minds, if not our mouths. The manufacture of national identity might reasonably be regarded as the attempt to diminish people's consciousness of their individuality and distinctiveness, and to superimpose over this a consciousness both of their similarity to their co-nationals and their difference from others.

The rhetoric of nationalism attempts to create a homology between the individual and the nation. From the top downwards, the individual is represented as the nation writ small; from the bottom up, the nation is the individual writ large. As Handler argued in his study of Quebec (1988), the relationship between the individual and nation has to be engineered and actively maintained, with the nation depicted as the realization of individuals' aspirations for their selves, and individuals' aspirations tailored to what the nation is able to deliver. The iconic intimacy of Scottish collective identity, its proximity to the circumstances of everyday life, would suggest that such an association of selfhood with nationalism should be plausible and persuasive. Yet my case shows that it might well founder on the flawed decision about what to say, where, and to whom, and thus illustrates the sheer difficulty of accommodating a convincing collective identity to the plurality of interests which it must represent.

But however ingeniously contrived rhetoric or other celebrations of the nation may be, they are still viewed from the unique vantages of sectarian local interest or of the self. Politicians and the state overestimate their abilities to culture thought and to subordinate, even to eliminate these more fundamental interests. The symbols they use may be persuasive: the flag, the language, "Scottishness," "culture" itself. But the power which these symbols exercise lies in providing us with the means by which to think, rather than in compelling us to think specific things. Their assumption to the contrary privileges culture over thinking selves, instead of seeing it as the product of thinking selves. The problem for nationalist discourse is simultaneously to leave the individual (and the locality) with the sense of having interpretive space within which to manoeuvre and to experience and express difference, while also contriving to define, or at least, to limit the space as "national."[6]

Notes

1. This chapter is based substantially on an article forthcoming in a special issue of *Anthropological Forum*, and entitled "Ownership, responsibility, and the rhetoric of nationalism: a Scottish case." I am most grateful to the editors, Noel Dyck and Philip Moore, for their permission to incorporate large parts of the text here. For their comments on earlier drafts, I am espe-

cially grateful to Frank Bechhofer, Ladislav Holy, David McCrone, Tom Nairn, Lindsay Paterson, and Robert Storey.
2. I have explored this distinction extensively in many publications and over many years, but most exhaustively in Cohen 1994a.
3. In a recent book, Lindsay Paterson (1994) has argued powerfully that the extent of this discretion has been seriously underestimated.
4. Space here does not permit the citation of pertinent literature, which is so extensive that any selection would be merely arbitrary. However, in my *Personal Nationalism* (Cohen 1994b), I deal explicitly with a specific body of contemporary nationalist writing to which these themes are central.
5. The occasion of the lecture closely followed the collapse of the Bank of Credit and Commerce International, as a result of which the Western Isles Council lost virtually its entire cash reserve of £24 million. For a community which was already regarded as marginal, indeed as anachronistic, this calamity was widely regarded as having left the Islands defenceless.
6. The same problem applies to attempts to contrive ethnic identity.

References

Cohen, A.P. (1987). *Whalsay: symbol, segment and boundary in a Shetland island community*. Manchester: Manchester University Press.

———. (1994a). *Self consciousness: an alternative anthropology of identity*. London: Routledge.

———. (1994b). *Personal nationalism: a preliminary view of some rites, rights and wrongs*. Distinguished Lecture to the Society for the Anthropology of Europe, Annual Conference of the American Anthropological Association.

Dahl, R.A. (1962). *Who governs? Democracy and power in an American city*. New Haven: Yale University Press.

Goodlad, J. (1993). *Shaping the future – a Shetland perspective: the Sabhal Mor Lecture 1992*. Stornoway: Acair.

Handler, R. (1988). *Nationalism and the politics of culture in Quebec*. Madison: University of Wisconsin Press.

Parkin, D.J. (1984). "Political language." *Annual Review of Anthropology* 13:345-65.

Paterson, L. (1994). *The Autonomy of Modern Scotland*. Edinburgh: Edinburgh University Press.

12

The Multiple Landscapes of Transnational Asian Women in the Diaspora

Parminder Bhachu

In this paper, I discuss the complex nature of migration and settlement. I point to the variations in migration and settlement trajectories, which produce a range of diasporic cultures in which Asian women are situated internationally. The vast majority of literature available on the subject treats migration as a single first movement of direct migrants to their destination economies. Yet there are direct, twice, and thrice migrant women, many of whom are involved in fourth movements, especially in the 1990s. These multiple migrations are important to the ways different migrants view themselves, to their orientations to a homeland, and to the impact of these movements on cultural reproduction in local, regional, and transnational contexts. I propose a more complex conceptualization of their economic and cultural locations than is conveyed in the literature and by media images, where Asian women are frequently represented as "working-class victims" forced to struggle with what are constructed as their "oppressive cultural systems." However, Asian women actively engage with international economies and occupy a range of class niches, which is further reflected in their negotiation of their cultural landscapes and consumption styles.

I want to suggest that in a way all of us speak only from the perspective of the local, even though we are all positioned in the spaces of the global. Perhaps the local and the global are the same moment. The moment of the production of new diasporic spaces, of new cultural forms, and new landscapes results in the creation of national and local identities that are increasingly being contested from the margins. Immigrants and migrants – the new nationals – are generating new versions of the local and producing new versions of local knowledge in the new spaces in global economies. These novel textures are produced in existing cultural geographies (what I am doing too) through the interpretation of local spaces.

What are the cultural consequences of dislocation and displacement through migration? How is cultural baggage relocated? I examine some of these issues by focusing my work on cultural reproduction, especially as related to consumption through the wedding economy. I focus on the new forms, the new rhythms and impetuses, which are as much products of globalization as they are of the local and regional contexts. For example, what is the impact of electronic technology on this and the electronic mediation of the diasporic world? What are the new resources that are mobilized by immigrants in the production and reproduction of their cultural bases in diasporic settings? My interest, in particular, is in the production of the local in these settings. For example, what is the nature of cultural identities as they are produced in global conditions which are, in a way, highly local spaces?

I focus on South Asian women in Britain in the 1990s to present a gendered discussion about the production of the diasporian aesthetic through an examination of their cultural patterns in the 1990s in global contexts of Asian diaspora. I point to the transformative role of British Asian women in the construction of their identities and the local diasporic spaces they occupy. These cultural spaces emerge from their simultaneous location in the local, the national, and the global, to innovatively reconstitute and produce new cultural forms and images. I emphasize their agency and their role as cultural entrepreneurs and identity makers who play a transformative role in engaging with their cultural systems and arenas of consumption to produce new cultural forms in Britain. These patterns are as much part of their ethnic cultural base as they are of their socialization to particular local and regional and class cultures in Britain. Such diasporic cultural production is, for me, a form of the production of the local in the new spaces generated by the enormous motion and movements of people in the 1990s.

Diasporic Cultural Spaces: global networks and local productions

Cultural products have multiple sites of production, but are essentially locally produced. They have a social and cultural life that emerges from specific places, migration histories, and local political and symbolic economies. For example, there is a local specificity to the consumption style of a Brummie (from Birmingham in the British Midlands) Asian woman and the interpretation of her identity and dowry which grows out of her socialization to the codes of her locality. These specificities have widespread global currency and are locally produced. Another example of this is the music of Apache Indian in Britain, which has the specificity of a young Punjabi man raised in multi-ethnic, working-class Birmingham. His music topped both the reggae and bhangra charts in 1991, a year in which he was also voted Best Newcomer at the British Reggae Industry Awards. He has played to packed stadiums in India and is famous and controversial in the international South Asian diaspora whilst at the same time being authenticated by African Caribbean diasporic communities. Apache himself is Steven Kapur, whose Hindu Punjabi parents migrated from the Jalandhar district of Punjab, which has produced the majority of Punjabi migrants internationally. Anthropologist Les Back, who has known and written about Apache Indian's music, states:

> Apache's music is a cultural crossroads, a meeting place where the languages and rhythms of four continents intermingle producing a culture that cannot be reduced to its component parts. Rather, it needs to be understood in the context of the global passage of linguistic and cultural forms and the localities where they converge; the culture is simultaneously both local and global ... *The new form was dubbed bhangramuffin* ... The types of 'fusion' that Apache's music personifies is not arbitrary. What his music demonstrates is a series of departures, identifications which traverse a number of continents then return, and pause at Birmingham's cultural crossroads only to re-depart again.... Apache Indian, answering the call of black music, heralds a subcontinent with a *diasporic triple consciousness* that is simultaneously inside and beyond the nations through which it passes. (1995: [forthcoming]; first emphasis mine)

Similar cultural products include the books of British Indian writer Salman Rushdie, products of his "mongrel self" (he states) and a hybrid space in the diaspora which are potently produced in his literature. He characterizes his latest book, *The Moor's Last Sigh*, as one centred on an "image of miscegenation of cultural hybridity." We could look also at the music of PBN – Punjabi by Nature – a Toronto-based group of Canadian-born South Asians whose music has been influenced by Apache Indian's bhangramuffin, his innovative combination of Rap and Bhangra (Britishified Punjabi harvest music). PBN produces these sounds through their socialization to the Toronto scene. This new music is as much a reflection of their diasporic Punjabiness, as it is of their Canadianness, as it is of their location in the subcultures of Toronto, as it is of the trends of global music! It is a product of "quadruple diasporic consciousness," to extend Les Back's metaphor. So what is the local in such a case?

It is precisely those spaces that are also the most challenging to the notions of citizenship, national identities, and character. We could also think about the production of the local without necessarily referring to national character and the textures of the nation-state. In the case of Britain, as Stuart Hall (1991:20-21) has stated, "The 'English eye' sees everything else but is not so good at recognizing that it is itself actually looking at something ... That is to say, it is strongly centred; knowing where it is, what it is it places everything else. And the thing that is wonderful about English identity is that it didn't place the colonized other, it placed *everybody* else." In a post-colonial British context, the colonized other is in England and is "English" – a *new European* – an identity produced without reference to the "Englishness" manufactured for the colonies and colonial domination. This latter was an identity that grew out of power and which negated all sorts of internal class, regional, and local differences. In a way, this was a highly local phenomenon of the construction of an exclusive commanding identity which could place all "others." It is precisely this type of identity that is being contested by, and through, the new textures of the diaspora, through the reproduction of the cultural baggage brought in by migrants as a result of movement and displacement. Such textures are having a fundamental impact, through the contestations of the migrants' second- and third-generation children, who in representing themselves are usurping hegemonic spaces to create new spaces and notions of citizenship.

For example, Southall, in West London, is an early site of South Asian (mainly Punjabi Sikh) settlement. This is an arena of the production of specific local versions of British identities, some of which concern working-class diasporic Punjabiness. This, indeed, is a version of Britishness in the late twentieth century that is not a product of Britain's colonies and its commonwealth but that is a local, home-grown identity. Of course, it is derived from a colonial context, but in Britain the baggage is locally reproduced, reconstituted, and resynthesized, especially by the young who are locally born. Their Punjabiness is as much a facet of their Britishness as it is of the cultural base with which their parents migrated and which is reproduced in specific sub-class and sub-cultural British contexts. So, what does it mean to be a new European, a new American, a new Norwegian person? What are the implications of Paul Gilroy's statement (the title of his 1987 book): "There ain't no black in the Union Jack?" So much of this has to do with the local and its impact on dominant models of knowledge production and constructions of identities, notions of citizenship, and nationality.

I will examine some of the above further in the context of my work on the wedding economy and the transformative role of Asian women in negotiating this. I will also refer to work that I have been doing on the commoditization processes of the wedding economy. I focus on the content of dowries, and in particular, the Punjabi suits. These clothing items constitute a large section of this gift exchange system and are commodity forms which have a local specificity and are locally interpreted. Although these cultural forms have become greatly standardized through global markets in the past five years, their interpretation has been fundamentally influenced and determined by sub-class and sub-cultural styles and the cultural baggage of migration.

Place and Space: my location in an American town

Firstly, some background on my own position in generating my own "local": my point is that the local is fluid and that local knowledges are being continuously generated. One cannot take the local for granted as it is constantly manufactured. But what is the local for me? I am a thrice migrant European woman of East African Asian descent, who is now a permanent resident of the U.S. So what sort of multiple diasporic networks and multiplicities of diasporic consciousness produce my "local"?

I have started a new life twice in the United States, first in Los Angeles and then in Worcester, Massachusetts. In both these places, I initially knew no one at all. Hence, much of my local is fundamentally tied to the diasporic cultural base to which I was socialized and which was reproduced in Britain by the twice migrant groups to which my family and extended kinship group belong. The subcultures and the British class cultures to which I was socialized as a South Londoner have an influence in the production of my "American" local. This production of a relocated local, of course, does have a territorial space. However, its production is not territorially located in the U.S., but is generated through the landscape that I alone have created for myself. It is produced through the networks that I carry with me and which sustain me, the majority of which are not based in Worcester or in Massachusetts or in the U.S. generally. These transnational networks are multi-located, and are vigilantly maintained through the use of modern electronic technology such as the telephone and cyberspace. Thus, the specificity of relocated identity reflects multiplicity of movements, yet at the same time it is very much a facet of the production of the local.

Direct, Twice, and Thrice Migrants: transnational Asian women

Direct, twice, and thrice migrant women represent different histories of migration and settlement in the diaspora. In previous work (Bhachu 1985, 1993; Gibson and Bhachu 1988) on the twice migrant British Asians who migrated from the Indian subcontinent to East Africa, and thence to Britain in the late 1960s, I demonstrated that migrants and settlers have differential skills and experiences of migration and settlement. This diversity is further reflected in their destination economies in cultural reproduction, in economic participation rates, and in the varying speeds with which the infrastructures of their communities are established. I explored the dynamics of migration through an analysis of the migrants' cultural base as it is reproduced through the axes of race, caste, and class in the British scene.

Experienced settlers, twice (that is in Britain) and thrice migrant women (in the United States context) possess considerable expertise in the management of their minority status, in the reconstruction of their ethnicities, and in the negotiation of their cultural systems. Their communities migrated from rural India in the late nineteenth century to East Africa, where they urbanized and established defined East African Asian identities. From Africa, they migrated to metropolitan Britain in the late 1960s, after their jobs were Africanized in post-independence East Africa. Many of them further migrated to the United States, Australia, and other European countries in the 1980s and 1990s. As relatively prosperous twice migrants in Britain with great command of mainstream skills (in comparison to the less experienced direct migrants who are not as skilled at the "game of migration"), they also occupy separate class as well as caste positions and maintain exclusive marriage and community circuits. These are precisely some of the people who constitute the thrice migrants in the United States. As expert migrants, they were able to enhance their already considerable migration skills initiated and developed in Africa, established and refined in Britain, and further reproduced efficiently in the United States and in other tertiary destination economies in the diaspora.

Twice, thrice, and quadruple migrants possess powerful communication networks, which are facilitated by the ease of global communications. Their command of European and global bureaucratic skills and of the English language has given them considerable expertise at reproducing their cultural bases and community infrastructures in a range of countries. Such a scenario is in complete contrast to that of the less "culturally and ethnically skilled" direct migrants, who are often characterized in the early stages of settlement by home orientation and a "myth of return." An important consequence of the latter characteristic is that the resources they generate in their destination economies are frequently remitted to a country of origin, where their positive (or for that matter negative) reference groups and status hierarchies remain. For direct migrants, migration, especially in the initial stages, is frequently a temporary economically goal-orientated move. For twice and thrice migrants, however, migration is not a sojourn but a more permanent move to settle. They lack home orientation and are geared toward staying in their destination economies from the point of entry and retaining their capital and resources. The phases of settlement that apply to direct migrants, from preliminary bachelor households to the later reconstitution of their communities, and then family unification many years later, are highly condensed in the case of multiple migrants. Twice and thrice migrants often migrate with three-generation family units or are united with their families within a year or two of settlement. Their communities possess a balanced age profile, unlike the direct migrants who often have a much younger age profile and only two-generation nuclear families.

This pattern of migration involving a series of moves is applicable to a wide range of groups in the United States: for example, the Vietnamese, Armenians, Iranians, and so on. It also applies to migrants in other countries, especially Canada, Australia, New Zealand, and prosperous European and Asian countries such as Germany and Japan. Situated as these experienced migrants are in an international milieu, migration in the 1980s and 1990s is for them no longer a first move, but a second, third, or even fourth movement; thus they constitute a transnational people with established international, national, and local connections. These features are critical to the reproduction of their cultural bases and ethnicities and to their engagement with the economies and polities of their countries of settlement. In all these processes of the construction and reconstruction of their identities and the reproduction of diasporic cultures, migrant women are the key actors. I turn now to my examination of Punjabi suits, one particular commodity form that constitutes a very large part of the *daaj* – the dowry.

Female Economic Activity and New Cultural Forms

The new cultural patterns and identities generated by these diasporic women are evident in their consumption patterns, which are analyzed here through the wedding economy. This wedding gift exchange system has become more elaborate since migration, especially as a result of women's entry into the waged labour market in Britain. The translation of their earnings, especially by the brides into specific parts of dowries, has transformed and reinterpreted a "traditional" cultural arena that has existed for centuries. One reason for this development is more financial control by young Asians than ever before, a situation evidenced by recent labour market statistics.

Asian women actively engage in the British economy, contrary to popular stereotypes. In fact, in certain cases they have higher economic activity rates than indigenous white women: twice migrant East African Asian women have slightly higher rates of employment (69 per cent) than either indigenous white women or the directly migrant Indian and Pakistani women (*Employment Gazette* 1987). This higher rate of economic activity among East African Asian women in Britain is a product of their urban experiences in formal employment sectors in Africa, in contrast to the mainly rural background of the majority of the directly migrant women from the subcontinent. It is also a consequence of the continuation of the employment trends established prior to migration from metropolitan Africa to metropolitan Britain. For example, the number of Asian female employees in Kenya had risen from 600 in 1948 to 3,750 in 1962, which was 10 per cent of the total Asian labour force there (Ghai 1965:95). By 1967, this statistic had risen to 18 per cent (Ghai 1970). This period coincided with the most intense amount of Asian migration to Britain from Africa after the full impact of the Africanization policies on them in the mid-1960s.

Labour market figures from the 1990s point to a great variation amongst ethnic groups and also emphasize that unemployment rates for Indian women have changed little since the 1980s. This is the case even when unemployment for men has increased twofold for most minorities, except for African Asians (*Employment Gazette*, May 1994:147-160). For example, in the years 1984, 1985 and 1986, and again in 1992 and 1993, the International Labor Organisation (ILO) unemployment rate for the minority groups was roughly twice that for the white population. Unemployment rates rose most for men of Pakistani/Bangladeshi and black origin. "*For Indian women, however, unemployment rates have increased very little since 1989 – little more than those of women in the white population*" (157; emphasis mine). The other interesting factor that emphasizes the class variations of Asian women (who are, as stated earlier, commonly portrayed as working class) is that a greater percentage of Asian women are professionals: "Among women in employment, the proportion in non-manual occupations are around two thirds in each of the ethnic groups. The proportion of women in the professional social class was lower than for men, but *women in all the main minority groups were a little more likely than their white counterparts to be professionals (5% overall compared with 2%)*" (53; emphasis mine).

There is definitely more money *controlled* by women since migration, with the increase in waged labour market participation (Bhachu 1988). It should also be emphasized that Indian and African Asian women have generally more employment than men, even if not in "appropriate for qualifications" jobs. This increases the possibility of certain types of consumer behaviour and ability to expend cash according to women's own choices. This situation is a more salient facet of the diaspora, where expenditures and spending choices are not dependent on parental income only, and where there is a certain amount of control over disposable income. However, it is also important to bear in mind that there is generally low employment for minorities and two incomes are necessary for the viability of a household unit. In a number of cases it is dependent on one, which is currently often the female income. However, despite this lack of male employment, it is also the case that the labour market profile of Asian women is complex. They occupy a range of class positions and regional opportunity structures, and many more are proportionally in the professional/managerial sectors than are their white and Afro-Caribbean and black counterparts. These varied economic activity rates and economic histories of Asian women fundamentally determine the reinterpretation and reproduction of the wedding gift exchange system in the diaspora.

Migration and Dowries in the Diaspora

As I have discussed, dowries, which represent the legitimate and recognized property rights of women, have become more elaborate since migration to Britain, as a result of women's entry into the waged labour market. Young Sikh women play a central role in manufacturing dowries, and the arena of dowry in the 1980s and 1990s in Britain has become a more important realm of creative consumption and reinterpretation than ever before (Bhachu 1985; 1986; 1988). It is a cultural idiom that has always been relevant and has seen significant inflation. Its commoditization is determined by the specificities of women's class positions and subcultural consumption styles, especially during the 1980s and 1990s, when most brides and younger Punjabi Sikh women are either locally born or have arrived as youngsters, and are therefore educated and socialized to regional and local British cultures. I first provide some brief background (detailed in Bhachu 1985; 1986) on the development of dowries as related to the migration process and settlement.

There is a close similarity between Punjabi Sikh notions of dowries – *daajs* – and those of high-status North Indians. The high-caste North Indian ideology of *kanyadaan*, the pure gift of a maiden for which no return is expected, and the accompanying *stridhanam*, exclusive female property, in the form of movable goods presented as pre-mortem inheritance from the patrimony (Goody 1975:1), also applies to Punjabi Sikhs regardless of their place within the migration chain and diaspora. Even though the same complex of beliefs as that of the high-caste Brahmans is widely accepted, these Sanskritic terms are rarely used by the Punjabi Sikhs. The four components of the *daaj* are clothes; gold for the bride; household goods including utensils, furniture, linen, quilts, kitchen gadgets, crockery, and consumer items; and affinal gifts. Large monetary gifts such as bridegroom price are non-existent, although the groom and his mother and father receive substantial wedding gifts, some of which are accompanied by small cash gifts.

These four major components, constituting the external framework of *daajs*, have remained stable with migration and diasporic cultural reproduction, although there have been content changes in the specific gifts presented. The designated recipients of wedding gifts have also shifted according to the various phases of migration and in response to structural changes in the household and power relations within families. For example, the *daajs* of the 1920s through 1940s presented in India and Africa were designated for the mother-in-law, the most powerful and senior female decision-maker within the domestic domain. She could redistribute the *daaj*, often using it for further gift-giving. The bride of this period had direct control only of her *muklawa* (a presentation of a smaller volume of much higher quality gifts similar to those presented in the *daaj*), which was received from her parents at the consummation of the marriage, often anywhere from three to seven years after the wedding ceremony and the presentation of the original *daaj*. It was after this rite of passage that the bride took up permanent residence in her affinal home.

But the *daajs* of the 1950s and 1960s in Africa, and of the 1970s through 1990s in Britain in the case of the twice migrant women, have acquired a different meaning. Affinal gifts were separated so that the mother-in-law had little control over bridal clothing and gold, though household goods in the 1950s and 1960s were often absorbed into extended family households which were then quite prevalent. Bridal control over her sectors of the *daaj* increased, undermining the mother-in-law's redistributive authority over them. This development coincided with the *daajs* presented in Africa during the late 1940s and 1950s. The previous *daajs* belonged to brides whose marriages had taken place in India, where the joint family system was stronger and when families were less fragmented by migration. None of these Indian-married brides had her own separate household, though an increasing number were establishing nuclear residences in urban Africa, a trend reproduced by the vast majority of twice and thrice migrant brides in the 1970s through 1990s in Britain and the United States.

By the 1970s, the British *daajs* – unlike the African and Indian Punjabi ones – contained fewer heavier household goods (such as bedroom, dining-room, and sitting-room furniture), which had been increasingly replaced by expensive, portable consumer items. Also around this time, affinal goods were separated totally from those reserved for the bride. This trend of earmarking affinal gifts began in 1950s Africa and was the norm by the 1970s among twice migrant brides in Britain. This separation of affinal and bridal gifts partly reflected household changes but was also a consequence of shifting residential patterns, which facilitated the establishment of a separate home immediately after marriage. The dramatic increase in the earning powers of the brides in Britain catalysed this process; wives became contributors to house mortgage payments and sometimes initiators of house purchases. Also, because they helped to make the *daaj*, they expected to control it. None of the pre-1970s brides could exercise such options since their command over economic resources, if any, was considerably lower.

Thus changes in the structure and control of the *daaj* are a product of the migration process. Some of these trends are obvious among urban households in India as well, and are a consequence of changing female employment patterns and residential patterns. In East Africa, these processes had already begun (although they have become more firmly established in Britain) as families separated into nuclear units and as women became cash contributors to family incomes. Furthermore, the erosion of control by the affines over the redistribution of bridal gifts and of the residential choices of couples is a result of increased couple-orientation as opposed to the kinship group-orientation characteristic of the previous phases of migration. Spouse selection criteria have also shifted to take more account of couple suitability and personal demands rather than extended family expectations (Bhachu 1985).

Dowries that consisted of minimal items both for the bride and for her affinal kin in the late 1950s and 1960s have escalated in size in the 1970s, 1980s, and 1990s. The three components of the *daaj* are always adhered to rigidly for caste-endogamous East African Asian marriages. Nor has the structure of the *daaj* changed over time, even though there have been internal changes in the items presented, reflecting the move to urban Britain. The designation of certain components of the *daaj* has also shifted, reflecting structural changes in the organization of the household and the various power relations within it. It is clear that migration, changing residential patterns, and increased female economic activity in the diaspora from the late 1960s onward have favoured the brides.

Diasporic Dowries

I present here a brief summary of the escalation of the dowry system among Punjabi Sikhs since migration to Britain not so much to detail the process of elaboration within it (Bhachu 1985; 1986; 1988), but to point to the significant inflation within it of those spheres that directly concern the brides themselves.

The wedding economy has been greatly elaborated since the 1970s as the twice migrants have become increasingly settled. This inflation applies both to the rituals of the wedding procedure and to the dowry system, to which young brides are significant contributors. For example, as mentioned earlier, the clothing included in the dowries has become more extravagant in quantity and quality. Dowries have increased from eleven to twenty-one clothing items in the 1950s and 1960s in Africa, to twenty-one items in Africa and Britain, to anything from twenty-one to fifty-one items in the 1970s, 1980s and 1990s in Britain and the U.S. Some of the clothes are high-quality silk saris and prestigious designer clothes, which are designed by leading European and Bombay-based Indian designers, and which are accompanied by expensive Gucci and Bally shoes and bags, especially in the case of high-earning professional brides. The "standard" East African Punjabi Sikh dowry of twenty-one clothing items and a whole range of accompanying accessories and exclusive consumer items for the bride are always presented in Britain. This norm persists regardless of the standing of the families involved and has been further reproduced in the United States. Twenty-one clothing items are also commonly presented in the Indian subcontinent and Pakistan.

Although a twenty-one-item *daaj* constitutes the British/American/East African Sikh pattern, there are major qualitative differences in its content, depending on the earning powers of the brides themselves. A bride who has not earned wages in her own right before marriage invariably has the basic twenty-one pieces, but the wage-earning brides' *daajs* are much more elaborate and voluminous. Even though the latter *daajs* may be of twenty-one clothing items, they are characterized by the inclusion not only of higher quality garments and personal accessories but also of a larger range of consumer durables – china sets, silver cutlery, electronic music equipment, and exclusive linen, which the brides have purchased from their own earnings and which they themselves are likely to utilize and also control.

Much more than were the 1970s dowries in Britain or the earlier ones in Africa, the late 1980s and 1990s dowries of the Asian women born and raised in Britain are particularly reflective of the British subcultural and regional styles, especially in the interpretation of their traditional ethnic garments. Now there are dowries that are "very London," emerging from the various areas and subcultures of the capital and according to the class positions occupied by the brides and their kinship groups. Similarly, there are dowries that reflect the various regional styles and cultures and accord with dominant consumption choices of the areas in which the brides have been raised and the local cultures to which they have been socialized. These variations also apply to the identities and ethnicities negotiated and generated by these diasporan Asian women according to their situation in specific localities. London Asian women identify themselves differently from those in Northern Ireland and Scotland and according to the class positions and local subcultures they occupy.

These regional patterns are also obvious from the marriage circuits – an informal metropolitan hypergamy – which operates in Britain. London girls tend not to marry outside London and the southeast. If they are married out, in a majority of cases they move back to London to set up a nuclear residence within a couple of years of marriage. This is not a new phenomenon. In East Africa, Nairobi Sikh girls tended not to marry men living outside the capital, who were considered to be more orthodox and less socially skilled – *paindoos* – in comparison to the Nairobi-wallahs. In India, a number of women from the larger cities such as Delhi and Bombay prefer not to marry into the small-town, provincial families.

I have considerably simplified a complex procedure mainly to point out the elaborations in the bridal spheres that have seen the most significant inflation. By focusing on a cultural trait, I have tried to show that the *daajs* presented to and manufactured by young South Asian women are influenced by and are responsive to class and regional trends, being products of particular consumption patterns which encode facets of their experiences and locations and reflect lifestyles that shift continuously. All this also applies to the identities negotiated and generated by Asian women. These too have their specificities, which are multifaceted and activated differently according to the various contexts. They are products of particular periods and of symbolic and material economies. Just as the dowries of these women are ethnically assertive, so too are they assertive of local, regional, and class trends and of subcultural consumption styles. Thus, they have a local specificity, even though they are influenced by all the standardization processes that occur within global economies. However, their uptake of globally available products is specifically locally interpreted.

Commoditized Wedding Consumption

Some of the processes that are commoditizing the wedding economy include the mushrooming of ready-made clothes boutiques that have sprung up all over London and the Midlands, mostly in areas of high concentration of British Asians, although they are also found in other areas such as Park Lane, St. John's Wood, etc. The outfits sold in these shops cost anything from a lower range of £30 to £100 to an upper range that reaches £800. They are run by the wedding service providers – mostly Asian women – some of whom are locally born, whilst others are either raised here, or are from India and have excellent Indian connections which provide them with Indian-made goods and access to services.

What is interesting is the entry of high-prestige white British designers who have been prominent interpreters of consumption trends among British Asians. These include designers like Katherine Hamnett, Katherine Walker, and Zandra Rhodes (now bankrupt), who have designed Punjabi suits and saris, some of which are sold in high-status Indian clothing stores in London. There are also locally produced Punjabi clothes by young, British-trained, British Asian designers, mostly young women in their mid to late 20s. A global cultural and consumer flow which was unexpected in its impact but very important in determining wedding consumption for large metropolitan centres of the Asian diaspora – London, New York, Los Angeles, Sydney, etc. – is the ready availability of Bombay-based designer clothes. These consumer flows, which have a strong local impact, also include British-trained Bombay Indian designers – also mostly women, though there are a number of important male players – whose mail-order clothing catalogues have led to the ready accessibility of their clothes for mass-market consumption.

Reconceptualizing Asian Women in the Diaspora

Whole facets of the existence of Asian women are subject to and determined by common economic, class-based, and regionally specific forces, which have as much impact on the lives of white British women as they do on Asian women, regardless of their various ethnicities. My purpose in referring to Asian women's translation of their earnings into a cultural trait — thus commoditizing "traditional" patterns, which are as controlled by their locations within the "ethnic" social structures as by their British class niches and regional locations — is to show that their identities are produced and governed by the same range of forces and are activated differentially in varying contexts. They do not remain static and unchanging, but are negotiated according to the conditions in which they are situated, and in direct relationship to the powers of negotiation that the women can muster in shifting economic and political conditions.

These transnational women transform traditional cultural forms to manufacture newer and newer cultural forms which derive from their ethnic traditions and which are continuously formulated in the context of their class and local cultures. Yet there is little perception of these migrant women as active agents or as negotiators of their cultural values, which are frequently presented as non-negotiable entities enforced on them as passive victims by patriarchies and capitalist producers. The latter agencies are indeed powerful in determining cultural patterns and cultural reproduction; however, these women also have agency, which plays an important role in their choice of lifestyles and their function as innovators and originators of new cultural forms and new diasporic spaces.

And not only is the role of Asian migrant women as active agents in the transnational diaspora one that is largely absent in the literature, but the cultural locations and ethnicities of these women are represented as fixed and "ethnically absolute" (Gilroy 1987:13). The forces that are given analytic supremacy in the definition of their identities and ethnicity are those of exclusion and of external and contrived enforcement of their cultural values. In all, Asian women are portrayed as divorced from the influences of local trends and from other homogenizing forces that emanate from popular culture and are internationally applicable.[1] The assumptions found in the literature are that the crucial determinants of their identities and cultural bases, especially in the context of migration and settlement, are the nurturing forces of a homeland culture, which at least in the early stages of migration and settlement provide cultural reinforcement; the maintenance of ethnic boundaries through the exclusionary forces of racism; confrontations that are said to lead to identities of resistance and defiance; and the desire of diasporan Asians to emulate and aspire to particular "white" class cultures and their symbols. There is a great deal of emphasis on boundary maintenance and on the perpetuation of what are presented as clearly organized, homogeneous, and fixed cultural values. Importance is attached to the impact of rejection, with racism and discrimination as the fundamental forces in structuring their identities and cultural locations in diaspora. Ethnicity is presented as a characteristic that has fixed components and symbols and is considered to be the primary agent controlling and generating migrants' various identities and migrant cultures. Indeed, all these social mechanisms are important in structuring their lives and in determining their life chances. My concern, however, is the many other forces that are equally important in framing their experiences and that lead to diasporic cultural reproduction.

International forces have a strong impact on migrants' engagement with global economies and on the cultural patterns negotiated in local economies. Thus particular ethnicities and identities are not stable, despite a common core of fundamental religious and cultural values that constitute cultural roots but which shift according to the forces operating on them. In the case of direct, twice, and thrice migrant Asian women, these identities are products not solely of confrontation and rejection, and the wholesale transference of homeland culture, but also of the vibrant and changing European and international cultures in which Asian women are situated and over which they have *genuine unselfconscious command*. Their cultural locations and styles are not "wholly defined by exclusion" (Hall 1989:46) or by consciously emulating particular subcultures, but through their natural familiarity with particular economies and with their symbolic and material culture, which they appropriate from, transform, reinterpret, and reproduce in local, national, and international contexts to generate new cultural forms in continually changing transnational settings.

New Cultural Geographies: a problematized local

I have focused in particular on the reconstitution of culture and a cultural base in diaspora to form newer and newer cultural landscapes. This is all the more apposite when the local for a large number of people in the world shifts frequently over their lifetime. These novel cultural textures are a result of the transformative role that immigrant and diasporic populations – often marginal people – negotiate amongst them. These marginal spaces are becoming some of the most powerful arenas of cultural creativity.

I have examined the wedding economy as a facet of consumption to point to the continuous reinterpretation of a "traditional" cultural form – the dowry system – that has existed for centuries. This pattern is being continuously resynthesized and reproduced innovatively according to the specific local codes, as well as through the forces that influence women internationally. Yet diasporic European Asian women's lifestyles, cultural locations, and consumption styles are specifically rooted in the local knowledges that their parents have produced since migration. These cultural baggages are continuously reinterpreted through the codes of their peer subcultures and the localities in which they were raised.

Thus, I have proposed a more complex model of the conceptualization of the economic and cultural locations of British Asian women in the 1990s as seen through wedding consumption and general consumer styles. I have pointed to their *transformative* roles in cultural reproduction in Britain to generate *new cultural forms* that are products of their British and *European identities*. British Asian women, by engaging with their "ethnic" cultural base – as seen by their creative interpretation and reinterpretation of their dowries and other wedding expenditures – in the context of their regional and national cultures and class codes, transform that base. Globalizing agencies also have a considerable impact on generating local interpretations of their consumption and cultural styles.

By examining their consumption patterns and cultural styles through an analysis of the wedding economy, in particular the dowry system, I have emphasized their role as cultural entrepreneurs who choose their cultural forms and create new ones. Migrant women's agency and their self-defining roles are largely ignored in the literature and in mainstream portrayals, which describe them as passive recipients of their cultures. I have also explored the construction and reconstruction of their ethnicity and diasporic identities to show that these are contextualized products of time and space occupied by these women in the migration process. Their marriage and dowry patterns are as elastic as are their identities: not only continuously negotiated and determined by their migration histories but powerfully shaped by the codes of their local and national cultures and also by their class positions. Equally important are international forces, which have a strong impact on the women's engagement with global economies and on the cultural patterns that are negotiated in these contexts. Their identities as new European women are not only continuously negotiated and determined by the migration histories of their families but also powerfully filtered through the codes of their peer cultures, class, and regional locations in national and global economies. In these economies, the women are active agents and cultural and consumer negotiators who are affected by the forces to which all Europeans are subject.

I have also discussed the complex nature of migration and settlement trajectories which produce a range of diasporic cultures. The vast majority of literature available on the subject treats migration as the single, first movement of direct migrants to their destination economies. Yet there are direct, twice, and thrice migrant women, many of whom are further involved in fourth movements, especially in the 1990s. These multiple migrations are important to the ways different migrants and settlers view themselves, to their orientations to a homeland, and to the impact of these movements on cultural reproduction in local, regional, and transnational settings. An analysis of the wedding economy has been traced through the multiple migrations that these groups have followed. Current theories of diaspora and diasporic cultural reproduction and reconstitution of cultures assume single sites – geographical sites and points of origin – as definitive in shaping diasporic cultural forms. Diasporic wedding economies are products of multiple sites; their textures have been influenced by their location in various migration histories and through the baggage that is reproduced in diasporic settings in Europe and elsewhere. But they are also locally interpreted and have many local specificities.

Notes

1. Hebdige (1987, 1988), in developing a cartography of taste in Britain, talks about the Americanization (homogenization) of cultural styles and patterns. This powerful universalization process is currently a burning topic with retail chain store bosses and consumer market analyzers: "There are 50 million kids in Europe, and they have *converging* lifestyles in music labels and Big Macs. The international market is a reality and consumers are becoming more similar globally" (*New Statesman and Society Magazine*, Sept. 8, 1989: 26).

References

Back, Les (1995). "X amount of Sat Siri Akal! Apache Indian, Reggae Music and the Cultural Intermezzo." In *New Formations*, Dec. 95 (forthcoming).

Bhachu, Parminder (1985). *Twice Migrants: East African Sikh Settlers in Britain*. London and New York: Tavistock.

———. (1986). "Work, Marriage and Dowry among East African Sikh Women in the United Kingdom." In Rita J. Simon and Caroline B. Brettell (eds.), *International Migration: The Female Experience*. Totowa, N.J.: Rowman and Allanheld, pp. 229-240.

———. (1988). "Home and work: Sikh women in Britain." In Sallie Westwood and Parminder Bhachu (eds.), *Enterprising Women: Ethnicity, Economy and Gender Relations*. London and New York: Routledge, pp. 76-103.

———. (1989). "Ethnicity Constructed and Reconstructed: The Role of Sikh Women in Cultural Elaboration and Educational Processes in Britain." *Gender and Education* 3:147-62.

———. (1991). "Culture, Ethnicity and Class among Punjabi Sikh Women in 1990's Britain." *New Community* 17(3):401-412.

———. (1992). "Identities Constructed and Reconstructed: Representations of Asian Women in Britain." In Gina Buijs (ed.), *Migrant Women: Crossing Boundaries and Changing Identities*. Oxford and New York: Berg Publishers.

———. (1994). "New Cultural Forms and Transnational Asian Women: Culture, Class and Consumption among British Asian Women in the Diaspora." In Peter Van der Veer (ed.), *Nation and Migration: The Politics of Space in the South Asian Diaspora*. Philadelphia: University of Pennsylvania Press.

Employment Gazette (1987). *Ethnic Origin and Economic Status*. London: HMSO, pp. 18-29.

———. (1988). *Ethnic Origin and the Labour Market*. London: HMSO, pp. 164-77.

———. (1994). *Ethnic groups and the labour market* (Report by Frances Sly). London: Harrington Kilbride, pp. 147-60.

Ghai, Yash (1965). *Portrait of a Minority: Asians In East Africa*. Nairobi: Oxford University Press.

———. (1970). *Portrait of a Minority: Asians in East Africa*, rev. ed. Nairobi: Oxford University Press.

Gibson, Margaret A., and Parminder Bhachu (1988). "Ethnicity and School Performance: A Comparative Study of Sikhs in Britain and the United States." *Ethnic and Racial Studies* 11(3):239-262.

Gilroy, Paul (1987). *'There Ain't No Black in the Union Jack': The Cultural Politics of Race and Nation*. London: Hutchinson.

Goody, J. (1975). "Bridewealth and Dowry in Africa and Eurasia." In Jack Goody and Stanley Tambiah (eds.), *Bridewealth and Dowry*. Cambridge: Cambridge University Press, pp. 1-58.

Hall, Stuart (1987). "Minimal Selves." *Identity Documents*. London: Institute of Contemporary Arts, pp. 44-48.

___. (1991). "The Local and the Global: Globalization and Ethnicity." In Anthony D. King (ed.), *Culture, Globalization and the World System*. London: Macmillan, pp. 19-40.

Hebidge, Dick (1987) "Toward a Cartography of Taste: 1935-1964" In Bernard Waites, Tony Bennet and Graham Martin (eds.), *Popular Culture: Past and Present*. London: Croom Helm, in association with Open University Press.

___. (1988). *Subculture: The Meaning of Style*. London and New York: Methuen.

Jones, Trevor (1993). *Britain's Ethnic Minorities: An analysis of the Labour Force Survey*. London: Policy Studies Institute.

Index

Note: "n" refers to endnotes

Abella, Rosalie 141
Aboriginals *see* First Nations
Abu-Laban, Yasmeen 91, 92
academic parochialism 9-16
ACCESSS (Alliance des Communautés Culturelles pour Egalité et Services Santé et Sociaux) 94
action: and identity 174; and norms 168-69; in social identity model 170; political, 13, 14
Adenauer, Konrad 195-96
ADISQ (Association du Disque et de l'Industrie du Spectacle et de la Vidéo du Québec) 119
Adorno, Theodor 181n22
Africa, South Asian migration to 287-90
African Americans and Canadians *see* Blacks
African Diaspora 163-66
Afro-Caribbean culture *see* Black culture
agency, cultural 86-87, 210-211, 283-301
Alleyne, Mervyn 166
ambivalence, concept of, in black cultural criticism 161, 166
Amerindians, and European Discovery 188-89, 240-62. *See also* First Nations
Amit-Talai, Vered 15, 86, 109
Anderson, Benedict 68-9

anthropology, philosophical 172-74, 178
anti-racism 77-79
anti-Semitism: and domestic imagery 79, 80-81; and visualism 154-55; black 35; European 30-31; in Canada 145-46; in Germany 188, 190-213. *See also* Jews
Anzaldúa, Gloria 148-9
Apache Indian (Steven Kapur) 285, 286
Appadurai, Arjun 89
Arabs, in Canada, as visible minority 137-40, 142, 143-45
Arens, W. 255n7
Aristotle 244-45, 248, 256n11
Aronowitz, Stanley 85, 108
Asian: culture and identity 163-64, 171-72, 175; Diaspora 163-66, 283-301
Asians 137-45
assimilation 12, 50, 74, 80, 91
Atkinson, Allene and Harry 220-24
autonomy, political, in Scotland 275, 277-81

Back, Les 285
Bacon, Francis 252-53, 258n29
Balint, Michael 73
Ballard, Willie Pugh 220-24, 225
Banton, Michael 28-29
Barham, P. 56, 61
Barkan, E. 26-27
Barth, Fredrik 107, 109, 110
Bauer, Bruno 201
Benhabib, Seyla 14

Benjamin, Walter 193-94
Berger, Thomas 148
Bernstein, J.M. 56, 66n6
Bhabha, Homi 207
Bhachu, Parminder 15, 265-66, 288, 291-92, 294-95
Birnbaum, Philip 213n3
black: culture, and values 87, 161-79; Diaspora 163-66; identity 171-72, 175; women 188, 228, 229; youth, in Britain 175-79; category of, defined 163
blackness 55; attitudes towards 48, 52, 62, 65; as membership norm 163; meanings of 47, 56, 64
Blacks: and "Inner City" 71-72; and race relations in Georgia 218-31; as cultural agents 87-88, 172; identity construction of 147; in Canada, as visible minority 137-40; in residential space 71-73, 78, 80-81; in U.S. civil rights movement 188; racism towards 23, 35, 47-65, 142, 145-46, 163, 175
Blauner, B. 35
Bolster, Paul 227
Börneplatz Konflict 192-93, 203, 207
Britain: black youth in 175-79; study of race in 26-34; race relations paradigm 29-32; racial identity 39; racism in 21-23, 175; the Left in 30. See also immigration; South Asian women
British Columbia, and native land claims 253-54
British race sociology, 12-13, 37, 40
British Union of Fascists 79
Brown v. Board of Ed 227, 228
Brown, Cynthia 234n47
Browne, Con and Ora 220-24
Buckner, Taylor 142, 146

Cambridge, Alrick 87-88, 167
Canada, visible minorities in 137-57. See also under racism
Canadian Charter 90
Canadian Human Rights Commission 138
Cancian, Francesca 167, 168-70, 174
capitalism 31, 44, 70-71, 78, 91, 200
Cashmore, E. E. 158n4
Cassidy, F. 254
chanson Québécoise 118-19
Chappell, David 234n47
Chicago School 29
children, in Canada, as disadvantaged group 141
Chinese, in Canada, as visible minority 137-40, 142, 145-46, 147
citizenship, and residential rights 74, 75
Civil Rights Act (U.S.) 229
civil rights movement (U.S.) 29-30, 188, 218-31
Classen, Constance 158n4
Clifton, Rodney A. 90
co-optation 11, 98-99, 103-104
Cohen, Anthony P. 13, 15, 265-66, 268-72, 282n2, n4
Cohen, Philip 22-23
Collingwood, R. G. 209
Columbus, and the Discovery 241, 243, 247, 252
Commission on Equality in Employment 141, 142
community: and race relations 218-31; defined 219; in ethnic studies, 110; types of 219
Confino, Alon 235n51
Congress of Black Lawyers and Jurists of Québec 93-94
conservation, of fishing stocks 272-73, 275, 278
Copernicus 248
Craton, Michael 180n13
Crawford, Vicki 234n47
Cruse, Harold 180n6
Culhane, Dara 254
cultural agency, 86-87, 210-11, 283-301
cultural identity, and localism 285-87
cultural norms & values, black 87, 161-79
cultural studies 9-14, 170, 177-78

culture, concept of, in ethnic studies 110. *See also* Asian culture, black culture, diasporic culture

daaj see dowry system
Dahl, Robert 279
Davis, Murphy, Rev. 224-26
Delegamuukw et al. v. R 253-54
Dene Indians *see under* First Nations
Deux Montagnes School Commission, racism in 50, 53-61
Diaspora, Asian and African 163-66, 283-301
diasporic culture 283-301
Diaz, and the Discovery 247
difference: and nationalism 274, 280-81; cultural forms of, 49-50; in the Discovery 248-53; racial 55
Diner, Dan 193
Dion, Céline 119
disabled, in Canada, as disadvantaged group 140
discourse: local 273-81; of home 68-81; on race and racism, 24-44
Discovery, and European identity 240-54
Dittmer, John 228
diversity 9, 162
domestic metaphors: and racism 68-81; gendered 69, 76-77
Douglass, Frederick 153-54
dowry system, of South Asian British women 266, 290-301. *See also* Punjabi suits
Driedger, Leo 145

economic development strategy, in Scotland 271-81
education levels, of visible minorities in Canada 139-40
Elliott, J. H. 251, 252
Elliott, Jean Leonard 91, 111n2
Ellison, Ralph 158n3
Elster, Jon 166, 173
employment, of visible minorities in Canada 100-101, 138-40

Employment Equity Act (1986) 137
England, Martin 219
equity legislation 137, 155-57. *See also* visible minority legislation; multiculturalism
Esman, Milton J. 85
Essed, P. 33
ethnic activism, professionalization of 89, 93-110
ethnic categories, in cultural studies 9-14
ethnic identity, of immigrants 170-71. *See also* identity construction; cultural identity
ethnic inequality, and visible minorities 143-46
ethnic leaders, marginalization of 104-105
ethnic minorities 21-22; and residential space 68-81; and the media 95-99. *See also* multiculturalism; racism; religious minorities; visible minorities
ethnic movements, urban, study of 104
ethnic music *see* world music
ethnic organizations, funding of 104-105
ethnic politics *see* identity politics
ethnic representation *see* minority representation
ethnic studies 9-17, 107-110
ethnic voluntary organizations, in Montreal 89, 93-110
ethnicity: as commodity 106; as contingent and invented 109-110; as distinct from race 35-36; and economic inequality 143-46; and world music 122-24, 127; in Québec 134n13
European Discovery of America *see* Amerindians
exclusion, racial 51, 52, 68-81
exclusion zones, urban/residential 71-72

Fairclough, Adam 234n45

Federal Contractors Program 137
Félix Awards 117, 118, 119-20
Fernandez-Armesto, Felipe 252
Fest, Joachim 213n9
Feuchtwang, Stephan 167
Fields, B. J. 38, 39
First Nations 115-32; Dene 148; Gitsksan 253-54; identity construction of 146-47, 148; as disadvantaged group in Canada, 140; Innu 120, 122-24, 125-26, 130-31; Mohawks 115, 127-31; Montaignais see Innu; Wet'suwet'en 253-54. *See also* Amerindians; Kashtin
fishing economy, Scottish 272-81
fishing stocks, depletion of 272-73, 275, 278
Fleras, Augie 91, 111n2
Fothergill, Anthony 254n6
Foucault, Michel 209-10
fragmentation, of racial and ethnic studies 12-14
Francofolies de Montréal 124-25, 134n11
Frankfurt Jewish Ghetto 190-213; and memory 187-88; as esthetic form 211-12; history of 199-206
Frankfurt Stadtwerke 191-2, 202-205, 211-12
Frederickson, George 181n18
French, Scot A. 229, 235n51
Frideres, James 134n14
Friedlander, Saul 196
Frith, Simon 122, 126, 127
Fuentes, Carlos 256n13

Garrow, David 234n47
Gates, Henry Louis, Jr. 179n4
German Social Democratic Party (SPD) 202
German State, and Jewish Question 194-98
Germany: anti-Semitism in 188, 190-213; history of Jews in 190-213; and "Otherness" 187-88; relations with Israel 195-96; the Left in 196
Gertz, Jochen 211-12, 215n32, n33
Ghai, Yash 290-91
Gibson, Margaret A. 288
Giddings, Paula 234n47
Gilroy, Paul 37, 164, 178, 179n5, 181n20
Gipsy Kings 121
Gitsksan *see under* First Nations
global/globalization 9, 11, 13, 14, 265-66; and migrant culture 266, 283-303; and racism 73-74. *See also* local
Goffman, Erving 155
Goldberg, D. T. 24, 37
Goodlad, John 265, 274-79
Goody, J. 292
Goulbourne, Harry 180n6
Grafton, Anthony 247, 248, 249, 254n2
Grayson, Paul 147
Greer, Germaine 151-2
Grégoire, Dr. M. 58
Grenier, Line 118-19, 124, 134n12
Groll, Klaus-Michael 197
Guérin, Dr. M. 58-63, 66n8
Guilbault, Jocelyne 121, 131
Guillaumin, C. 32
Gutzmore, Cecil 164, 179n5

Habermas, Juergen 213n9
Hagopian, Patrick 233n35
Halbwachs, Maurice 207-209, 252n24, n28
Hale, John 245, 246
Hall, Stuart 13, 286, 299
Handler, R. 268, 281
Hannerz, Ulf 104
Harley, Brian 249-50
Harris, Wilson 164-65
Harrison, Faye 108-109
Hayward, Philip 132
Hernstein, Richard J. 32
Hersog, Roman 198
Heuss, Theodor 195
Hibbits, Bernard 154

INDEX 307

Higham, John 107
history: and absence 209-211; and identity, in Judengasse Museum 207; and memory 187-261; as institution for constitution of social memory 207-211; problem of power in 188, 209-211
history, oral *see* oral history
Hodgen, Margaret T. 245, 246, 250
Holocaust, impact on European race concept 30-31
home: and capitalism 70-71; as private space 68, 69, 72-73, 77-78, 81; images of 68-81
Home Alone 77
home ownership, symbolic meaning of 72
homely racism 71-81
hooks, bell 34
House of Commons Select Committee of Race Relations and Immigration (UK) 176
Howes, David 87, 158n4
Hu-Dehart, Evelyn 91-92
Hulme, Peter 255n9
human rights, and race in Quebec 21, 49-65
humanism, and identity 172-74
Hunter, Mead 121
hybridity, cultural 161, 164-66

identity: and action 174; and ethnic culture 274; and history, in Judengasse Museum 207; and humanism 172-74; and memory 187-261; and normative change 169; and race 39-41; and the self 173-74; changes in 173-74; local, 267-81; mediated 115-32; religious 55-56; social context of 173-74. *See also* social identity theory
identity construction: by visible minorities 146-51; and language 147-49; and the media 115-32
identity politics 85-183; and academia 10-12, 14, 86, 92-93, 107-110; and multiculturalism 90-92; and postmodernism 10-11, 108; and professionalization of ethnic activism 89-110; Asian 175; black 175; sociological study of 85
identity structure theory 170-72
immigrants, 27-31, 68-81, 283-301. *See also* migrant women
immigration: sociological study of 28-31; to Britain 27-31, 69, 79, 80-81, 283-301; to the U.S. 29, 30, 287-90. *See also* migration
income, of visible minorities in Canada 143-45
Indians *see* Amerindians; First Nations
Innu *see under* First Nations
institutionalization, of minority representation, 86, 89-110
Irwin-Zarecke, Ivona 215n24
Israel, relations with postwar Germany 195-96
Italians 145-46

James, C. L. R. 165
James, Winston 164
Japanese 137-45
Jaspers, Karl 196-97
Jean, Dr. C. F. 58
Jewish immigration 69, 79, 80-81
Jewish Question, and postwar German State 194-98
Jews: in Canada 145; in Frankfurt Ghetto 190-213; role in early pariah capitalism 200; tensions between Eastern European and German 198-99, 205-206, 211. *See also* anti-Semitism
Johnson, Howard 220-24, 225
Joint Concordia/UQAM Chair in Ethnic Studies 94
Jordan, Clarence 219, 223, 224, 225
Judengasse *see* Frankfurt Jewish Ghetto
Judengasse Museum 192, 203-207, 211-12

Kafe, William 47-65

Kahnawake Indian reservation 115, 127-31
Kahnesatake Indian reservation 115, 127-31
Karenga, M. 34
Kashtin: as Québécois 86, 115-32; as world music 122-25; during Oka crisis 129-31
Kelly, Karen 139, 140-41
Kennedy, Leslie 107
King, Martin Luther 228, 229
kinship systems 172
K'Meyer, Tracy E. 188
Knauft, Bruce M. 11
Knopff, Rainer 85
Knowles, Caroline 15, 23
Koinonia Farm 218-31; as part of civil rights movement 223, 226-31
Koreans 137-40
Krueger, Thomas 234n47
Kugelman, Cilly 199
Kupperman, Karen Ordahl 259n35

LaFontaine, Yves 95-99, 102
Lamming, George 180n7
Langer, Lawrence 211
language: and Québécois music 119-20, 125-26; in ethnic identity construction 147-49; in Quebec 134n13
Lasch, Christopher 181n18
Latin Americans 137-40, 143-46. See also Mexican Americans
Lawson, Steven 234n45
Le Pen, Jean-Marie 70
Left 11, 30, 109, 196
LeGoff, Jacques 208-209
Lerner, M. 35
Levin, David Michael 154
Lewin, Kurt 104, 105
Li, Peter S. 12, 111n3
Lieberman, L. 37
linguistic minorities 141
lived racism 47-65
local 11-15, 265-66; and migrant culture 266, 283-303; and racism 74; discourse 273-81; identity 267-81; meaning of 9, 15, 266; patriotism 79; power 68; space 72. See also global
Lord, Audre 153
Los Angeles riots, race in 42-44
Luebbe, Hermann 194
Lustiger-Thaler, Henri 15, 187-88

Macedo, Helder 243, 249, 253, 255n8
Malarek, Victor 111n3
Maliotenam Indian reservation 116, 125, 132. See also First Nations; Kashtin
Malm, Krister 118
marriage see South Asian women
Marx, Karl 70, 201
Marxist theory 109
Maxwell, Kenneth 247
McEachern, Allen 253
McGrane, Bernard 243, 249
McIntyre, Alisdaire 181n15
McKenzie, Claude 115-32. See also Kashtin
media: and Quebec minorities 95-99; role in identity construction 115-32
mediated identity 115-32; in music industry 126-27
Meintjes, Louise 121, 127
Memmi, Albert 259n35
memory: and Frankfurt Jewish Ghetto 187-88, 190-213; and history 187-261; and identity 187-261; and power relations 188, 209-211; and U.S. civil rights movement 188, 218-239; as form of agency 210-11; collective, 188, 219, 224-26, 230, 235; cultural 207-211; historical 223, 226-31; individual 188, 220-24, 229-30; social 207-11
Mercer, Kobena 162, 179n1, n4
Mexican Americans, identity construction of 148-49. See also Latin Americans
migrant women, as cultural agents 283-301

migration: and cultural identity 285-87; in the U.S. 29, 30. *See also* immigration
mikvehs 191, 202
Miles, Jack 42
Miles, Robert 22, 32, 37, 39, 42, 179n1
minority: activists, co-optation of 98-99, 103-104; representation 86, 89-110; rights 21, 49-65
minority circuit 94-110
Mohawks *see under* First Nations
mongrelization 162
Montagnais *see* First Nations—Innu
Montaigne 250-51
Montreal: minority representation in 86, 89-110; racism in educational system 48-65; visible minorities in 138
Montreal Minority Circuit *see* minority circuit
moral geography 248-51
Moreau, Joanne 140
Morrison, Toni 207
Morrison, Val 86, 134n12
Morton, F. L. 85
multiculturalism 48-50, 61, 65, 86, 87; and identity politics 90-92; and racism 49, 52; and the New Left 109; and visible minorities 137; debates over 90-93
Multiculturalism Act 90, 137
Munster, Sebastian 247, 248
Murray, Charles 32
music: black 181n20; ethnic *see* world music; industry 86, 120-27

Nagel, Joane 107
Naipaul, V. S. 172
Nasstrom, Kathryn 228, 229, 235n51
nation, as homeland 70
nationalism: and difference 274, 280-81; and the local 265-81; and transnationalism 265-303; in ethnic studies 110; and homely racism 70, 76, 79, 81; personal 268; Scottish rhetoric of 267-81

native land claims 127-31, 253-54
Natives, North American *see* Amerindians; First Nations; Kashtin
Neree, Dr. A. 58
NIMBYism 77-78
Nolte, Ernst 213n9
Nora, Pierre 213n4
normative change, and identities 169
norms 87, 169-70, 178
Ntolo, Mrs. 80-81
Nuremburg trials 194

O'Gorman, Edmundo 243
Oka crisis 115, 127-31
Omi, M. 37-40, 41
oral history 220-24, 230-31
Orkney and Shetland Movements 271, 276
Otherness: and Amerindian pagans 189; and British ethnic immigrants 286; and race 22-23; in German history 187-88, 191, 192; in historical narrative and memory 208-211

Pacini, Deborah Hernandez 121
Pagden, Anthony 244, 245, 248, 250, 252, 256n12
Paglia, Camille 152
Paine, Robert 188-89, 249
Parkin, David 279
parochialism, in race and ethnic studies 9-16
Passerini, L. 187
Paterson, Lindsay 282n3
Pfeffercorn, Johans 200
Poles 145-46
political action 13, 14
politics of identity *see* identity politics
Popper, Karl 179, 181n22
Portelli, A. 187
Porter, John 143
postmodernism 10-14, 108, 170, 177-78
power: and identity construction 14, 86, 131, 147; and memory 188; and

psychiatry 56; and racism 35, 71, 155, 145-46, 153, 155; and the media 127; black 227-30; in cultural studies 10; local 68; of South Asian British women 293; problem of, in historical discourse 188, 209-211
private property, and racism 68, 69, 72-73, 77-78, 81
Pryce, Ken 164, 165, 177
psychiatry, and racism 47, 53-54, 56-65
Public Service Employment Equity Program 137
Public Service Reform Act 137
Punjabi by Nature (PBN) 286
Punjabi suits 290, 292-97

Quebec: and ethnicity 134n13; and language 134n13; and minority representation 86, 89-110; and minority rights 49-65; and native land claims 127-31; and multiculturalism 48-50, 65; and the media 115-32; and world music 124-25, 126
Quebec Code of Human Rights 50
Quebec education system, and racism 47-65
Quebec Human Rights Commission 49, 52, 58, 60-61, 63, 95-98
Quebec immigration policy 50
Québécois music 115-32; changing definition of 118-20; and minorities 86; *chanson* 118-19; language in 119-200, 125-26
Québécois, changing meaning of 134n13

Rabinbach, Anson 195, 213n9
race: and academic performance 32; and ethnicity 9, 35-36; and psychiatry 62-63; as analytical category 26-44; biological basis of 22, 25-34, 39-41; in black cultural criticism 161; in Los Angeles riots 42-44; in postwar Europe 30-31; in sociology 12-13, 25-44; and skin colour 33, 37, 40; spatialized 71-74; symbolism and imagery of 22-23; and difference 55. *See also* racism; visible minorities
race and ethnic studies 9-17, 37-40, 107-110
race relations paradigm 36, 41, 43-44; Chicago School 29; in Britain 29-32; in U.S. 29-33; and racism 33
race relations 24-46; and community 218-31
race sociology 12-13, 37-40
racial and ethnic categories 9-14, 40-41
racial: discourse 24-44; exclusion 51, 52; identity 39-41; markers 64, 65; space 22-23, 71-74, 187-88; violence 51-52, 53, 63
racialization process 34-42, 138, 151, 155
racism: administrative 47-65; and biography 47-65; and cultural hybridity 165; and human rights 21, 47-67; and multiculturalism 49, 52; and power 155; and psychiatry 47, 53-54, 65-66; and race relations paradigm 33; anti-black 23, 35, 47-65, 142, 145-46, 163, 175; at micro-level 48; concept of 33-34, 38, 44; coping methods 48; defined 21; existential 47-65; homely 71-81; in Britain 21-23; in Canada 21, 23, 48-65, 142, 145-46; in the U.S. 21-22; psychological consequences of 47-65; residential 68-81; resistance to 52-53, 56, 63, 65; study of 37; survey of 145-46; white/black dichotomy in 30, 31, 34-36, 38, 42-43; worsening of 22. *See also* anti-racism; anti-Semitism; race; visible minorities
Rapport, Nigel 259n32
Reed, Linda 234n47
religious freedom 80-81
religious minorities 141

Report of the Special Committee on Visible Minorities in Canadian Society (Daudlin Report) 142
representation 10, 14, 161. *See also* minority representation
residential space, and racism 68-81
retrieved subjectivity 210-211
Rex, John 28-29, 170-72, 174, 180n9, 181n18
Reynolds, L. T. 37
rhetoric, of local Scottish nationalism 267-81; and responsibility theme 277-81
Ricoeur, Paul 48, 181n14
rights *see* minority rights
Roberts, Lance W. 90
Robinson, Armstead L. 234n45
Rodriguez, Richard 149-50
Rogers, Kim Lacy 235n52, n53
Rorty, Richard 210
Rosaldo, Renato 92, 93, 108
Roy, Bruno 118
Rushdie, Salman 162, 285-86
Ryan, Michael T. 10, 250, 251

Said, Edward 250, 256n20, 257n23
Sanchez, Dr. M. A. 63
Sanjek, Roger 12
Sartre, Jean-Paul 154, 179n3
Satzewich, Vic 12
Schmidt, Helmut 196
Schneider, David M. 255n7
Schrager, Samuel 233n35
Schwartz, Barry 215n28
Scotland: economy 272-81; nationalism 265-66, 267-81; political autonomy 275, 277-81
Scottish National Party (SNP) 269-71, 276
segregation, residential 71-81
Serres, Michael 68
sexism, links to visualism and racism 151-55
Shalev-Gertz, Esther 211-12, 215n32, n33
shared memory *see* memory, collective

Shenker, Barry 223
Shetland Fisherman's Association 274
Shetland Islands 270-81
Simon, Paul 121
Sitkoff, Harvard 228
skin colour, and race 33, 37, 40, 59, 143, 147
Small, Stephen 176-77
Smith, Kenneth L. 234n43
SNCC *see* Student Non-Violent Coordinating Committee (SNCC)
social class, and identity construction 149-51
social identity theory 167-70, 172
sociology, and racial discourse 25-34, 39-44
sociology of youth culture 177-79
Sony Music 116, 117
Sosna, Morton 234n47
South Asian women: and changes to dowry system in Britain 266, 290-301; and economic activity in Britain 290-92, 294; as cultural agents 283-301; in sociological literature 298; migration—to Africa 287-90, to Britain 283-301, to the U.S. 287-90
South Asians 137-45. *See also* Asians
Sowell, T. 34, 36
space, racial 22-23, 71-74, 187-88
SPD *see* German Social Democratic Party (SPD)
Stadtwerke *see* Frankfurt Stadtwerke
Stasiulis, Daiva 91, 92
Stern, Frank 197
Student Non-Violent Coordinating Committee (SNCC) 227
Sullivan, Patricia 234n45
Synnott, Anthony 87, 158n4

Table de Concertation des réfugiés de Montréal 94
Takagi, Dana 93
Taylor, Charles 181n15
technology 271, 274, 275, 278
Todorov, Tzvetan 249, 252

Toronto, visible minorities in 138
Torres, Rudy 22
transnationalism 10, 15, 265-66, 283-303
Trigger, Bruce 259n35

unemployment *see* employment
UNESCO 29, 31
United States: identity politics in 10-11; and race 21-22, 29-33, 34-42; cultural studies in 10; migration 29-30, 287-90
Université du Québec à Montréal (UQAM) 94
urban ethnic movements, study of 104
urban space, racialized 22-23, 68-81

values: and black culture 87, 161-79; and cultural studies 170, 177-78
Vancouver, visible minorities in 138
Verdery, Katherine 92-93, 107, 110
violence, racial 51-52, 53, 63
visible minorities: and multiculturalism 137; and racism 138, 142, 144, 145-46, 151-55; and skin colour 143, 147; and white gaze 151-55; diversity among 140-46; educational levels of 139-40; employment of 140; identity construction 146-51; in Canada 137-57; income of 143-45; research on 142; statistics on 138-41.
visible minority legislation 87, 137-57. *See also* equity legislation
visual markers, and identity construction 149-51

visualism 151-55
Vollant, Florent 115-32. *See also* Kashtin
Voting Rights Act (U.S.) 229

Wallis, Roger 118
Waterman, Christopher 131
Weber, Max 200
Weiner, Kay 218
Weinreich, P. 171-72
Weisbrot, Robert 228
Wellman, D. 34, 38
Werbner, Pnina 104
West, Cornel 24-25, 33-37, 42-43, 154, 151
Wet'suwet'en *see under* First Nations
white flight 72-73
white gaze 151-55
white/black dichotomy, in racism 30, 31, 34-36, 38, 42-43, 144
Wilson, Seymour 91
Wilson, W. J. 34
Winant, M. 37-40, 41
Wittkamper, Margaret 220-24
Wolf, Eric 254n3
Wollheim, Richard 180n10
Wollstonecraft, Mary 151
women: Asian *see* South Asian women; black 188, 228, 229; in Canada 140; migrant 283-301
world music 120-127

Young, James 215n32
youth, black 175-79

Zepp, Ira G. 234n43